Software Engineering for Real-time Systems

Volume 1 - Foundations
2nd Edition

Jim Cooling

Published by Lindentree Associates © 2019

From the Lindentree series 'The engineering of real-time embedded systems'

For my grandson

Finnian James Cooling

CONTENTS

Chapter 3
First steps - Requirements analysis and specification 55

Chapter 4
Software and program design concepts 105

Chapter 5
Multitasking systems - an introduction

Glossary of terms

ADC	Analogue to digital
ANSI	American National Standards Institute
ASIC	Application-Specific Integrated Circuit
BDM	Background Debug Mode
BSP	Board Support Package
CASE	Computer-Aided Software Engineering
CISC	Complex Instruction Set Computer
CORE	Controlled Requirements Expression
CPU	Central Processing Unit
CRC	Class-Responsibility-Collaboration
CT	Control Transformation
DAC	Digital to analogue
DDT	Dynamic Debugging Tool
DFD	Data Flow Diagram
DMA	Direct Memory Access
DOS	Disk Operating System
DP	Data Processing
DSD	Design Structure Diagram
DSP	Digital Signal Processor
DT	Data Transformation
EEPROM	Electrically Erasable Programmable Read Only Memory
EPROM	(UV)Erasable ROM
ERD	Entity Relationship Diagram
FIFO	First-In First-Out
FPGA	Field Programmable Gate Array
FRAM	Ferroelectric Random Access Memory
FSM	Finite State Machine
FFD	Functional Flow Diagram
GDP	Graphics Display Processor
GUI	Graphical User Interface
HCI	Human-Computer Interface
HLL	High-Level Language
I/O	Input/Output
ICE	In-Circuit Emulator
IEEE	Institute of Electronic and Electrical Engineers
IP	Intellectual Property
ISO	International Standards Organisation
ISR	Interrupt Service Routing
JSP	Jackson Structured Programming
JTAG	Joint Test Action Group
LOC	Lines Of Code

MBD	Model-based Design
MDA	Model-driven Architecture
MDS	Microprocessor Development System
Mflops	Mega floating point operations per second
MIPS	Millions of Instructions Per Second
MSC	Message Sequence Chart
MTBF	Mean Time Between Failures
MTTF	Mean Time To Fail
MTTR	Mean Time To Repair
NMI	Non-Maskable Interrupt
OCD	On-Chip Debug
OED	Oxford English Dictionary
OLTP	On-Line Transaction Processing
OOAD	Object-Oriented Analysis and Design
OOD	Object-Oriented design
OS	Operating System
OSI	Open Systems Interconnection
OT	PROMOne Time PROM
PC	Personal Computer
PCI	Peripheral Component Interconnect
PDF	Program Development Facility
PROM	Programmable Read Only Memory
PSD	Program Structure Diagram
QA	Quality Assurance
RAM	Random Access Memory
RISC	Reduced Instruction Set Computer
ROM	Read Only Memory
RT-IDE	Real-Time Integrated Development Environment
RTOS	Real-Time Operating System
SAP	Service Access Point
SBC	Single-Board Computer
S-H	Sample-Hold
SC	Structure Chart
SDL	Specification and Description Language
SOC	System-On-Chip
SOR	Statement Of Requirements
SP	Structured Programming
STD	State Transition Diagram
TOD	Time Of Day
UML	Unified Modelling Language
VDU	Visual Display Unit
VHDL	Very High Level Description Language
VME	Versa Module Europa

Preface

Software Engineering for Real-time Systems is a three-volume book-set; the preface here applies to the complete set.

What are these books about?

These books set out to provide a firm foundation in the knowledge and skills needed to develop and produce real-time (and in particular, embedded) systems.

   Let us be clear right up front what they do not aim to do. They don't teach you how to be a designer. They do not show you, in fine detail, how to design real-time software. They are not programming texts. What they do, however, is actually more fundamental (and in reality, more important); they deal with the *engineering* of real-time systems.

Who should read these books?

Those working - or intending to work - in the field of software development for real-time systems. They have been written with four audiences in mind:

- Students.
- Engineers, scientists and mathematicians moving into software systems.
- Professional and experienced software engineers entering the embedded field.
- Programmers having little or no formal education in the underlying principles of software-based real-time systems.

Why should you read these books?

First let's assume that your major interest is in the real-time area. Why should you part with your hard-earned money (though for students it may be somebody else's money) for this textbook? Well, it's essential to realise that many skills are needed to produce quality real-time software. Being able to program is but one step. The whole process involves a range of activities, involving (among others) problem analysis, software and program design, testing, debugging, documentation, reviews and configuration management. This book covers the essential features of such topics.

At what level is this book pitched?

Taken as a whole, few assumptions are made about the background of the reader. Ideally he (shorthand for he/she) will have a broad grasp of microprocessor systems, a basic understanding of programming and an appreciation of elementary digital logic. These aren't essential but they help in understanding the reasoning used at many points in the text. Some experience of assembly language and high-level language programming would also be helpful here.

How is this book-set organized?

The material is organized to cater for both new and experienced readers. It provides full coverage for those new to software engineering and real-time systems. At the same time it allows experienced software engineers to move rapidly onto the more practical-oriented aspects of the subject. This it does by grouping the material into three books:

Volume 1: Foundations.
Volume 2: Designing and developing real-time software.
Volume 3: Implementation and performance issues.

In general there is a logical progression from start to finish (hardly startling but useful). Chapters, where possible, have been written to stand alone. Thus some repetition and duplication will be found (see also later remarks concerning diagramming aspects). Occasionally forward referencing will be met, but this is used mainly as a pointer to future topics.

What are the objectives and contents of Volume 1?

The aim of volume 1 is to give a good grounding in the basics of the subject. The material, which forms the foundations for later chapters, is essential reading for those new to real-time software.

It begins by describing what real-time systems are, their structures and applications, and the impact of these on software design in general. This should be especially useful to readers having a software background only.

Following this is a chapter that shows clearly that to achieve reliable, safe and correct operation, a professional approach to software design is imperative. It explains how and why software errors occur, what qualities are desirable (e.g. feasibility, suitability, robustness, etc.), discusses error avoidance and defensive programming and finishes by looking at design styles.

The problems of deducing and defining system specifications and performance requirements are covered next, including the topics of rapid and animation prototyping. This leads into the basic concepts of software and program design, including modularization, structured programming and mainstream design methods (specifically functionally structured, functional flow and object-oriented (OO) techniques).

Rounding off Part 1 is an introduction to multitasking systems together with the basics of real-time operating systems. This covers the fundamentals of the topic, including the tasking model of software, scheduling, mutual exclusion and inter-task communication.

What are the objectives and contents of Volume 2?

The purpose of Volume 2 is to introduce key practical issues met in the analysis, design and development of real-time software. It is especially relevant to those actively involved in such work.

Opening Volume 2 are two chapters concerned with a core aspect of modern software development: diagramming. Chapter 1 is a groundwork chapter. It explains why diagrams and diagramming are important, what we achieve by using diagrams and the types used in the software development process. Chapter 2 extends this material showing diagrams that are in common use, are integral to mainstream design methods and are supported by computer-based tools. For sound practical reasons the topic is set in the context of functionally structured and object-oriented design techniques.

Next to be covered (chapter 3) are essentially code-related topics, including code development, code organization and packaging and the integration of program units. Issues handled include fundamental program design and construction techniques, the use of component technology in software development, the programming needs of embedded systems, and how mainstream programming languages (Ada, C, C++ and Java) meet these requirements. It concludes by showing how the Unified Modelling Language (UML) can be used to document code-related work.

The concluding chapter of Part 2 (chapter 4) shows the application of these aspects to practical software development. It looks at the overall specification-to-coding process using a variety of techniques: functionally structured, object-oriented, model driven, model based and Agile design methods.

What are the objectives and contents of Volume 3?

Volume 3 has two objectives. One aim is to cover important implementation subjects, including analysing and testing source code in both host and target systems and documenting development work. This work applies to all real-time software developments. The second aim is explain why criticality and performance are key design-drivers in many applications and to give a sound grounding in these topics.

Opening this final section is the chapter 'Analysing and testing source code'. It explains the underlying concepts of source code testing, describes static and dynamic analysis, introduces code complexity metrics and coverage analysis, and deals with OO-specific issues. Following this, chapter 2, is a description of the last stage of software development, that of producing debugged code in the target system. Topics include software debugging on host and target systems, debugging in host/ target combinations, the use of performance analysis tools, emulators and progammers, and integrated development environments.

The next two chapters are essentially stand-alone ones (although their content has a major impact on practical design, development and implementation methods). Chapter 3 explains what critical and fault-tolerant systems are and why their design strategies differ from run-of-the-mill software systems. It is a very wide-ranging chapter, dealing with many diverse aspects important to the development of critical systems. These include the categorization of critical systems, formal specification methods, numerical operations, the development of robust software, dealing with real-world interfacing, operating systems, handling processor and memory malfunctions, and using hardware-based techniques to limit the effects of software failures.

Chapter 4 sets out to show why it is important to design for performance, especially where systems have demanding timing requirements. It shows where such requirements come from, how software performance relates to system performance, and how performance targets get translated into deliverables. It also shows the value of modelling and simulation for analysis, prediction and evaluation of software performance. Lastly it illustrates the techniques of top-down, middle-out and bottom-up performance analysis.

Chapter 5, which deals with documentation, rounds off this section. It describes the relevance and importance of system test and documentation, from functional specification through module description and test operations to maintenance documents. The importance and implementation of configuration management and version control techniques are also covered.

Why is diagramming covered so extensively?

Diagramming is the one area where there may appear to be a fair degree of repetition of material (so I think it's important to discuss this just in case you think it's a ploy to produce a larger book and make more money). One of the reasons for coming up with the structure of this book is that it worked well in its predecessor. However, at that time the major battle was to convince software designers that diagramming really is an integral part of the design process. Ten years on (and 33 years after my first use of flow charts) things have changed. We find (from our commercial software engineering training courses) that where diagramming is concerned there are fundamentally three groups of people:

1. One: those who don't see the need for diagrams and who use expressions like 'the code is my design' (frequently made by those producing write-only C++ programs).
2. Two: those who, because of the influence of UML, see that diagramming is 'good', but appear to have little understanding of its effective use.
3. Three: those who truly understand the value of diagramming, practice it and attempt to integrate it within their design processes.

We have also had a sea-change in attitude with UML becoming the de-facto standard for OO-based designs.

Volume 1 deals with fundamentals, not diagramming *per se*. As you can see, 'pictures' are used to demonstrate and illustrate points through this section. It just seemed common-sense to use standard notation rather than *ad-hoc* methods wherever appropriate. The material here is aimed at demonstrating, by example, how useful diagramming is. Moreover, it is hoped that readers new to software will have gradually absorbed information making it easier to assimilate the material in later stages.

In volume 2 the intent of chapter 1, 'Diagramming – an introduction', is to show exactly why we should be using diagrams. As the material is mostly conceptual, it could have been placed in volume 1. However, there are a number of reasons for putting it here. First, if the lessons (many implicit) of volume 1 have been taken on board, then there is little need to sell the 'message' of the chapter. Second, by covering the material at this point, the reader can readily see how it relates to software processes introduced earlier. Third, it acts as a natural lead-in to practical diagramming methods, the subject of the next chapter. You will find diagrams from earlier work repeated here but set in a different context; the intent is to describe the syntax and semantics of diagrams used for functionally structured and object-oriented design work. Repeating material also allows chapters to be self-contained and complete, so eliminating the need for constant backward references. More experienced readers who choose to skip Part 1 will appreciate this feature.

The intent of chapters 3 and 4 is to show how diagrams can be used when developing real systems. Chapter 3 uses them to model code-specific aspects such as component dependencies, class packaging and software deployment. In contrast chapter 4, 'Software and program design concepts', uses diagrams to model design-specific aspects of the development process.

Good reading, ladies and gentlemen.

Jim Cooling
Markfield, December 2019

Chapter 1

Real-time systems - setting the scene

Forty years ago software development was widely seen as consisting only of programming. And this was regarded more as an art than a science (and certainly not as an engineering discipline). Perhaps that's why this period is associated with so many gloomy tales of project failure. Well, the industry matured. Along the way we had new languages, real design methods and, in 1968, the distinction between computer science and software engineering.

The microprocessor arrived circa 1970 and set a revolution in motion. But experienced software developers played little part in this. For, until the late 1970s, most developers of microcomputer software were electronic, electrical or control engineers. And they proceeded to make exactly the same mistakes as their predecessors. Now why didn't they learn from the experience of earlier workers? There were three main reasons for this. In the first place, there was little contact between electronic engineers (and the like) and computer scientists. In the second place, many proposed software design methods weren't suitable for real-time applications. Thirdly, traditional computer scientists were quite dismissive of the difficulties met by microprocessor systems designers. Because programs were small the tasks were trivial (or so it was concluded).

Over the years the industry has changed considerably. The driving force for this has been the need to :

- Reduce costs.
- Improve quality, reliability and safety.
- Reduce design, development and commissioning timescales.
- Design complex systems.
- Build complex systems.

Without this pressure for change the tools, techniques and concepts discussed in this book would probably still be academic playthings.

Early design methods can be likened to hand-crafting, while the latest ones are more like automated manufacture. But, as in any industry, it's no good automating the wrong tools; we have to use the right tools in the right place at the right time. This chapter lays the groundwork for later work by giving a general picture of real-time systems. It:

- Highlights the differences between general-purpose computer applications (e.g. information technology, management information systems, etc.) and real-time systems.
- Looks at the types of real-time systems met in practice.
- Describes the environmental and performance requirements of embedded real-time systems.
- Describes typical structures of modern microprocessors and microcomputers.
- Shows, in general, how software design and development techniques are influenced by these factors.

The detailed features of modern software methods are covered in later chapters.

1.1 Categorizing computer systems.

How are computer systems categorized? There are many answers to this, sometimes conflicting, sometimes overlapping. But if we use speed of response as the main criterion, then three general groups emerge:

- Batch: I don't mind when the computer results arrive, within reason (the time taken may be hours or even days in such systems).
- Interactive on-line: I would like the results with a fairly short time, typically a few seconds.
- Real-time: I need the results within definite time scales, otherwise the system just won't work properly.

Let's consider these in turn.
   An example of a modern batch system is shown in figure 1.1. Methods like this are used

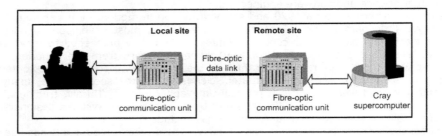

Figure 1.1 Modern batch system

where computing resources are scarce and/or expensive as it is a very efficient technique.
Here the user usually pre-processes all programs and information, perhaps storing data on a local computer. At some convenient time, say at the start of an evening shift, this job is passed over the data link to a remote site (often a number of jobs are transmitted as a single job-lot). When all jobs are finished the results are transmitted back to the originating site.
   Interactive on-line computer systems are widely used in banking, holiday booking and mail-order systems. Here, for private systems, access to the system is made using (typically) PC-based remote terminals, figure 1.2. Local processing of data isn't normally done in this instance. Instead, all

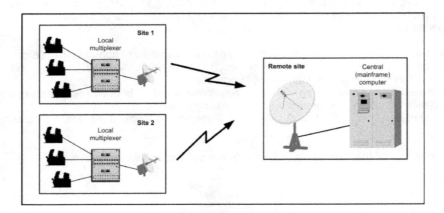

Figure 1.2 Typical interactive on-line computer system

transactions are handled by the central computer in a time-sliced fashion. Routing and access control is the responsibility of the front-end processors and local multiplexers. Many readers will, of course, have experience of such systems through their use of the internet and the web (perhaps the importance of timeliness in interactive systems is summed up by the definition of www. as standing for 'world wide wait'). A further point to take note of is that response times depend on the amount of activity. All systems slow down as load builds up, sometimes seizing-up at peak times. For time-critical applications this type of response is unacceptable, as for example, in auto cruise-control systems, figure 1.3. Here the driver dials in the desired cruising speed. The cruise control computer

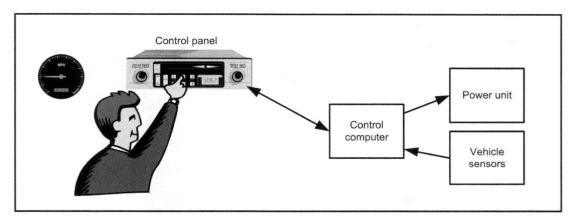

Figure 1.3 Real-time computer system

notes this and compares it with the actual vehicle speed. If there is a difference, correcting signals are sent to the power unit. The vehicle will either speed up or slow down, depending on the desired response. Provided control is executed quickly the vehicle will be powered in a smooth and responsive manner.   But if there is a significant delay in the computer, a kangaroo-like performance occurs. Clearly, in this case, the computer is worse than useless, it degrades the car's performance.

   In this book 'real-time' is taken to imply time-bounded response constraints. Should computer responses exceed specific time bounds then performance degradation and/or malfunction results. So, within this definition, batch and interactive on-line systems are not considered to operate in real-time.

1.2 Real-time computer systems.

1.2.1 Time and criticality issues.

From what's been said so far, one factor distinguishes real-time systems from batch and on-line applications: timeliness. Unfortunately, this is a rather limited definition; a more precise one is needed.   Many ways of categorizing real-time systems have been proposed and are in use.   One particular pragmatic scheme, based on time and criticality, is shown in figure 1.4.   An arbitrary boundary between slow and fast is one second (chosen because problems shift from individual computing issues to overall system aspects at around this point). The related attributes are given in figure 1.5.

   Hard, fast embedded systems tend, in computing terms, to be small (or may be a small, localised part of a larger system). Computation times are short (typically in the tens of milliseconds or faster), and deadlines are critical. Software complexity is usually low, especially in safety-critical work. A good example is the airbag deployment system in motor vehicles. Late deployment defeats the whole purpose of airbag protection.

Time → Criticality ↓	Slow	Fast
Soft	Machine condition monitoring	Man-machine interfacing
Hard	Missile point defence system	Airbag control system

Figure 1.4 Real-time system categorization.

Attribute → Category ↓	Execution time	Deadlines	Software size	Software complexity
Hard-Fast	****	****	*	*
Hard-Slow	*	****	* → ****	* → ****
Soft-Fast	****	**	* → ****	* → ****
Soft-Slow	*	**	* → ****	* → ****

Figure 1.5 Attributes of real-time systems.

Hard, slow systems do not fall into any particular size category (though many, as with process controllers, are small). An illustrative example of such an application is an anti-aircraft missile-based point-defence system for fast patrol boats. Here the total reaction time is in the order of 10 seconds. However, the consequences of failing to respond in this time frame are self-evident.

Larger systems usually include comprehensive, and sometimes complex, human-machine interfaces (HMIs). Such interfaces may form an integral part of the total system operation, as for instance, in integrated weapon fire-control systems. Fast operator responses may be required, but deadlines are not critical as in the previous cases. Significant tolerance can be permitted (in fact, this is generally true when humans form part of system operation). HMI software tends to be large and complex.

The final category, soft/slow, is typified by condition monitoring, trend analysis and statistics analysis in, for example, factory automation. Frequently such software is large and complex. Applications like these may be classified as information processing (IP) systems.

1.2.2 Real-time system structures.

It is clear that the fundamental difference between real-time and other (i.e. batch and interactive) systems is one of timeliness. However, this in itself tells us little about the structure of such computer systems. So, before looking at modern real-time systems, it's worth digressing to consider the set-up of IT-type mainframe installations. While most modern mainframe systems are large and complex (and may be used for a whole variety of jobs) they have many features in common. In the first case, the essential architectures are broadly similar; the real differences lie in the applications themselves and the application software.   Second, the physical environments are usually benign ones, often including air conditioning. Peripheral devices include terminals, PCs, printers, plotters, disks, tapes, communication links; and little else. Common to many mainframe installations is the use of terabytes of disk and tape storage.   The installation itself is staffed and maintained by professional DP personnel. It requires maintenance in the broadest sense, including that for upgrading and modifying programs.   In such a setting it's not surprising that the computer is the focus of attention and concern.

By contrast, real-time systems come in many types and sizes. The largest, in geographical terms, are telemetry control systems, figure 1.6.

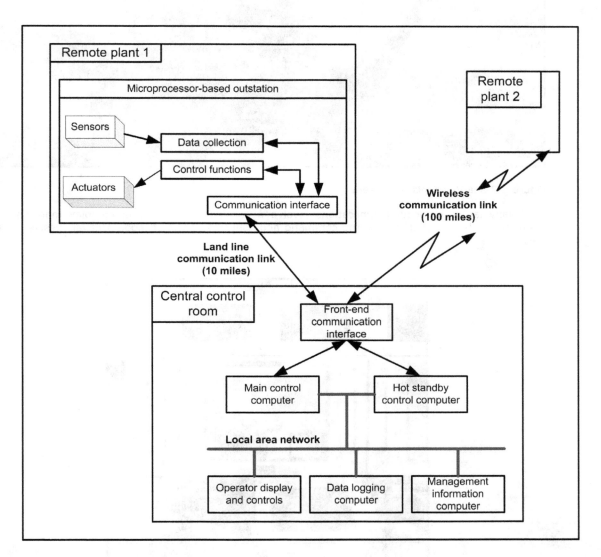

Figure 1.6 Telemetry control system

Such systems are widely used in the gas, oil, water and electricity industries. They provide centralized control and monitoring of remote sites from a single control room.

Smaller in size, but probably more complex in nature, are missile control systems, figure 1.7.

Figure 1.7 Sea Viper missile system

Many larger embedded applications involve a considerable degree of complex man-machine interaction. Typical of these are the command and control systems of modern naval vessels (figure 1.8).

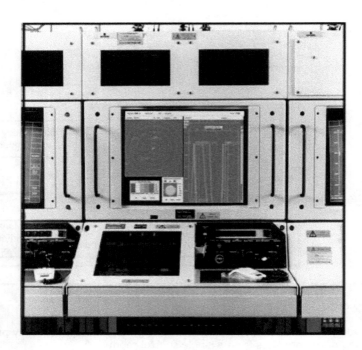

Figure 1.8 Submarine control system console (reproduced with permission from BAE systems).

And of course one of the major application areas of real-time systems is that of avionics, figure 1.9.

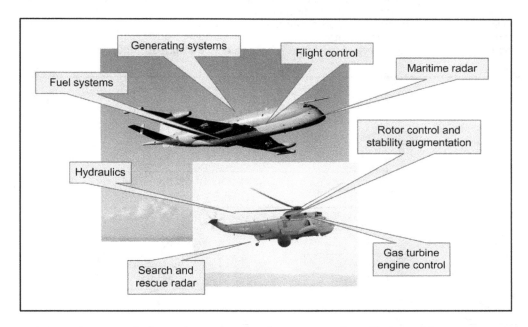

Figure 1.9 Typical avionic platforms (reproduced with permission from Thales Ltd.).

These, in particular, involve numerous hard, fast and safety-critical systems.
   On the industrial scene there are many installations that use computer-based standalone controllers (often for quite dedicated functions).   Applications include vending machines (figure 1.10), printer controllers, anti-lock braking, burglar alarms; the list is endless.

Figure 1.10 Microprocessor-based vending machine units

These examples differ in many detailed ways from DP installations, such factors being discussed below. There are, though, two fundamental points. First, as stated above, the computer is seen to be merely one component of a larger system. Second, the user does not normally have the requirements - or facilities - to modify programs on a day-to-day basis. In practice, most users won't have the knowledge or skill to re-program the machine.

Embedded systems use a variety of hardware architectures ('platforms'), figure 1.11.

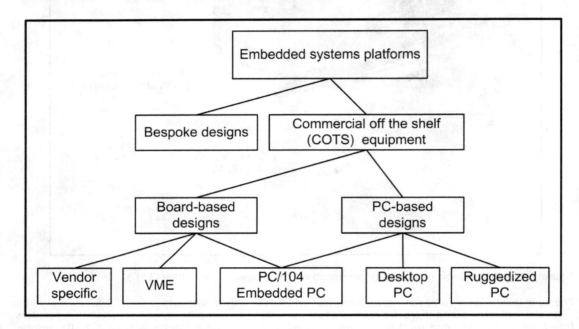

Figure 1.11 Embedded systems platforms

Many are based on special-to-purpose ('bespoke') designs, especially where there are significant constraints such as:

• Environmental aspects (temperature, shock, vibration, humidity, etc.).
• Size and weight (aerospace, auto, telecomms, etc.).
• Cost (auto, consumer goods, etc.).

The advantage of bespoke systems are that products are optimized for the applications. Unfortunately, design and development is a costly and time-consuming process. A much cheaper and faster approach is to use ready-made items, a commercial off-the-shelf (COTS) buying policy. Broadly speaking there are two alternative approaches:

• Base the hardware design on the use of sets of circuit-boards or
• Implement the design using some form of PC.

In reality these aren't mutually exclusive.

(a) COTS board-based designs.
Many vendors offer single-board computer systems, based on particular processors and having a wide range of peripheral boards. In some cases these may be compatible with standard PC buses such as PCI (peripheral component interconnect).   For embedded applications, it is problematic whether

boards from different suppliers can be mixed and matched with confidence. However, where boards are designed to comply with well-defined standards, this can be done (generally) without worry. One great advantage with this is that it doesn't tie a company to one specific supplier. Two standards are particularly important in the embedded world: VME and PC/104.

VME was originally introduced by a number of vendors in 1981, and was later standardized as IEEE standard 1014-1987. It is especially important to developers of military and similar systems, as robust, wide-temperature range boards are available. A second significant standard for embedded applications is PC/104, a cheaper alternative to VME. It is essentially a PC but with a different physical construction, being based on stackable circuit boards (it gets its name from its PC roots and the number of pins used to connect the boards together(104)). At present it is estimated that more than 150 vendors manufacture PC/104 compatible products.

(b) COTS PC-based designs.

Clearly PC/104 designs are PC-based. However, an alternative to the board solution is to use ready-made personal computers. These may be tailored to particular applications by using specialised plug-in boards (e.g. stepper motor drives, data acquisition units, etc.). If the machine is to be located in say an office environment, then a standard desktop computer may be satisfactory. However, these are not designed to cope with conditions met on the factory floor, such as dust, moisture, etc. In such situations ruggedized, industrial standard PCs can be used.   Where reliability, durability and serviceability are concerned, these are immensely superior to the desktop machines.

1.2.3 Characteristics of embedded systems.

Embedded computers are defined to be those where the computer is used as a component within a system: not as a computing engine in its own right.   This definition is the one which, at heart, separates embedded from non-embedded designs   (note that, from now on, 'embedded' implicitly means 'real-time embedded').

Embedded systems are characterized (figure 1.12) by:

• The environments they work in.
• The performance expected of them.
• The interfaces to the outside world.

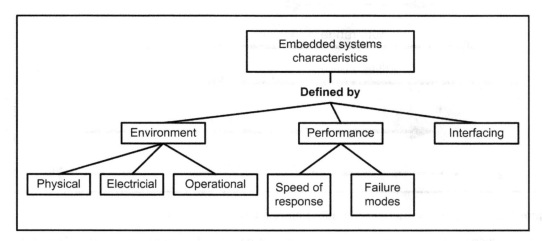

Figure 1.12 Embedded systems characteristics

(a) Environmental aspects.

Environmental factors may, at first glance, seem to have little bearing on software.   Primarily they affect:

- Hardware design and construction.
- Operator interaction with the system.

But these, to a large extent, determine how the complete system works   -   and that defines the overall software requirements. Consider the physical effects of:

- Temperature.
- Shock and vibration.
- Humidity.
- Size limits.
- Weight limits.

The temperature ranges commonly met in embedded applications are shown in figure 1.13.

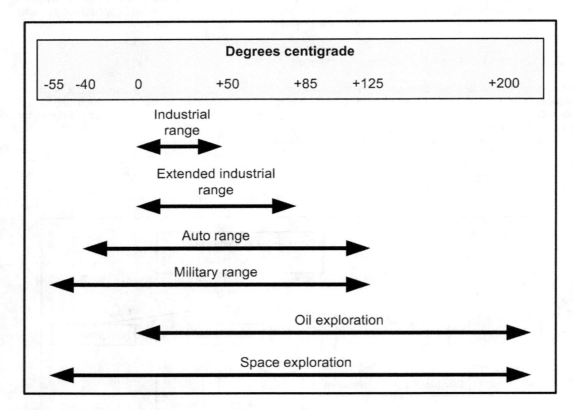

Figure 1.13 Typical temperature specifications for real-time applications

Many components used in commercial computers are designed to operate in the band 0-30 degrees centigrade. Electronic components aren't usually a problem. Items like terminals, display units and hard disks are the weaknesses. As a result, the embedded designer must either do without them or else provide them with a protected environment - which can be a costly solution. When the requirements to withstand shock, vibration and water penetration are added , the options narrow. For instance, the ideal way to re-program a system might be to update the system using a flash card. But if we can't use this technology because of environmental factors, then what?

Size and weight are two factors uppermost in the minds of many embedded systems designers. For vehicle systems, such as automobiles, aircraft, armoured fighting vehicles and submarines, they may be the crucial factors.   Not much to do with software, you may think.   But suppose a design requirement can only be met by using a single-chip micro (see later).   Further, suppose that this device has only 256 bytes of random access memory (RAM).   How does that affect our choice of programming language?

The electrical environments of industrial and military systems are not easy to work in. Yet most systems are expected to cope with extensive power supply variations in a predictable manner. To handle problems like this we may have to resort to defensive programming techniques (chapter 2). Program malfunction can result from electrical interference; again, defensive programming is needed to handle this.   A further complicating factor in some systems is that the available power may be limited.   This won't cause difficulties in small systems.   But if your software needs 10 gigabytes of dynamic RAM to run in, the power system designers are going to face problems.

Let's now turn to the operational environmental aspects of embedded systems. Normally we expect that when the power is turned on the system starts up safely and correctly. It should do this every time, and without any operator intervention. Conversely, when the power is turned off, the system should also behave safely. What we design for are 'fit and forget' functions.

In many instances embedded systems have long operational lives, perhaps from ten to thirty years. Often it is required to upgrade the equipment a number of times in its lifetime. So, the software itself will also need upgrading. This aspect of software, its maintenance, may well affect how we design it in the first place.

(b) Performance.
Two particular factors are important here:

● How fast does a system respond?
● When it fails, what happens?

(i) The speed of response.
All required responses are time critical (although these may vary from microseconds to days). Therefore the designer should predict the delivered performance of the embedded system. Unfortunately, with the best will in the world, it may not be possible to give 100% guarantees. The situation is complicated because there are two distinct sides to this issue - both relating to the way tasks are processed by the computer.

Case one concerns demands to run jobs at regular, pre-defined intervals. A typical application is that of closed-loop digital controllers having fixed, preset sampling rates. This we'll define to be a 'synchronous' or 'periodic' task event (synchronous with some real-time clock - figure 1.14).

Case two occurs when the computer must respond to (generally) external events which occur at random ('asynchronous' or 'aperiodic').   And the event must be serviced within a specific maximum time period.   Where the computer handles only periodic events, response times can be determined reasonably well.   This is also true where only one aperiodic event drives the system (a rare event), figure 1.15.

When the system has to cope with a number of asynchronous events, estimates are difficult to arrive at.   But by setting task priorities, good estimates of worst case performance can be deduced (figure 1.16). As shown here task 1 has higher priority than task 2.

Where we get into trouble is in situations which involve a mixture of periodic and aperiodic events - which are usual in real-time designs.   Much thought and skill are needed to deal with the response requirements of periodic and aperiodic tasks (especially when using just one processor).

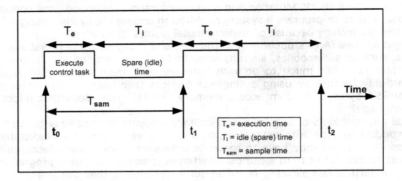

Figure 1.14 Computer loading - single synchronous (periodic) task

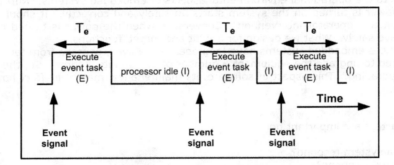

Figure 1.15 Computer loading - single asynchronous (aperiodic) task

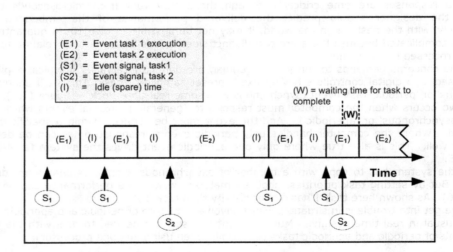

Figure 1.16 Computer loading - multiple asynchronous (aperiodic) tasks

(ii) Failures and their effects.

All systems go wrong at some time in their lives. It may be a transient condition or a hard failure; the cause may be hardware or software or a combination of both. It really doesn't matter; accept that it will happen. What we have to concern ourselves with are:

- The consequences of such faults and failures.
- Why the problem(s) arose in the first place.

Because a system can tolerate faults without sustaining damage doesn't mean that such performance is acceptable. Nuisance tripping out of a large piece of plant, for instance, is not going to win many friends.   All real-time software must therefore be designed in a professional manner to handle all foreseen problems, that is, 'exception' handling (an exception is defined here to be an error or fault which produces program malfunction, see chapter 2. It may originate within the program itself or be due to external factors). If, on the other hand, software packages are bought in, their quality must be assessed. Regularly claims are made concerning the benefits of using Windows operating systems in real-time applications. Yet users of such systems often experience unpredictable behaviour, including total system hang-up. Could this really be trusted for plant control and similar applications?

In other situations we may not be able to cope with unrectified system faults. Three options are open to us.   In the first, where no recovery action is possible, the system is put into a fail-safe condition.   In the second, the system keeps on working, but with reduced service. This may be achieved, say, by reducing response times or by servicing only the 'good' elements of the system. Such systems are said to offer 'graceful' degradation in their response characteristics. Finally, for fault tolerant operation, full and safe performance is maintained in the presence of faults.

(c) Interfacing.

The range of devices which interface to embedded computers is extensive.   It includes sensors, actuators, motors, switches, display panels, serial communication links, parallel communication methods, analogue-to-digital converters, digital-to-analogue converters, voltage-to-frequency converters, pulse-width modulated controllers and so on. Signals may be analogue (d.c. or a.c.) or digital; voltage, current or frequency encoding methods may be used. In anything but the smallest systems hardware size is dominated by the interfacing electronics. This has a profound effect on system design strategies concerning processor replication and exception handling.

When the processor itself is the major item in a system, fitting a back-up to cope with failures is feasible and sensible. Using this same approach in an input-output (I/O) dominated system makes much less sense (and introduces much complexity).

Conventional exception handling schemes are usually concerned with detecting internal (program) problems. These include stack overflow, array bound violations and arithmetic overflow. However, for most real-time systems a new range of problems has to be considered. These relate to factors such as sensor failure, illegal operator actions, program malfunction induced by external interference, etc. Detecting such faults is one thing; deciding what to do subsequently can be an even more difficult problem.   Exception-handling strategies need careful design to prevent faults causing system or environmental damage (or worse - injury or death).

1.3 The computing elements of real-time systems.

1.3.1 Overview.

In real-time systems, computing elements are destined for use in either general-purpose or specialized applications, figure 1.17.

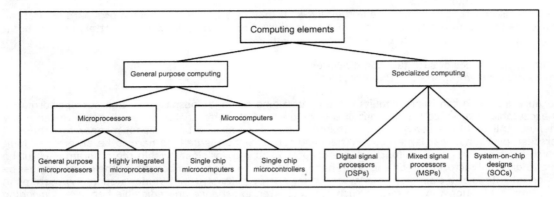

Figure 1.17 The computing elements of real-time systems

To use these effectively, the software designer should have a good understanding of their features. After all, what might be an excellent design solution for one application might be ghastly (or even unusable) in others.

1.3.2 General purpose microprocessors.

General purpose microprocessors were originally the core building blocks of microcomputer systems. Although they are much less common nowadays they form a good starting point for this topic.

By itself the processor is only one element within the microprocessor system. To turn it into a computing machine certain essential elements need to be added (figure 1.18). The program code

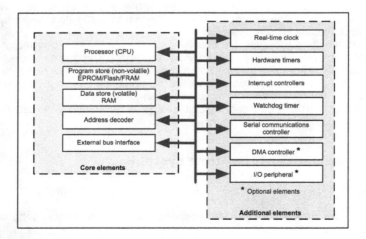

Figure 1.18 Elements of a microcomputer system

itself is stored in memory which, for embedded systems, must be retained on power-down. That is, the memory must be 'non-volatile'. Older designs typically used ultra-violet erasable (electrically) programmable ROM (EPROM). The drawback with this device is that (normally) it must be removed from the computer for erasure and re-programming. However, where in-circuit re-programming is required, code is located in electrically erasable/ programmable non-volatile storage, the alternatives being:

• Electrically erasable programmable ROM (EEPROM).
• Flash memory (a particular type of EEPROM technology).
• Ferroelectric random access memory (FRAM).

Flash memory has, to a large extent, replaced EPROM in new designs.
   When large production quantities are concerned, two approaches may be used:

• Mask-programmable devices.
• One-time programmable ROM (OTPROM).

In the first case the program is set in the memory by the chip manufacturer; as such it is unalterable. The second method is essentially an EPROM device without a light window. Nowadays this market sector usually uses single chip microcomputers rather that general purpose ones.
   All data which is subject to regular change is located in read-write 'random-access' memory (a confusing term, as memory locations, for most devices, can be accessed randomly). This includes program variables, stack data, process descriptors and dynamic data items.
   The final element is the address decoder unit. Its function is to identify the element being accessed by the processor.
   Taken together, these items form the heart of the microcomputer. However, to make it usable in real-time applications, extra elements need to be added. The key items are:

• Real-time clock.
• Hardware timers.
• Interrupt controller
• Watchdog timer.
• Serial communication controller.

Items which should also be considered at the design stage include:

• Direct memory access (DMA) controllers.
• I/O peripheral controllers (only where large volume data transfer is required).

These may be essential in some systems but not in others.

(a) Interrupt controllers.
As pointed out earlier, real-time systems must support both periodic and aperiodic tasks. In most designs "guaranteed" response times are obtained by using interrupts.

(b) Real-time clock.
The function of the real-time clock is to provide a highly accurate record of elapsed time. It is normally used in conjunction with an interrupt function. Real-time clocks shouldn't be confused with calendar clocks (although they may be used for calendar functions). When an operating system is incorporated within the software the clock acts as the basic timing element (the 'tick').

(c)Hardware timers.
Accurate timing, especially that involving long time periods, cannot normally be done in software. Without the timing support of the tick in an operating system, hardware timers have to be used. Even when an operating system is used, these timers provide great flexibility. Generally these are software

programmable (figure 1.19), both in terms of timing and modes of operation (e.g. square-wave generation, 'one-shot' pulse outputs and retriggerable operation.

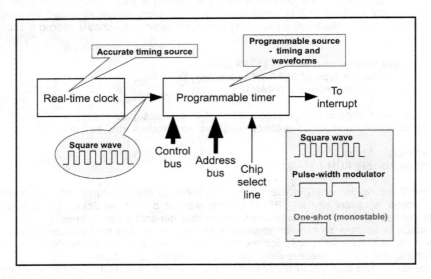

Figure 1.19 Timing in hardware

(d) Watchdog timer.

The purpose of the watchdog timer is to act as the last line of defence against program malfunction. It normally consists of a retriggerable monostable or one-shot timer, activated by a program write command (figure 1.20). Each time the timer is signalled it is retriggered, the output staying in the

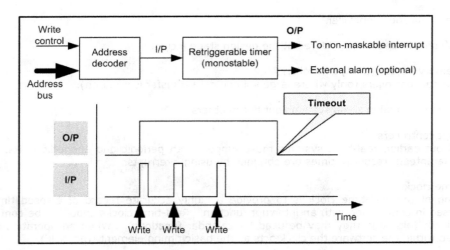

Figure 1.20 Watchdog timer

'normal' state. If for any reason it isn't retriggered then time-out occurs, and the output goes into alarm conditions. The usual course of action is to then generate a non-maskable interrupt (NMI), so setting a recovery program into action. In some instances external warnings are also produced. In others, especially digital control systems, warnings are produced and the controller then isolated from the controlled process.

Address decoding of the watchdog timer is, for critical systems, performed over all bits of the address. In these circumstances the address is a unique one; hence retriggering by accident is virtually eliminated.

(e) Serial communications controllers.

Serial communications facilities are integral parts of many modern embedded systems. However, even where this isn't needed, it is well worth while to design in a USB and/or an RS232 compatible communication channel. These can be used as major aids in the development and debugging of the application software (see Book 2).

(f) DMA controllers.

The DMA controller (figure 1.21) is used where data has to be moved about quickly and/or in large

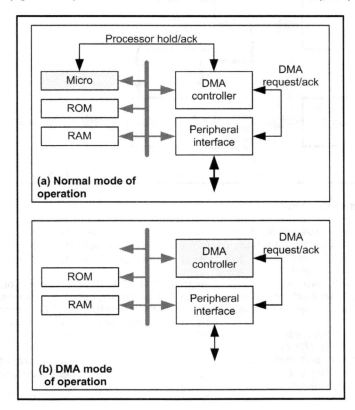

Figure 1.21 DMA operation

amounts (data rates can exceed 1 Gbyte/sec). DMA techniques are widely used in conjunction with bulk memory storage devices such as hard disks and compact disks. For many real-time systems they are frequently used where high-speed serial communication links have to be supported.

   In normal circumstances (the 'normal' mode of operation, figure 1.21(a)), the controller acts just like any other slave device, being controlled by the processor. However, when a DMA request is generated by a peripheral device, control is taken over by the DMA controller (figure 1.21(b)). In this case the micro is electrically disconnected from the rest of the system. Precise details of data transfer operations are usually programmed into the controller by the micro.

(g) I/O peripheral.

I/O peripherals are used either as controllers or as interfacing devices. When used as a controller, their function is to offload routine I/O processing, control and high-speed transfer work from the processor itself, figure 1.22.

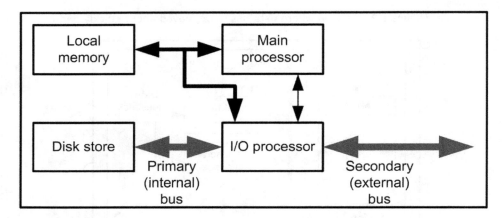

Figure 1.22 Intelligent I/O processing

One of the most common uses of such devices is to handle high-speed large volume data transfers to and from hard disk. They are especially useful in dealing with replicated memory storage units, as with replicated arrays of independent disk (RAID) technology. Other applications include intelligent bus, network and communications interfacing.

   The I/O controller's basic operation is similar to that of a DMA controller, but with two major differences. First, it can work co-operatively with the processor, using system resources when the processor is busy. Second, I/O processors are much more powerful than DMA devices. For example, the Intel i960 IOP includes (amongst other items) a high-speed parallel bus bridge, a specialized serial bus interface, internal DMA controllers and a performance monitoring unit.

   In other applications I/O devices are used to provide compact, simple and low-cost interfaces between the processor and peripheral equipment, figure 1.23. Input/output pins are user-programmable to set up the desired connections to such equipment. These interface chips function as slave devices to the processing unit.

1.3.3 Highly integrated microprocessors.

Highly integrated processors are those which contain many of the standard elements of a microcomputer system on a single chip. A typical example is the NXP MPC8240 integrated processor (figure 1.24).

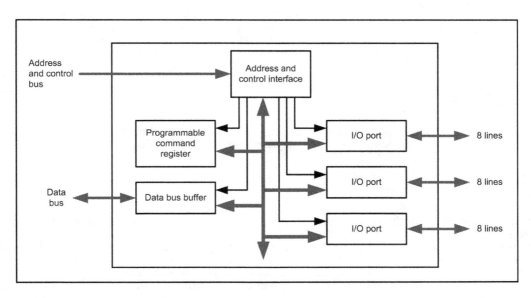

Figure 1.23 I/O interface peripheral

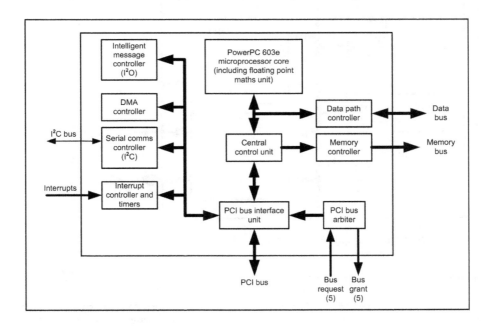

Figure 1.24 Highly integrated processor - NXP MPC8240

A comparison of figure 1.18 and figure 1.24 shows just what can be achieved on one chip (the MPC8240, for example, reduces the chip count from eight to one).   Naturally, such processors are more expensive than the basic general purpose device.   However, the integration of many devices onto one chip usually reduces overall system cost.   Moreover, it makes a major impact on board-packing densities, which also reduces manufacturing and test costs.   In short, these are highly suited for use in embedded systems design.

1.3.4 Single chip microcomputers.

With modern technology complete microcomputers can be implemented on a single chip, eliminating the need for external components.   Using the single-chip solution reduces the:

- Package count.
- Size.
- Overall costs.

One widely used device of this type is the 8052 microcomputer, a Microchip variant being shown in figure 1.25.
  By now all the on-chip devices will be familiar.   Note that the interfacing to the outside world may be carried out through the I/O port sub-system.   This is a highly flexible structure which, in smaller systems, minimizes component count.   But with only 8 kBytes of ROM and 256 bytes of RAM, it is clearly intended for use in small systems (the memory size can, of course, be extended by using external devices).

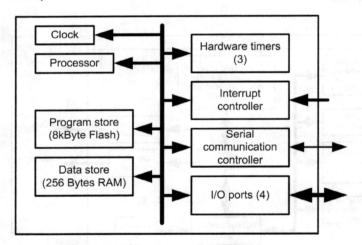

Figure 1.25 Single chip microcomputer - Microchip AT89C52

1.3.5 Single chip microcontrollers.

Microcontrollers are derivatives of microcomputers, but aimed specifically at the embedded control market (though the boundary between the two is becoming somewhat blurred).   Like single chip microcomputers they are designed to provide all necessary computing functions in a single package. Broadly speaking there are two categories: general-purpose (sector independent) and sector-specific. These differ only in the actual internal devices included on the chip.   For sector-specific units the on-chip devices are chosen to provide support specifically for that sector. In particular they try to provide all required functionality *on the chip*, so minimizing the need for (extra) external hardware.

An example of such a device, aimed at automotive body electronic applications, is that shown in figure 1.26, the STMicroelectronics SPC560 series chip.

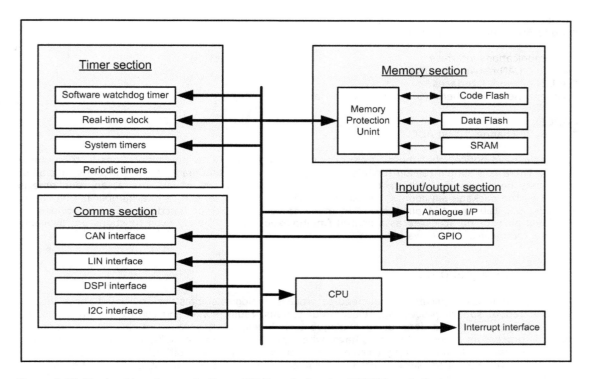

Figure 1.26 Single chip microcontroller - STMicroelectronics SPC560 main features

Like many modern microcontrollers it contains an impressive set of functions:

• Memory:
‾ Up to 512 Kbytes Code Flash, with error correcting code (ECC).
‾ 64 Kbytes Data Flash, with error correcting code.
‾ Up to 48 Kbytes SRAM, with error correcting code.
‾ Memory protection unit (MPU).

• Interrupts:
‾ Up to 24 external interrupts.

• GPIO:
Between 45 and 123, depending on the IC package type.

- Timers:
 - 6-channel periodic interrupt timers.
 - 4-channel system timer module.
 - Software watchdog timer.
 - Real-time clock timer.

- I/O:
 - Up to 56 channels counter-time-triggered I/Os.

- Communications interface:
 - Up to 6 CAN network interfaces.
 - 4 LIN network interfaces.
 - Others: Serial Peripheral (SPI) and I2C Interfaces.

- ADC:
 - Up to 36 channel 10-bit ADC.

You might have noticed that the diagram of figure 1.26 doesn't show any connections to the outside world. There is a simple reason for this. Although the device has many, many functions, not all of these may be accessed simultaneously. In practice what you can actually use at *any one time* is limited by the package pin count. The SPC560 series, for example, comes in a number of chip sizes, including 64, 100 and 144 pin types. In many cases a number of functions may be provided on individual pins, being accessed as a shared (multiplexed) item. Clearly such functions are available only in a mutually-exclusive way.

1.3.6 Digital signal processors.

There are numerous applications that need to process analogue signals very quickly. These include instrumentation, speech processing, telecommunications, radar, sonar and control systems. In the past such processing was done using analogue techniques. But because of the disadvantages of analogue processors (filters), designers have, where possible, moved to digital techniques. Central to this is the use of digital filtering calculations, typified by sets of multiply and add (accumulate) instructions (the so-called 'sum of products' computation). The important characteristics of such systems are that they:

- Have extremely high throughputs.
- Are optimized for numerical operations.
- Employ a small number of repetitive numerical calculations.
- Are usually low-cost.

These needs have, for some time now been met by a device specialised for such work: the digital signal processor (DSP).
    To achieve high processing speeds, the basic computing engine is organized around a high-speed multiplier/accumulator combination (figure 1.27) In these designs the Von Neumann structure is replaced by the Harvard architecture, having separate paths for instruction and data. The system form shown in figure 1.27 is fairly typical of digital signal processors. Obviously, specific details vary from processor to processor, see http://www.ti.com/processors/dsp/overview.html for further information.
    Programming DSPs is a demanding task, especially working at assembly language level. The instruction sets are carefully chosen to perform fast, efficient and effective arithmetic. Among those instructions are ones that invoke complex multipurpose operations. Added to this is the need to produce compact and efficient code if the whole program is to fit into the on-chip ROM. And finally,

there is the need to handle extensive fixed-point computations without running into overflow problems. It used to be said that, in fixed-point DSP programming '90% of the effort goes into worrying about where the decimal point is'. Fortunately this is much less of a problem nowadays as word lengths of 32 or 64 bits are commonplace.

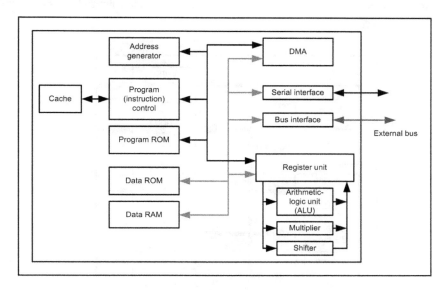

Figure 1.27 Digital signal processor structure

A final point: the classical DSP processor is being challenged by 'conventional' processors that include DSP instructions. One such example is the ARM NEON SIMD (single instruction multiple data) architecture extension for their Cortex series processors: see https://developer.arm.com/technologies/dsp

1.3.7 Mixed signal processors.

Mixed signal processors, as their name suggests, are designed to interface simultaneously to analogue and digital components. The Texas MSP430, for example (figure 1.28, the G2 variant), is aimed at battery-powered applications (such as multimeters, intelligent sensing, etc.) where low power consumption is paramount. Quoted figures (typical) for power requirements are:

(i)   Active: 230 µA at 1MHz, 2.2 volts.
(ii) Standby: 0.5 µA.
(iii) Off mode (RAM retention): 0.1µA.

Work like this could be done by a standard microcontroller, but this is a relatively costly solution. Hence mixed signal processors are optimized for use in low cost, high-volume products.

1.3.8 System-on-chip designs - overview.

A system on chip device (SOC) is an integrated circuit (IC) that integrates all components of a microcomputer or microcontroller (or other electronic system) into a single chip. Thus the Microchip AT89C52 (figure 1.25) and the MSP430 (figure 1.28) are, in fact, SOC devices. ICs like these have capabilities designed for *general* use within *specific* sectors (e.g. the 89C52 for embedded controller applications, the MSP430 for metering systems). Their place in the SOC technology range is shown in figure 1.29 (please note; this is a simplified view of the topic, being limited to the more important device types).

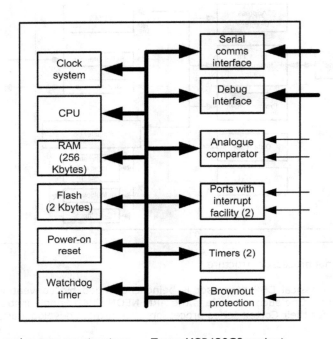

Figure 1.28 Mixed signal processor structure - Texas MSP430G2 variant

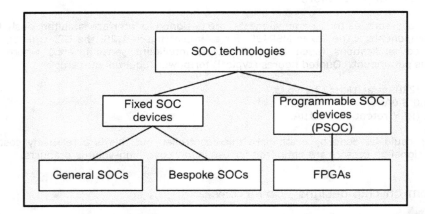

Figure 1.29 SOC technologies - simplified view

One of the key aspects here is that their hardware functionality is fixed by the manufacturer; it cannot be changed by the user. What these devices also have in common is that the processors themselves are company-specific. However, in the past few years there has been a major trend by chip designers to buy-in the processor designs. Such components are usually called 'virtual components', 'virtual cores' (VCs) or 'intellectual property (IP) cores'. Probably the most important company in this area is ARM (especially in the 32 and 64 bit field); you'll find their 'products' incorporated in many, many SOC devices.

One drawback with using general purpose SOC ICs is that designs may have to be extensively tailored to meet specific application needs.   Other factors may also be important, e.g. power consumption, temperature range, radiation hardness, etc. Such needs can be met by using bespoke system-on-chip (SOC) devices, these essentially being specialized single-chip *application-specific* designs.

Now, application-specific integrated circuit (ASIC) technology is not new. Electronic engineers have been using it for many years to produce specialized devices (e.g. ICs for advanced signal processing, image stabilization, digital filtering, etc.). Design itself is performed typically using computer-aided design (CAD) methods based on very high-level description language (VHDL) programming.   SOC design methods are fundamentally the same but the implementations are much more complex. In particular, they incorporate microprocessor(s) and memory devices, etc. to form full on-chip microcomputers or microcontrollers. Applications include digital cameras, wireless communication, engine management, specialised peripherals and complex signal processing. Typical of this technology is the Snapdragon SOC suite from Qualcomm Inc, intended for use in mobile devices (https://www.qualcomm.com/products/snapdragon).

Figure 1.30 is a representative structure of an SOC unit, though by definition there are many variations of such structures.

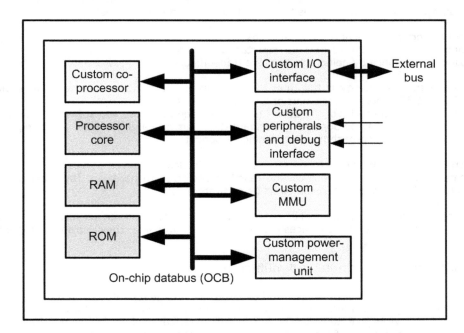

Figure 1.30 Example system-on-a-chip design

The sub-systems shown here fall into two groups, 'custom' and other. Anything designed by the chip-designer is labelled custom; the others represent bought-in items (e.g. microprocessor, RAM, ROM). Of course, because this is chip-fabrication, we cannot 'plug-in' such items onto the chip. What happens typically is that VHDL descriptions of the components are used within the overall design process. The end result of the design process is a 'manufacturing' file which is then sent to a chip manufacturer.

1.3.9 Programmable SOCs - FPGA embedded processors.

The customized SOC technology described above has some major drawbacks.   First, having a specialized chip manufactured can be quite costly. Second, it isn't exactly a fast process; typically the manufacturing process takes six to eight weeks, done in highly specialized semiconductor fabrication plants.   Third, modifying the design and producing a new chip is both costly and time-consuming. Fourth, it isn't suitable for low-volume product production because of the costs involved. Fortunately, for many applications, these obstacles can be overcome by using programmable SOC (PSOC) technology.   And one of the most important devices here is the Field Programmable Gate Array (FPGA).

An FPGA is a general-purpose digital device that consists of sets of electronic building blocks. You, the designer, set the functionality of the FPGA by configuring these blocks, typically using VHDL design methods. This, which requires specialized design knowledge, is normally done by hardware engineers. Software engineers haven't generally concerned themselves with the detailed aspects of FPGAs, treating them merely as peripheral devices. However, things have changed as a result of FPGA chip manufacturers embedding silicon cores into their devices, the 'FPGA embedded processor'. As a result we have some very compelling reasons to go down the FPGA route, such as:

- Producing custom products at a reasonable cost.
- Minimizing component count (especially important when size is constrained).
- Maximizing performance by being able to make tradeoffs between software and hardware.

An example of this technology is the Intel Nios processor, figure 1.31.   Its use in an application is shown in figure 1.32, where it forms part of a Cyclone V FPGA.

Here the overall functionality of the device is split between hardware and software. For devices like these all programming may be done in C: standard C for software and System C (or its equivalent) for the hardware. Such an approach has two significant benefits:

- It's much easier to get hold of C programmers than VHDL designers.
- Algorithms, etc. coded in software can be readily transferred to hardware (by making only minor changes to the C code and then recompiling using System C).

And remember: the device functionality can always be modified without us having to make actual physical hardware changes. Thus devices are not only programmable; they're also re-programmable.

1.3.10 SOC devices - single and multicore.

A single core device is defined to be a chip that contains just one CPU (thus all conventional microprocessors can be considered to be examples of single core designs). However, SOC technology has given rise to devices that consist of two or more cores, called multicore chips. This structure is now a very important feature of high-performance microcontrollers; at present the claimed record for the greatest number of cores on a single chip is 100 ARM CPUs, made by the company EZchip, www.tilera.com).

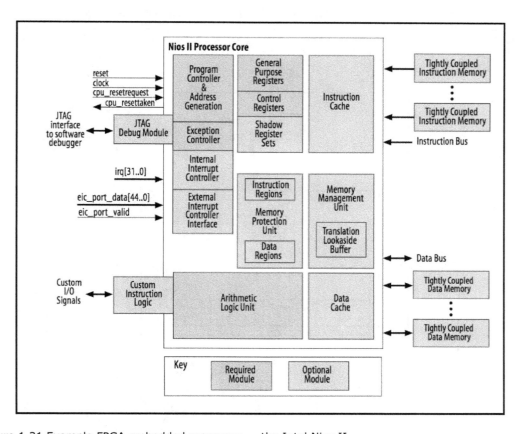

Figure 1.31 Example FPGA embedded processor - the Intel Nios II.

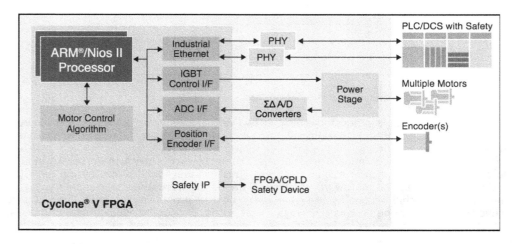

Figure1.32 Example embedded processor FPGA application.

Figure 1.33 shows the makeup of a typical small multicore-based SOC integrated circuit. Here the multicore processor consists of two CPUs together with key processor-related devices: interrupt management, memory and timers. This processor is embedded within a single chip microcontroller that also includes various real-world devices.

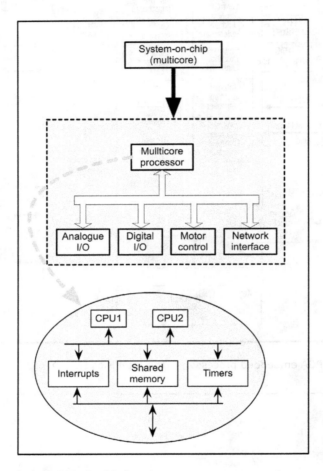

Fig.1.33 SOC multicore designs in embedded systems

From a hardware perspective processors come in two forms: symmetric and asymmetric. Basically, with a symmetric multiprocessor design, all the processing units are identical; with asymmetric multiprocessors the units differ.

An example of an embedded multicore symmetric multiprocessor is the Arm Cortex A9, figure 1.34 showing a simplified description of its key features. This has four identical processing units (cores), each one consisting of a CPU, hardware accelerator, debug interface and cache memory. It can be seen that several on-chip resources are shared by all the processing units.   From a software perspective the device can be used in two ways. First, each core can be allocated specific tasks, and hence is considered to be a dedicated resource.   Second, any core can run any task, thus being treated as an anonymous resource.

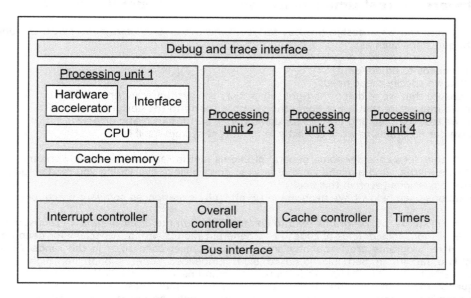

Fig.1.34 Example symmetric multiprocessor - multicore implementation

An example of an asymmetric multicore multiprocessor is the Texas TMS320DM6443, figure 1.35.

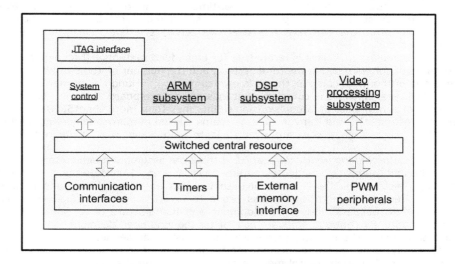

Fig.1.35 Example asymmetric multiprocessor - multicore implementation

In this device there are two distinct processing units, one for general purpose computing and the other for digital signal processing.

One final small point: cores are defined to be 'hard' or 'soft'. Where the actual silicon of a processor is used as the core it is said to be hard. But when the core is implemented using design file data then it is a soft one.

1.4 Software for real-time applications - some general comments

In later chapters the total design process for real-time systems is described.   We'll be looking for answers to questions such as:

- What truly needs to be done?
- How should we specify these needs?
- How we ensure that we're doing the right job (satisfy the system requirements)?
- How can we make sure that we're doing the job right (perform the design correctly)?
- How can we test the resulting designs for correctness, performance and errors?
- How do we get programs to work correctly in the target system itself?

Before doing this, let's consider some general problems met in real-time systems work and also dispel a few software myths. And a useful word of advice; don't believe everything you read - question any unsupported assertions (even in this book).

   The quotations used below have been made (in print) by experienced software practitioners.

'For real-time systems ..... programs tend to be large, often in the order of tens of thousands or even of hundreds of thousands of lines of code'. This generalization is wrong, especially for deep embedded systems. Here programs are frequently small, having object code sizes in the range 2-64 kBytes (however, two factors in particular tend to bloat embedded code: support for highly-interactive graphical user interfaces and support for internet communication protocols). It is a great mistake (one frequently made) to apply the rules of large systems to small ones.

   'At the specification stage .... all the functional requirements, performance requirements and design constraints must be specified'. In the world of real-time system design this is an illusion. Ideas like these have come about mostly from the DP world. There, systems such as stock control, accounting, management reporting methods and the like can be specified in their entirety before software design commences.   In contrast, specifications for real-time systems tend to follow an evolutionary development.   We may start with an apparently clear set of requirements.   At a much later stage (usually some time after the software has been delivered) the final, clear, but quite different specifications are agreed.

   'Software costs dominate ....' This is rarely true for embedded systems. It all depends on the size of the job, the role of software within the total system, and the number of items to be manufactured.

   'Software is one of the most complex things known to man   ... Hundreds of man years to develop system XXX'. Well, yes, software is complex. But let's not go overboard about it. Just consider that the development of a new nuclear propulsion for submarines took more than 5000 man-years (at a very conservative estimate).   And it involved large teams, skilled in many engineering disciplines, and based at various geographically separate sites.   Is this an 'easy' task compared with software development.

   'Software, by its nature, is inherently unreliable'. I think the assumption behind this is that software is a product of thought, and isn't bounded by natural physical laws. Therefore there is a much greater chance a making mistakes.   This is rather like saying that as circuit theory underpins electronic design, hardware designs are intrinsically less prone to errors.   Not so.   Delivered hardware is generally free of fault because design, development and manufacture is (or should be) rigorous, formal and systematic. By contrast, software has for far too long been developed in a sloppy manner in cottage industry style.   The industry (especially the industrial embedded world) has lacked design formality, has rarely used software design tools, and almost completely ignored the use of documentation and configuration control mechanisms. Look out for the classic hacker comment: 'my code is the design'.

   The final point for consideration concerns the knowledge and background needed by embedded systems software designers. In the early days of microprocessor systems there was an intimate bond between hardware and software. It was (and, in many cases, still is) essential to have a very good understanding of the hardware: especially so for the I/O activities. Unfortunately, in recent years a gulf has developed between hardware and software engineers. As a result it is increasingly difficult to find engineers with the ability to bridge this gap effectively. Moreover, larger and larger jobs are being implemented using microprocessors. Allied to this has been an explosion in the use of software-based real-time systems. As a result, more and more software is being developed by people who have little knowledge of hardware or systems. We may not like the situation, but that's the way it is. To cope with this, there has been a change in software design methodologies. Now the design philosophy is to provide a 'software base' for handling hardware and system specific tasks. This is sometimes called 'foundation' or 'service' software. Programmers can then build their application programs on the foundation software, needing only a minimal understanding of the system hardware. The greatest impact of this has been in the area of real-time operating systems.

1.5 Review

You should now:

- Clearly understand the important features of real-time systems.
- Know what sets them apart from batch and interactive applications.
- See how real-time systems may be categorized in terms of speed and criticality.
- Have a general understanding of the range of real-time (and especially embedded) applications.
- Realize that environmental and performance factors are key drivers in real-time systems design.
- Know the basic component parts of real-time computer units.
- Appreciate the essential differences between microprocessors, microcomputers and microcontrollers.
- Realize why there is a large market for specialized processors.

1.6 Useful reading material

Advanced HW/SW Embedded System for Designers 2017, Lennart Lindh Tommy Klevin Mia Lindh.
https://www.amazon.co.uk/

DSP benchmarking suite.
 http://www.bdti.com/procsum/index.htm.

EIA standard 232: Interface between data terminal equipment and data communication equipment employing serial binary data interchange, Electronic Industries Association, 1969.
https://en.wikipedia.org/wiki/RS-232#Related_standards

PC/104 embedded solutions, www.pc104.org.

System C tutorial.
https://embedded.eecs.berkeley.edu/Respep/Research/hsc/class/ee249/lectures/l10-SystemC.pdf

The designers guide to VHDL, Peter Ashenden, Morgan Kaufmann, ISBN 1558606742.
https://www.amazon.co.uk/Designers-Guide-VHDL-Systems-Silicon/dp/0120887851/ref=sr_1_1?ie=UTF8&qid=1521623316&sr=8-1&keywords=the+designer%27s+guide+to+vhdl

The mythical man-month, F.P.Brooks, Addison-Wesley.
https://www.amazon.co.uk/Mythical-Man-Month-Software-Engineering-Anniversary/dp/0201835959

VME - Versa Module Europa, IEEE Std. 1014-1987, www.vmebus-systems.com.

END OF CHAPTER

Chapter 2

The search for dependable software

Many steps have to be taken to combat the problems of poor software. Proper system specification, defined design methods, high-level language support and good development tools all contribute toward a solution. But to appreciate their use (instead of merely knowing what they do), we must understand what they aim to achieve. To answer that we need to know where, why and how software problems arise. Then at least we can define the features of software and software design which can eliminate such problems.

 The aims of this chapter are to:
- Show where, why and how software errors arise.
- Explain why, in the real world, development of fault-free systems cannot be achieved.
- Distinguish between correct, reliable and safe software.
- Establish that dependable software should be a primary design aim.
- Highlight the importance and influence of the software operating environment.
- Establish the basics of good software.
- Describe the need for, and use of, defensive programming.
- Show that, in a professional software design environment, codes of practice are a key element.

2.1 What do we want in our software?

In an ideal world, what do we look for in our software? There are many answers to this question, but, more than anything else, one stands out: the production of totally fault-free software. We look for that because, we reason, given such software, our systems should work exactly as planned. But will they? Unfortunately not necessarily so, as will be shown later. When designing software a total system view must be taken. There are too many opportunities to get designs and implementations wrong; it isn't just confined to the code writing stage.

 In this chapter we'll first look at the root problems of such errors. Then we'll define the qualities of software which attempt to eliminate these. One must be realistic about them, however. Given the current state of design tools it is impossible to guarantee the delivery of fault-free systems (on a personal note, I believe that totally fault-free systems are a myth).

 Therefore, if fault-free systems are unattainable, what should we aim for? A different, realistic, criterion is needed, that of 'dependable software', having the qualities shown in figure 2.1. Many people, when asked to define fault-free software, talk about 'correct' software. But what is correct software? The *Dictionary of Computing* defines correctness as 'the static property that a program is consistent with its specification'. In other words, if we check the code against the job specification, it does exactly what is asked of it.

 On the other hand, reliability is concerned with the intended function of the system. The IEEE definition of software reliability is 'the extent to which a program can be expected to perform its intended function with required precision'. That is, it defines how well a program carries out the required task when asked to do so. Thus it is a measure of the dynamic performance of the software.

 Can a correct program be unreliable? Conversely, can an incorrect program be reliable? The answer in each case is, surprisingly, yes. Consider the first question. Let's suppose that a program

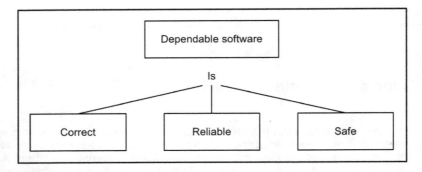

Figure 2.1 Qualities of dependable software

has been checked out statically and shown to be correct. Subsequently, when installed in a system, it behaves in an unexpected way. In this situation it hasn't performed its intended function. So the program is deemed to be unreliable. This really means that the design specification wasn't right in the first place.

Now let's turn to the second one. Assume that we've written a program to implement a control algorithm in a closed loop control system. This should produce results with a given, predefined, accuracy. If it fails to do this then clearly it is incorrect. Yet, if the errors are small, the control loop will work quite well. In this instance it performs its intended function satisfactorily. Thus the program is deemed to be reliable.

The terms 'safe software' and 'reliable software' are often used loosely to mean the same thing. They are, in fact, very different. In extreme cases, the aims of reliability and safety may conflict.

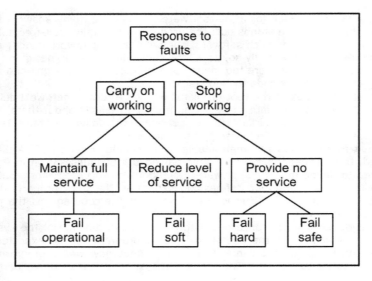

Figure 2.2 System behaviour under fault conditions

Where software is designed with safety in mind, it is concerned with the consequences of failure. Such consequences usually involve injury or death and/or material damage. Reliability is concerned with failures per se. A system can be 100% reliable, yet be totally unsafe. And, as a ludicrous example, a system can be 100% safe but 0% reliable if it is never switched on.

All designs aim for high reliability (it goes without saying that we would like our programs to be correct as well). By contrast the emphasis put on safeness depends on each particular task. Any real system will throw up a fault at some point in its life. Therefore, we need to decide at the design stage exactly how they system should behave when faults occur. The broad division is between those which carry on working and those that don't (figure 2.2).

Within the first group are two sub-groups. First there are those that provide full service even in the presence of faults ('fail-operational'). These are usually found in highly-critical applications where failure would be catastrophic (e.g. a passenger aircraft flight control system). Second are 'fail-soft' systems (also called 'fail-active'), designed to keep on working with faults present, but with reduced performance. For instance, some automobiles use simplified back-up engine management systems to cater for failures of the main unit. Both systems (fail-operational and fail-soft) are defined to be fault-tolerant ones, described in detail in volume 3 of this book set.

Those that stop working can be grouped into two types, fail-hard and fail-safe. Hard failures are those which, while they persist, may well cause the whole system to grind to a halt. These problems are often met in personal computers. In such applications they usually don't cause damage (though they are extremely irritating). This failure mode may be acceptable in some applications.

Fail-safe systems make no effort to meet normal operational requirements. Instead they aim to limit the danger or damage caused by the fault. Such techniques are applicable to aircraft weapon stores management systems, nuclear reactor control equipment and the like.

Most real-time software needs some attention paid to its safety aspects. In many applications hard software failures are tolerable because external devices are used to limit their effects. For more stringent functions, or where external back-ups aren't available, fail-soft methods are used. Finally, fail-safe methods are generally used only in safety-critical operations, an important area of real-time systems (aviation, auto, medical, railways, robotics and power generation, for example).

On a last note, although we talk about 'unsafe software', in fact only hardware (or people) can do physical damage.

2.2 Software errors.

2.2.1 Overview.

In this text a software error is defined to be 'any feature of a program which produces a system malfunction'. This is a very broad definition, really quite unfair to software developers. In many instances of system misbehaviour the code is blameless; but we still talk of 'faulty software'. What it does, though, is emphasize that it isn't sufficient to eliminate errors At the software design stage; other factors need to be taken into account (figure 2.3). These are looked at in more detail below.

2.2.2 System design errors.

System design takes place right at the front end of a project. Quite often software engineers are excluded from this stage. Many system designers have the attitude of 'well, we'll go out and buy a box to control the plant (once we've worked out how to put it together)'. Mistakes made here usually show only when system trials begin (or worse still, when the system is in service). It doesn't matter whether we're talking about mechanical, electrical or software designs; getting it wrong at this point can have dramatic consequences. For instance, on one type of Royal Navy destroyer the radar mast was located just aft of the funnel. During sea trials the paint burnt off the mast. Only then was it realized that the design was suitable for steam propulsion, not gas turbines (as fitted).

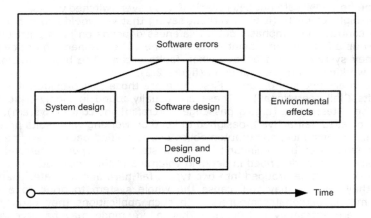

Figure 2.3 Types of software errors

During the system design phase the designer has to make many assumptions about the system and its operational environment. These form the basis for the specification against which the software is designed. If this is wrong then everything else from then on is also wrong (no matter how many times the program is validated and verified). The following examples illustrate this:

- 'A wing-mounted missile on an F18 aircraft failed to separate from the launcher after ignition because a computer program signalled the missile retaining mechanism to close before the rocket had built up sufficient thrust to clear the missile from the wing. An erroneous assumption had been made about the length of time that this would take. The aircraft went violently out of control' [LEV86].
- 'HMS Sheffield radar system identified an incoming Argentine Exocet missile as non-Soviet and thus friendly. No alarm was raised. The ship was sunk with considerable loss of life' [SEN3].

The moral for the software designer is to make the software flexible because you never know when you'll need to change it.

2.2.3 Design and coding errors.

In software design, a concept is translated into computer code without any sign of a physical product. In essence it is an intellectual effort by the designer. Thus errors introduced at the point must be due to faulty thinking about the problem or its solution.

Design and coding errors fall into four categories, figure 2.4. The only way we can catch mistakes of this type is to force the designer to externalize his thinking (a rather up-market way of saying 'get it out of him'). That is the essence of modern software design practices.

(a) Syntax errors.
The Oxford English Dictionary defines syntax to be 'the grammatical arrangement of words in speech or writing' (figure 2.5).

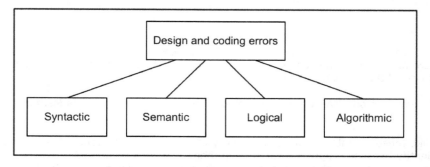

Figure 2.4 Errors in the design process

Figure 2.5 A problem of syntax

In software terms, syntax is the definition and arrangement of program symbols that the computer will accept. Such symbols include program words and delimiters – semicolons, full stops (periods), brackets, etc.

There are two distinct types of syntax error. In the first, the wrong symbol is used. In the second the symbol is used wrongly. As an example of the first suppose that, in an Ada program, we write:

    ShaftSpeed: Integer:

Here the final delimiter, ':' is incorrect. It should be ';'. Mistakes like this are, almost without exception, picked up by the compiler. So although they're frustrating, no damage is done.

However, consider writing

    X = Y . . .

in a C program when what was wanted was:

    X = = Y . . . . .

Both are valid constructs; yet they produce quite different results.   If it so happens that the statements are accepted by the compiler then the program is guaranteed to malfunction. This may not appear to be all that significant, except that:

'a misplaced comma in one NASA program sent a Voyager spacecraft towards Mars instead of Venus' [HAM86].

   Problems like these fall into the general category of 'errors of user intent'. They can be extremely difficult to identify because programs that contain them appear to be correct.
   The best way to combat syntax errors is to use the right language for the job. This doesn't mean that one, and only one, language should be used.   It's more a question of having the right basic features to support good design practices (discussed later).   Nowadays, unless there are special reasons, code should be written in a modern high-level language (HLL).   The text produced is compact and readable, two very good reasons for using such languages. Furthermore, the less we write, the fewer chances there are of making mistakes. And the less there is to read, the easier it is to grasp its meaning.   On top of this, modern HLL compilers usually have powerful error-checking features.   Executable code produced in this way should be syntactically quite trustworthy – but never forget that compilers themselves can have residual errors.

(b) Semantic errors.
Semantics 'relate to the meaning in language' (Oxford English Dictionary).   Semantic errors (figure 2.6) can arise in two ways. First, we may not properly understand what the

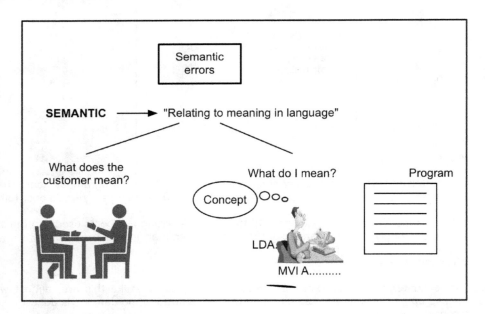

Figure 2.6 A problem of semantics

software is supposed to do. So we end up translating the wrong solution into code. Second, we may understand the problem but translate it wrongly into code. This second point is the one most often talked about under the heading of semantic errors (the Dictionary of Computing defines these to be 'programming errors that arise from a misunderstanding of the meaning or effect of some construct in a programming language').

An example of the first type of mistake is that which resulted in an accident involving a chemical reactor [KLE83]. Due to human and software problems a reactor overheated, discharging its contents into the atmosphere.   Afterwards, during the accident investigation, the system specifications were examined. In these the programmers were told if a fault occurred in the plant, they were to leave all controlled variables as they were and sound the alarm. But it was also found that they didn't properly understand this directive. Did this mean that the valve which controlled the flow of cooling water to the reactor should freeze its position? Or, should the temperature of the reactor itself be held steady? The systems engineers clearly thought they'd specified the second response. Unfortunately the programmers had done it the other way round.

Problems caused by not having a full and proper understanding of programming languages are very common. Mistakes are made mostly by inexperienced programmers. But they also crop up when software teams begin to use new programming languages. An example of such a mistake was made by a fairly experienced assembly language programmer when using an HLL for the first time. The design task was to produce a series of recursive filter algorithms, implemented as procedures. But because he didn't appreciate the difference between static and dynamic variables, these algorithms just refused to work.

Both problems described here are also 'errors of intent'. As pointed out earlier, these are extremely hard to catch before software is tested. To eliminate the first we need to set down an agreed design specification. And to do that we have to extract full and correct information from the system designers. Then we have to show them that we understand it.

Having a set specification helps us attack the second issue. From such specifications we can produce the source code. This can then be checked against the original requirement to verify that it is correct. In safety-critical systems we may have to use formal mathematical techniques in the verification process. The more complex the language the more likely it is that blunders will be made (and the longer it'll take to find them). Assembly language working certainly produces many more problems of this type compared with HLLs.

(c) Logic errors.
These are also errors of user intent, made during program design and coding phases (figure 2.7).

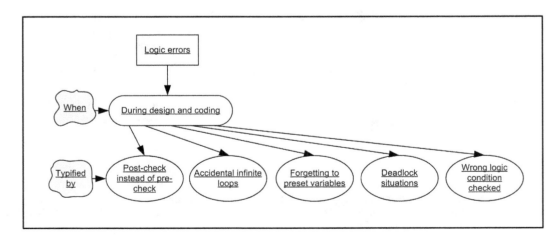

Figure 2.7 Logic errors – when and what

As a result these programs don't behave in a logically correct manner. This can show up in a number of ways. For instance, the program may appear to run correctly but keeps on giving the wrong answers. Doing post-checks instead of pre-checks leads to this. Forgetting to preset variables produces similar results; we may violate assumptions upon which the logic operations are built. In other cases systems hang-up as a result of carrying out logical actions. Infinite loops and deadlocks in multiprocessing/tasking are well known examples. Mistakes of logic aren't always found in test. And when they do who the results can be costly:

'Mariner 18 lost due to missing NOT statement in program' [SEN2].

It's important to realize that logical errors are easily made. And, when programs are coded in assembly language, the errors are quite difficult to detect before the test stage. Fundamentally this is due to the highly detailed nature of low-level coding methods. When using these it is almost impossible to see the structure of the logic. Hence it is difficult to spot logical errors just by reading through the source code. By contrast, when using a high-level language, such errors are less likely to be made in the first place; the inbuilt constructs ('while-do', 'repeat-until') force us to do the right thing. Even when mistakes are made they are much easier to find and correct because of improved program readability.

(d) Algorithmic errors.
These occur during mathematical operations (figure 2.8), for a variety of reasons.

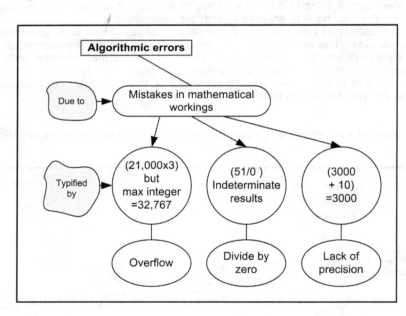

Figure 2.8 Algorithmic errors

In some situations basic mathematical rules are broken, as in trying to divide by zero. In other cases the capabilities of the computer system are exceeded. Every machine has limits on the size and range of its number system, affecting:

● The largest number that the machine can hold.

- The smallest number.
- The ratio of the largest to the smallest number that can be manipulated simultaneously.
- The degree of precision (resolution) of numbers.
- The range of values that input-output devices handle.

What are the effects of algorithmic errors? Here are some examples:

- 'A Shuttle laser experiment failed because the computer data was in nautical miles instead of feet' [SEN3].
- 'The Mars Climate Orbiter spacecraft was destroyed (a 'fly-by' became a 'fly-into') owing of failure to translate English units into metric units in a segment of the mission software [NAS99]
- 'The Vancouver Stock Exchange Index rose by 50% when two years of round-off errors were corrected' [SEN4].
- 'The first Ariane 5 launch ended in disaster with the destruction of the launcher itself. It was a result of number overflow of the horizontal velocity value' [ARI96].

Algorithmic errors are a significant factor in control system and signal processing work. When coding is done at assembler level it is a painstaking and time-consuming task. These tasks are much more controllable and testable when working in an HLL. But designers still needs to understand fully the number system used by their machines.

2.2.4 Environmental factors.

This is a broad-ranging topic because it concerns how software behaves within its normal working environment. Far too often designers regard software as something which is complete in itself. They forget that it is just one part of a larger process. And, in most real-time applications, this involves not only hardware but also humans. For such designs it's not good enough to produce software that is correct. We must also ensure that the system in which it is incorporated also works correctly.

These problems often surface for the first time when full system testing is carried out. In other cases they lie dormant for long periods until the right set of circumstances occurs; then they can strike catastrophically. There is no way that we can eliminate environmental problems at the design stage; there are just too many different ways in which they can occur (see below). All we can do is to minimize the number of potential trouble-spots by deep and extensive design analysis. It also helps, as a matter of sanity, to accept Murphy's law ('anything that can go wrong, will').

- A computer issued a "close weapons bay door" command on a B-1A aircraft at a time when a mechanical inhibit had been put in place in order to perform maintenance on the door. The "close" command was generated when someone in the cockpit punched the close switch on the control panel during a test. Two hours later, when maintenance was completed and the inhibit removed, the door unexpectedly closed. Luckily nobody was injured. The software was later altered to discard any commands not complete within a certain time frame, but this situation had never been considered during testing' [FRO84].
- A mechanical malfunction in a fly-by-wire flight control system set up an accelerated environment for which the flight control computer was not programmed. The aircraft went out of control and crashed [FRO84].
- Just before the Apollo 11's moon landing, the software sent out an alarm indicating that it was overloaded with tasks and had to reset itself continually to service critical functions. The program was still functional, so the landing went ahead.   Later it was found that an astronaut had mistakenly been instructed to turn on a sensor that sent a continuous stream of interrupts to the processor, causing the overload [HAM86].

- An F16 autopilot flipped the plane upside down whenever it crossed the equator' [SEN2]. The fact that this occurred in a simulator doesn't lessen the gravity of the mistake.
- As the F-22 Raptors reached the International Date Line, the navigation computers locked up. "Apparently we had built an aircraft for the Western Hemisphere only," says a senior U.S. Air Force commentator. http://www.f-22raptor.com/news_view.php?nid=267
- In one case, a 62 year old man died abruptly during treatment. Interference from the therapeutic microwaves had reset his pacemaker, driving his already injured heart to beat at 214 times a minute. It couldn't do it. [SEN5].

2.2.5 Why do we get poor software?

There isn't a formal definition for 'poor' software. This term is meant to cover all aspects of the problem, including software that is:

- Incorrect.
- Unreliable.
- Unsafe.
- Late.
- Expensive.

The last two items are usually closely bound up with the first three.

What gives rise to poor software? Many answers to this question will by now be obvious. What doesn't always show is that, frequently, more fundamental problems exist. There are three general aspects to this (figure 2.9).

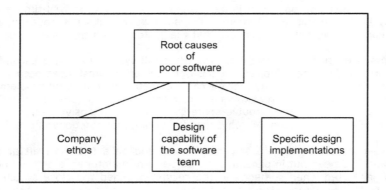

Figure 2.9 Poor software – the reasons

(a) Company ethos.
This is all tied up with how software activities are understood at a senior level within a firm. Basically, the characteristic spirit of a company determines how well jobs are done. A company with negative attitudes has:

- Poor senior management response to problems.
- Lack of formal and rigorous company software design and documentation procedures.
- Inadequate tools.
- Lack of professionalism and discipline in the software team.

If senior management doesn't (or doesn't want to) understand the needs of software development then poor software becomes endemic. No effort is made to bring formality and rigour into the design and development process. No specifications are set for documentation. No provision is made for the costs of design documentation. Development tools are obtained only with the greatest of difficulty, often much later than needed. The inevitable consequences are that design teams become demoralized. Good people opt out, either by leaving or just by giving in to the system. It is no accident that one very large company which epitomizes these qualities had - in its 'management by accident phase' - lost money, contracts and prestige in large amounts. It had government contracts terminated. It had one of its major projects investigated and evaluated by a rival software house (this being paid for by a highly disillusioned customer). And its software effort on one defence project was described as being run by 'one man and his dog'.

(b) Design capability.
Management decisions have a strong bearing on the levels of competence and expertise achieved by software teams. You don't get good software by accident. It requires experienced, professional and dedicated designers. And you don't hold such people without the right support and encouragement from senior management. Indicators of a suspect design team are:

• Lack of appreciation of software complexity.
• Little formal documentation.
• Little use of software design tools.
• No system prototyping.
• Designing from scratch (no reuse of software).

These directly affect just how well individual jobs are handled.

(c) Specific design implementations.
Given the situation outlined above, it isn't surprising that inferior software designs commonly have:

• Hazy system requirements specifications.
• An overrun on time.
• An overrun on budget.
• Faulty delivered software.
• Negligible documentation.

Contributory factors are:

• Simultaneous development of hardware and software.
• Incorrect trade-off of resources.

Let's look at how these all combine to turn a software project into a nightmare.
    In the first place it's not unusual to find that nobody can define exactly what the system is supposed to do. Everybody thinks they know what should happen, but frequently these just don't add up. Because little is committed to paper during the design stage such discrepancies fail to surface.
    As the design progresses, three factors cause it to become late. It often turns out that the software is much more complex than first envisaged. Second, much more effort is required. Finally, implementing it without decent software design tools makes it a long (and often error-prone) task. And, because no use is made of reusable software, all of it has to be designed from scratch.
    The overall system may involve new hardware. This presents the software designers with a task over and above that of writing the application software; that is, the need to develop programs to interface to the physical level, the 'service' software. It's not enough just to allow for the time and effort needed to do this. In these circumstances the development phase takes on a new dimension. System programs can't be tested out until the hardware is ready. And application software can't be

fully tested until both these are complete. Concurrent development of hardware, system software and application software is a recipe for long, long development timescales.

During this period various trade-offs have to be made which affect the resulting software. For instance, an early decision concerns the choice of a programming language and/or compiler. This has a profound impact on productivity, visibility and, ultimately, dependability. At the same time the hardware-software balance has to be decided on. Later, specific effects of the language have to be checked out, concerning items such as memory usage and program run-time. It takes experience and knowledge to get these right.

All of these combine to make the job late, and as a result it costs more than planned. And, the first set of software is delivered as the final item: there is no prototyping effort as in normal engineering design. So it is not surprising that the software fails to work correctly on delivery. It then takes a massive effort to eliminate all the faults (this last items seems to be a way of life in much commercial software; it has been said that some firms regard customers as extensions to their software teams, acting as fault finders).

The factors outlined above influence the general nature of software design in a company. As an analogy, visualize management as providing hygienic facilities, the software teams being hygiene attendants. If facilities are poor then the attendants are unlikely to produce a safe environment – no matter how hard they work. The end result is that the user's health is under threat.

2.2.6 Testing – how useful?

The testing of software is a contentious issue, particularly for safety critical applications. Testing is an important part of the development process but its limits must be recognized. Design flaws can often be picked up early on by running the program in an emulated environment. Consider, for instance, where source code is written, compiled and linked using a personal computer (PC). It may be possible to exercise it subsequently under the control of the PC operating system. The behaviour of the program can be examined and any faults rectified. But there is a limit to what we can do at this point; some errors will always get through to the final hardware. Unfortunately, these errors tend to be the really difficult ones to sort out. The only solution then is to use specialized test gear such as In-Circuit Emulators.

There are sound objections to using tests for proving that software works. Consider the flow-chart example of figure 2.10.

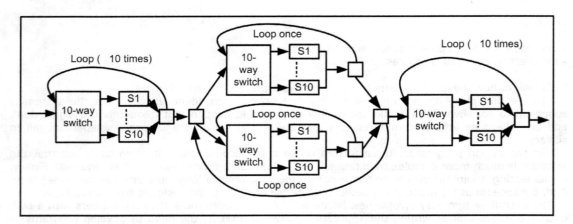

Figure 2.10 A flow-chart problem

The questions are:

- How many paths through this section of program?
- How long would it take to check out each and every path at 10 μsec per path?

The answers are (approximately) 4×10^{10} and 111 hours (almost five days of fully automated testing).

   This shows that statements which say that 'full and complete testing of the program has been carried out' must be treated with scepticism. Fortunately, in practice, things are not quite so gloomy. Usually a smaller number of tests exercises a sufficient, statistically significant number of paths through the program. While this is very encouraging it has a profound implication. That is, testing of this kind cannot prove that the software is error-free.

   There is a second, more fundamental, point implicit in this technique. What we have tested is the correctness of the program. But this, as has already been pointed out, is not sufficient. Correctness testing only shows how well the program meets its specification. It cannot point out where the specifications may be wrong. Further, such testing is static. We really need to verify that it will behave reliably. Consequently, many real-time systems developers use simulation as a test method. This gives much greater confidence in the behaviour of the software. But it still leaves questions unanswered because:

- Most testing is done by simulation of the environment.
- It is difficult to provide realistic test exercises and set-ups.
- In many cases the test strategy is based on assumptions about the total system and its environment. There is no guarantee that these are right.
- It is difficult to predict and simulate all failure modes of the system. Hardware failures complicate the matter.
- The behaviour of the software may vary with time or environmental conditions. This requires testing to be dynamic.
- Following on from this, it may become impossible to carry out complete and exhaustive tests for real-time systems.

Don't get paranoid about software problems. Be assured that all engineering project managers would instantly recognize the difficulties listed above. Just be realistic about what can and can't be achieved by the testing of software.

2.3 The basics of good software.

2.3.1 General.

'Good' software is dependable, is delivered on time and is done within budget. Whether we can achieve this depends on many factors. Some relate to major sections of the development process. Others affect quite specific design activities.

   What then, do we need to do to create a quality software product? At the minimum, we should:

- Develop a clear statement of requirements for the software.
- Ensure that the design solution is capable of satisfying these requirements.
- Organize the development so that the project is manageable.
- Organize the development so that the time scales can be met.
- Make sure that the design can be changed without major rewrites.
- Design for testability.
- Minimize risks by using tried and trusted methods.
- Ensure that safety is given its correct priority.

- Make sure that the project doesn't completely rely on particular individuals.
- Produce a maintainable design.

Mind you, there is a bit of the 'wish' element here.
   Let's now look at items that determine precisely how well we can achieve these aims.

2.3.2 Specification correctness.

There is only one way to make sure that the software specification is right. Talk to the users. Explain what you're doing. Put it down on paper in a way that they can understand. Get to know the job yourself. Keep on talking to the users. And never delude yourself that the requirements' documents are set in concrete. In reality they never stop changing.
   Specification methods and related topics are covered in detail in chapter 3.

2.3.3 Feasibility and suitability.

Here we seek to answer the general question 'will it work?' (feasibility) and 'how well?' (suitability). Specifically we need to assess the:

- Time allowed to complete tasks.
- Accuracy and completeness of input information.
- Required accuracy of mathematical operations.
- Operator interaction with the system.
- Special operating conditions, such as data retention on a power loss.
- Power supply parameters.
- Special performance parameters, such as radiation hardness.

   It may seem that decisions concerning the last two items should be left to hardware engineers. But these can have a major impact on the software development. For instance, if a battery-powered system is specified then a low power processor will have to be used. Likewise, if radiation hardness is required it may be that very specific technologies *have* to be used. Any choices made must take into account their effects on the software aspects of the project. So they need consideration at the feasibility design stage.
   We then need to consider the overall hardware and software structure, and determine:

- Is the language correct for the job?
- Are there proper support tools for the chosen language?
- Is there enough code and data store space?
- Will task execution times meet their specifications?
- If, at test time, task execution times are excessive, how can we handle to problem?
- Will the system be able to respond sufficiently fast to asynchronous events?

   This part of the development process isn't easy to get right. It is carried out at an early stage when there are many unknowns in the project. Frequently the size of the problem is under-estimated. Combine that with the usual optimism of designers and it's not surprising that so many projects have problems.

2.3.4 Modularization.

One of the most highly refined structures for the handling of major projects in set time scales is that of the military (figure 2.11).

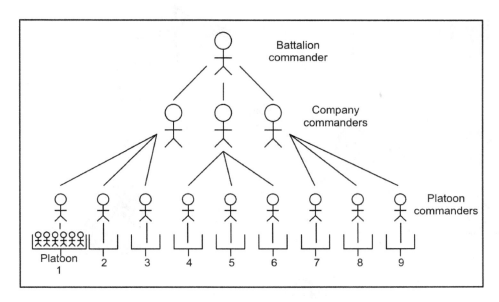

Figure 2.11 Hierarchical modularized structure

The military command structure is hierarchical, grouping men together as a set of distinct units (or 'modules'). Without this structure all we'd have would be a disorganized rabble. But with it, the organization becomes manageable and effective. With this simple chain of command, control is easy to maintain. Large jobs can be tackled by the group as a whole. Yet, at the lowest level, the jobs taken on by separate platoons are 'visible'. Individual progress and performance can be monitored and assessed. When troubles arise they can be dealt with quickly and effectively.
Software which is organized in a modular way exhibits the same properties:

• The overall project is manageable and flexible.
• Low-level tasks can be made small enough for one person to work on.
• Software can be designed as a set of parallel (concurrent) actions.

Even within the work of one person, modularization gives the same sort of benefits.
What is not so obvious is that modularization can make a program very stable. That is, localized changes produce very little of a ripple-through effect in the program as a whole. For exactly the same reasons a modular program is much easier to test and maintain (but this is also closely tied up with program design methods, chapter 4).

2.3.5 Portability and reusability.

Most manufacturers of microprocessor systems produce a range of products (figure 2.12).

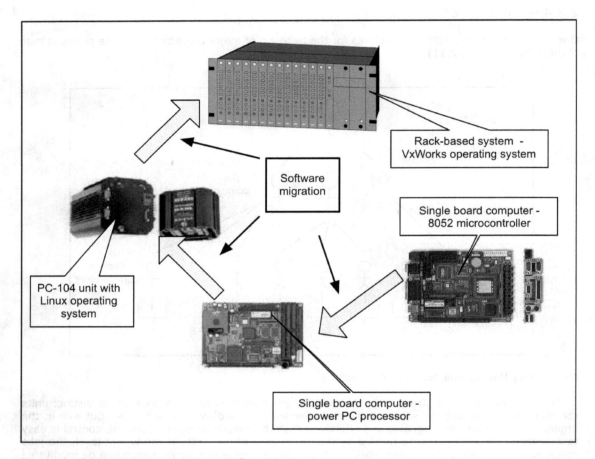

Figure 2.12 Microprocessor system configurations

Typically these range from simple single board computers (SBCs) through to multiple rack units. In many cases a number of microprocessor types are used. To a lesser extent different operating systems may be in use. If each configuration requires unique software, development is expensive and time-consuming – and threatens to generate a whole new range of software faults. Ideally we would like one set of programs capable of running on all configurations – fully portable software. Portability is a measure of the effort needed to transfer programs between:

• Computers which use different processors.
• Different configurations based on the same processor.
• Configurations which use different operating systems.
• Different compilers, given the same language and same hardware.

If programs need a complete rewrite before being transferred they are totally non-portable.

It is true that, in the past, most real-time software was non-portable. Now there is much greater emphasis on portability, especially for professional work. There are still many barriers to achieving this goal, the major ones being:

- Computer hardware.
- Number representation, range and precision.
- Programming language.
- Operating system structures.
- Communication structures and protocols.

For embedded systems, fully portable software can never be attained. The stumbling block is that hardware structures almost always differ from job to job. But, given the right design approach and the right programming language, very high levels of portability can be achieved.

Reusability is a measure of how easily we can use existing software, especially that which is tried and trusted. Doing this saves us from (to quote a very hackneyed but true cliché) 're-inventing the wheel'. There's no doubt that high portability produces high reusability (and vice versa).

What exactly do we gain by having a suite of portable and reusable software? The advantages are that:

- Design and coding times are reduced.
- Development effort is reduced.
- Less manpower is needed.
- Less debugging is needed (use of proven software).
- Costs are reduced.
- Correct and reliable designs are more easily achieved.

In recent years one item has emerged as being key to the development of reusable software: the component (CB15). Unfortunately, trying to precisely define what this is - and get everyone else to agree with you - seems difficult to achieve. We'll somewhat fudge the issue by using the following definition: 'a component is an independent part of a larger ('parent') system. It is intended to carry out specific functions; these may or may not depend on the nature and/or role of the parent system. It may be implemented as a single software unit or as a logical collection of such units. In all cases it must provide a set of clearly specified interfaces'.

Components by themselves are not a universal remedy for poor design techniques. They must be organized in terms of clearly defined functions, and be easy to use. Otherwise they are likely to make it more, not less, difficult to implement a design. How, though, can components be categorized? Many ways are possible; the criteria given in figure 2.13 are those of our choice. This gives us eight groups:

1. General application, source code form, vendor independent. Example: Linux operating system.
2. General application, source code form, vendor specific. Example: Altia Design GUI Editor, http://www.altia.com/products/design/.
3. General application, linkable code form, vendor independent. Example:CORBA, the Common Object Request Broker Architecture, http://www.corba.org/.
4. General application, linkable code form, vendor specific. Example: DCOM, the Distributed Component Model from Microsoft, https://msdn.microsoft.com/en-us/library/6zzy7zky.aspx.
5. Sector specific, source code form, vendor independent. Example: CAMP, the Common Ada Missile Packages project, https://archive.org/details/DTIC_ADB102655.
6. Sector specific, source code form, vendor specific. Example: PEG graphics software, https://www.nxp.com/support/developer-resources/run-time-software/peg-graphics-software:PEG-HOME.
7. Sector specific, linkable code form, vendor independent. Example: embedded TCP/IP stacks, https://www.hcc-embedded.com/embedded-systems-software-products/tcp-stack-networking.
8. Sector specific, linkable code form, vendor specific. Example: Windows Operating System, Dynamic Link Libraries (DLLs), https://msdn.microsoft.com/en-us/library/windows/desktop/ms682589(v=vs.85).aspx.

Closely related to these developments is the growing use of commercial off-the-shelf (COTS) components as a way of building software systems. These are especially useful in large or/and complex projects.

Just to clarify things:

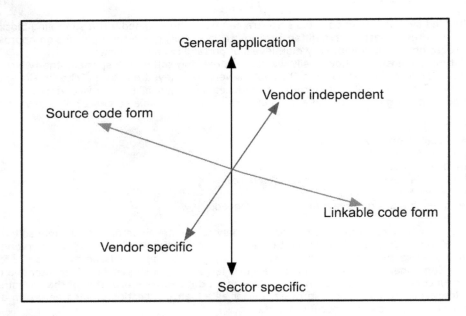

Figure 2.13 Component categorization

- 'Vendor independent' means that any vendor may produce the product in accordance with a defined specification or standard.
- 'Linkable code form' includes binary files which are linked into the application code and 'software in silicon' object code provided in programmable devices.

2.3.6 Error avoidance and defensive programming – robust programs.

How can we deal with error situations? Start off by accepting that, in any real project, mistakes will be made. Therefore we need to design software to limit the effects of such mistakes – damage limitation. But to do this we must have some idea of the general (and sometimes specific) nature of error sources. Exactly how, when, why and where do these problems arise? Generally they are due to:

- The human factor.
- Computational problems.
- Hardware failure.

(a) The human factor.
The problem can originate outside the system due to the behaviour of people (assuming they can interact with the software). For instance, consider using a processor as a controller for a closed loop control system.   Normally the controller is expected to carry out tasks additional to that of

controlling the loop. So, under normal conditions, the control task runs at regular and preset times; other tasks are executed in the remaining time. Assume that the operator can set the system sampling rate as desired. If this is set too fast the processor will execute nothing but the loop control algorithm; all other tasks are ignored. Despite the fact that the software may be faultless, the system fails to work correctly.

(b) Computational problems.
One of the well-known mistakes here is not allowing for invalid mathematical operations. These, such as dividing by zero, produce indeterminate results. Other items, such as going outside the correct limits of array bounds, also fall into this category.

(c) Hardware failure.
The following example typifies the problems of hardware failure. A control program instructs an analogue-to-digital converter to begin conversion. It then polls the converter, looking for the end of conversion signal. But for some reason the converter fails to generate this signal. The result is that the program just sits there ad infinitum (or until the power is switched off); control of the system is completely lost.

   The technique used to handle these situations is called 'defensive programming'. Fundamentally, this method accepts that errors will occur, originating inside the computer system and/or external to it. It aims to:

• Prevent faults being introduced into the system in the first place.
• Detect faults if they do occur.
• Control the resulting response of the system.

   Software which behaves like this combines the attributes of fault resistance with fault tolerance.
   In the case of (a) above we would limit the range of sample times that are accepted as valid. In (b) and (c) we can't control the occurrence of a fault. Instead, once having detected the fault, we must put the system into a safe mode ('exception handling'). An ideal design includes a specific test and a corresponding response for each possible error condition. In practice this is very unlikely to be achieved. But, for real-time systems, this isn't our chief concern. If we can identify the cause of the problem, fine. But it's usually much more important to respond to faults quickly, safely, and in a deterministic manner.
   All these factors are summed up in a quality called the 'robustness' of the program. This is defined by the Dictionary of Computing as 'a measure of the ability of a system to recover from error conditions, whether generated externally or internally, e.g. a robust system would be tolerant to errors in input data or to failures of internal components. Although there may be a relationship between robustness and reliability, the two are distinct measures. A system never required to recover from error conditions may be reliable without being robust. By contrast a highly robust system that recovers and continues to operate - despite numerous error conditions - may still be regarded as unreliable. The reason?. Quite simply it fails to provide essential services in a timely fashion on demand'.

2.3.7 Design codes of practice – style, clarity and documentation.

First, it is important not only that software specifications and the corresponding design solutions are correct; they must be seen to be so. Second, the resulting program must be understandable and unambiguous. And not just to the original designer. Finally, the ability to assess the effects of program modifications easily and quickly is very desirable.
   These items are not so concerned with how well we do a design (design quality is considered to be an implicit requirement). Rather, it relates to the quality and completeness of design methods and documentation.

Design style defines the way in which the development as a whole is tackled. It covers all aspects of the work, from initial feasibility studies to post-design services. Most engineering firms have, for many years, used 'codes of practice' to establish design styles. In large organizations such practices are fairly formal; small companies can afford to work informally. The purpose is to create working conditions and attitudes which:

• Encourage the production of high quality work.
• Ensure that time scales are met.
• Ensure that budgets are met.

Codes of practice may be written for detailed as well as general design activities. For instance, one company which used C++ as a programming language was concerned about the quality of their existing implementations. As a result company standards were issued limiting the language constructs that its programmers could use. The purpose of this was to:

• Eliminate unsafe programming practices.
• Get rid of 'clever' (i.e. obscure) programming tricks.
• Produce understandable programs (clarity).
• Avoid (or minimize) the use of undefined, unspecified and locale specific language constructs (affects portability).

This aspect of design is normally termed 'programming style'.
    Clarity is not just restricted to program writing; it is essential that the design as a whole should be easy to understand. At all stages we should be able to answer the 'what, why and how' questions. This is why good, clear, comprehensive documentation is such an important item.

2.4 A final comment.

It is only in the last few years that the ideas and methods described here have been put into action by the software industry. Much still remains to be done, especially in view of the 'cottage industry' mentality of many developers. It's not as if professionals didn't recognize the problems of software design and development. In fact, many tools and techniques have been proposed with a fervour normally associated with evangelical rallies. Most of the early developments came from the DP field, a trend that has continued with OO technology. Unfortunately, these have little to offer for real-time work. Now the sheer size of the software problem (time, cost, reliability, etc.) is acting as the driving force for the development of:

• New and better tools specifically for the real-time market.
• Powerful integrated development environments.
• Design formality.
• Defined documentation standards and
• High standards of professionalism (as exhibited by software engineers)

All these are combining to raise software quality standards.

2.5 Review.

Having finished this chapter you should now:

• Realize why, in the real world, we can never guarantee to produce fault-free systems.

- Know what is meant by correct, reliable and safe software.
- Know what is meant by dependable software and why it should be a primary design aim.
- Understand that software errors arise from problems to do with system design, software design and environmental factors.
- See that developing real-time software without taking system factors into account can lead to major problems.
- Appreciate some of the root causes of poor software.
- Recognize what has to be done to produce a quality software product.
- Be aware of the need for and use of codes of practice in a professional development environment.
- Be able to describe the need for, and use of, defensive programming.

2.6 References.

[AND88] The CAMP approach to software reuse, C.Anderson, Defense Computing, pp25-29, Sept./Oct. 1988.

[ARI96]: ARIANE 5 Flight 501 Failure Report by the Inquiry Board, http://www.mssl.ucl.ac.uk/www_plasma/missions/cluster/ariane5rep.html July 1996.

[CB15] Component-Based Software Engineering 2015, https://www.slideshare.net/DEVANSHI12/component-based-software-engineering-46462727

[FRO84] System Safety in Aircraft Management, F.R.Frola and C.O.Miller, Logistics Management Institute, Washington, D.C., January 1984.

[HAM86] Zero-defect software: the elusive goal, M.H.Hamilton, IEEE Spectrum, pp48-53, March 1986.

[KLE83] Human problems with computer control, hazard prevention, T.Kletz, Journal of the System Safety Society, pp24-26, March/April 1983.

[LEV86] Software safety: why, what and how, Nancy Leveson, ACM Computing Surveys, Vol.18, No. 2, pp125-163, June 1986.

[LEV95] SAFEWARE - SYSTEM SAFETY AND COMPUTERS, Nancy Leveson, ,Addison-Wesley, ISBN 0-201-11972-2, 1995.

[NAS99] Mars climate orbiter failure, NASA release H99-134, http://spaceflight.nasa.gov/spacenews/releases/h-99-134.html.

[OED16] Dictionary of Computing (2016), Oxford University Press, Oxford, https://www.amazon.co.uk/Dictionary-Computer-Science-Oxford-Reference/dp/0199688974

[SEN1] ACM Software Engineering Notes, Vol.8, No.3.

[SEN2] ACM Software Engineering Notes, Vol.5, No.2.

[SEN3] ACM Software Engineering Notes, Vol.10, No.3.

[SEN4] ACM Software Engineering Notes, Vol.9, No.1.

[SEN5] ACM Software Engineering Notes, Vol.5, No.1.

[WIE94] Digital Woes - Why We Should Not Depend on Software, Lauren Ruth Wiener, ISBN 0-201-40796-5

END OF CHAPTER

Chapter 3

First steps - Requirements analysis and specification

One of the most difficult tasks in any project is to establish precisely what the system requirements are.   This is a problem faced by project managers from time immemorial, who recognize that getting it right at the start of a job is of the utmost importance.   Engineers have long realized that a disciplined, organized and formalized approach must be used when evaluating systems requirements (whether that's always been practised is another matter).   This hasn't been done through a sense of 'doing the right thing;'.   No.   Experience, frequently painful, has shown that such methods are necessary. In particular, with projects of any real size, they are essential.

   What is the situation concerning software projects? Considering the number of major failure stories in circulation, the answer must be 'pretty awful'.   In the past this situation has frequently been condoned on the grounds that software is inherently highly complex; one can't expect anything else in such projects.   This is nonsense.   The real problem was that anything smacking of organization and discipline was considered to impinge upon the programmer's creativity.   Eventually, though, the point came when such an approach to professional software couldn't be tolerated any longer.   Consequently, requirements analysis and software specification are now regularly practised as a formal aspect of quality software design.   The purpose of this chapter is to:

- Distinguish between mythical and realistic software life cycle models.
- Show where requirements analysis and software specification (the requirements stage) fits into the life cycle.
- Highlight the importance of the requirements stage.
- Explain why and how mistakes are made during this period.
- Discuss practical analysis and specification methods.
- Introduce the topic of software prototyping.

In reality this isn't about software; it's project engineering.

3.1 The software life cycle.

3.1.1 Introduction.

There is a long path between recognizing the need for a product and satisfying this need.   Many activities take place along this 'life cycle' path, involving system, software and hardware designers.   In an attempt to formalize the process, models have been developed describing what the process consists of and how it functions.   Although these cover all aspects of system development they nave generally become known as 'software life cycle models'.   Software engineering textbooks describe these in varying degrees of detail, such descriptions usually being quite plausible.   Regrettably many suffer from the 'wish' syndrome – as in 'I wish it was like this' – ignoring the realities of life.   Consequently, models usually belong to one of two distinct groups – mythical and real.   And, for the inexperienced engineer, it can be difficult to tell them apart on a first meeting.

3.1.2 A mythical model of the software life cycle.

The simplistic 'waterfall' structure shown in figure 3.1 is an example of a mythical software life cycle model.   Let's see how this model is supposed to function.   The process begins when a prospective customer arrives looking for a solution to a clearly-defined requirement.   Frequently this is a desire to automate an existing manual system, such as accounts handling, stock control, or bookings and reservations.   The computing task is seen primarily as a software one, even though hardware forms part of the design solution. Hardware is subordinated to software because the equipment fit is usually based on standard items, configured specifically for each application.   Moreover, by using standard hardware, there isn't a need to develop system software; the primary objective is the production of application software only.

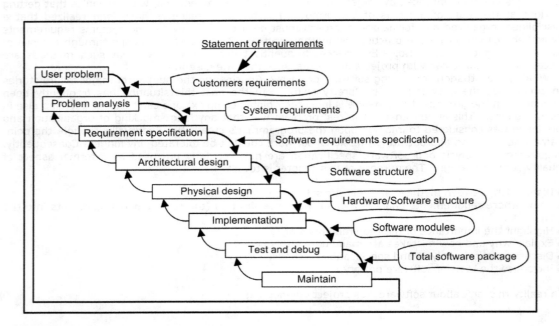

Figure 3.1 The mythical software life cycle model

   At this point the software house sends its top men – the system's analysts – to investigate the client's existing system. Their objectives are to:

• Analyse the problem presented to them (i.e. the existing system).
• Establish precisely what the new system is supposed to do.
• Document these aspects in a clear and understandable way.

   The output from the problem analysis phase is the system's requirements' document. Using this the system's analysts, together with senior software designers, define what the software must do to meet these requirements. This includes the:

• Objectives of the software.
• Constraints placed on the software developers.
• Overall software work plan.

Such features are described in the software specification document, issued at the end of the requirements specification phase.   Note that usually there is iteration around the analysis and specification loop, to resolve errors, ambiguities, etc. Note also that similar iterations take place at all stages in the model.

Only now does software design commence, in a neatly compartmentalized manner, figure 3.2. Experienced designers, working with a clear, complete and correct software specification document, begin software architectural design.   Their purpose is to identify and model the overall software structure, based on the software specification supplied to them.   The resulting software structure document defines the essential components of the system, how these fit together and how they communicate.   In essence it describes an abstract model of the software, ignoring implementation aspects (i.e. processor hardware, communication links, etc.).

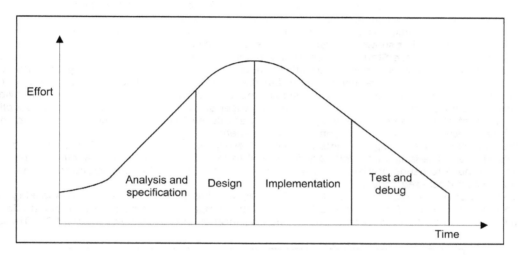

Figure 3.2 Project effort distribution – another myth

During the next stage, that of physical design, the abstract structure is partitioned or 'mapped' onto actual system hardware.   In some applications this may be a complex task – but it is considerably simplified by using standard hardware.   The outcome of *this* work is a hardware/software structure-defining document, forming the input to the implementation phase.   The function of this phase is to take the physical design structures and translate them into source code.   Once the code is written it can be tested and debugged.   Normally this is first done on a host development system; later it is tested in the target system (in most cases the host and target computers are identical).

One of the assumptions underlying this simplistic approach is that system hardware requires configuration, installation and commissioning: but not development.   It also assumes that such activities proceed in parallel with the design task; that the hardware is fully functional when application software tests commence on the target system.   Such testing is, of course, always needed to show that the finished code performs as specified. Thus the integration of software and hardware is a straightforward and fairly painless task.

Once the customer is convinced that the system performs as required it is put into operational use; the maintenance phase begins.   This involves two major factors.   First, not all errors are detected during the testing phase; such residual bugs need to be eradicated from the software.   Second, upgrades and enhancements are usually demanded by the customer during the life of the system. Minor changes involve tinkering with the source code (the minor iteration). But significant alterations take us back to the analysis stage of the life cycle model, the major iteration loop.

3.1.3 Bringing realism to the life cycle.

So, what's wrong with the model described so far? It seems reasonable, clearly describing the major activities and outputs relating to software production. It also defines what these involve, where they occur and how they relate to each other. Quite true. The problem is not with the definition and use of the individual activities.   These are perfectly valid, forming a sound basis for software design methodologies. Fundamentally it is due to many underlying false assumptions within this model, the first relating to the customer's requirements.

Most real-time software designs form part of larger systems (it's also worth pointing out that software costs dominate hardware costs only if a very narrow view of hardware is taken, i.e. the computer installation itself). In such applications it isn't a case of putting processor-based equipment into a company to perform a computing task; the problems are much more complex.   Moreover, although there may be a single end user, other bodies often have vested interests in the project. It isn't easy to generalize about real-time developments because projects are so diverse. But let's take the following example that shows how complex the situation can become.

Assume that the Defence Staff have perceived a potential air warfare threat. Decisions are made to develop a new air interceptor fighter aircraft to counter this, its requirements being stated in very general terms. At this stage the need is seen, but the solution isn't. Studies are then carried out by defence procurement agencies, research establishments and the end user.   Aircraft and avionic companies are invited to bid. They in turn perform tender studies that involve their system suppliers (e.g. flight control, weapon management, etc.). Only at this level are hard decisions made concerning mechanical, electrical, electronic and software systems, etc.

One can define system requirements at each and every point in this chain. The content of such requirements and the issues involved vary from level to level. So when we talk about requirements analysis, we have to define precisely the issues which concern us. In this text attention is focused on the lowest level discussed above.

The customer (in this case the aircraft manufacturer, say) has a perceived need, and is looking for a way to meet this need. Internal discussions within the company – and possibly external studies by consultants – lead to the production of an informal specification of requirements (figure 3.3). These

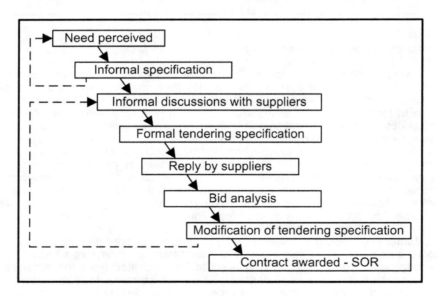

Figure 3.3 Formulating the user statement of requirements (SOR)

are firmed up in terms of concepts, achievable targets, online costs, etc., during informal discussions with potential suppliers of equipment.   The process is repeated until the customer is sure that the requirements are realizable, both technically and financially – and within desired time scales. Eventually he produces a formal tendering document requesting bids by suppliers.   Replies are analysed, the responses usually leading to changes in the tendering document. This is then re-issued in modified form, requesting further bids. Finally, a single supplier is identified as the best contender and nominated for the job. When contracts are awarded, the tendering document is converted into a statement of requirements (SOR) for the task. This then becomes the binding legal document for all further developments.

Note that even before the design process proper begins many decisions have already been made. These concern system structure, performance targets, size, weight, time scales, as well as project management functions.   So although work hasn't yet started many constraints apply to the job – compounded by one major factor. The specifications *always* change in such complex systems. This is an immutable rule which can't be proved but always holds true. It is inherent in the evolutionary aspects of the design process.

So, we start the life cycle with what appears to be a complete, correct and full statement of requirements of the problem; in reality, it is nothing of the sort. It is, though, the best we can do given the nature of the problem.   Consequently much greater effort is needed at the requirements analysis stage to clarify the customer's requirements. The effect of this is to introduce a new major iteration step between the analysis and problem definition (the SOR) stages, figure 3.4.

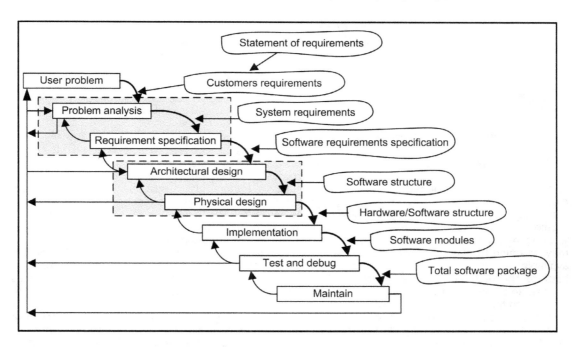

Figure 3.4 A more realistic software life cycle model

The steps through requirements specification and architectural design tend to follow the earlier pattern.   In practice there may be a major change in design methodology between these steps. Problems encountered in these stages are usually reasonably easy to solve, unless they are fundamental (for instance, it just won't work).   It's at the physical design stage that some really difficult problems surface, involving computer power, speed, memory, size, weight and cost. If the designer had a free hand there wouldn't be a problem; but he hasn't. Constraints set at the tendering phase act as a straitjacket, limiting the designer's choices. If the effects are significant they usually lead to a major iteration, going right back to the user problem. Surprisingly, critical problems at the physical design level can often be eliminated by making simple changes to the SOR.

During the implementation phase minor changes may be made in the physical design structure. For instance, tasks may be partitioned in more efficient ways, better modular structures formed, etc. Generally this part of the work doesn't raise real difficulties, provided proper development tools are available. However, the next set of major stumbling blocks occur in the test, integration and debug phase. This is a wide-ranging activity which includes:

- Testing software in a host environment.
- Testing software in a target environment.
- Integrating separately designed software packages.
- Integrating software and hardware.
- Integrating subsystems.
- System trials.
- System commissioning.

This phase, which embraces much more than just software, is often *the* major activity in the development of processor-based systems, as shown in figure 3.5 [FAR75].

PROJECT	Requirements and design	Implementation	Test, debug and integration
SAGE	39	14	47
NTDS	30	20	50
GEMINI	36	17	47
SATURN V	32	24	44
OS/360	33	17	50
TRW Survey	46	20	34

Figure 3.5 Distribution of software effort

There are many reasons for the size of this activity. Testing and debugging software in a target environment is a difficult and time-consuming process. This is compounded by the fact that target systems are usually quite different from the hosts. Integration of systems, whether software, electronic, mechanical, etc. is always fraught with problems. Some system testing *can* take place in a simulated environment. Mostly it has to be done within the real environment, with all its attendant problems. Like, for instance, operating hundreds of miles from base, with limited test facilities, working long hours in arduous conditions, trying to meet near impossible time scales. Grave problems may be found for the first time at this stage, particularly concerning processing power (not enough), available memory size (too small) and response times (too slow). Solving these involves iteration back to the architectural design stage (at the very least). In really dramatic cases it may be impossible to meet the user requirements under any circumstances. So we need to go right back to the SOR to try to resolve the problem.

Maintenance aspects are similar to those described earlier, only the whole process is more difficult to carry out. It may be tedious to hunt for bugs in an accounts recording system. By contrast, trying to pin down a fault in the flight control software of a supersonic fighter can be a Herculean task. Upgrading systems can also present major problems. With DP systems the emphasis is on software upgrading; for real-time applications it includes software, hardware, subsystems and even whole systems.

Lack of precision in the initial SOR, together with continual changes in this document, alters the way a project progresses. Project effort distribution become more like that shown in figure 3.6 than that of figure 3.2

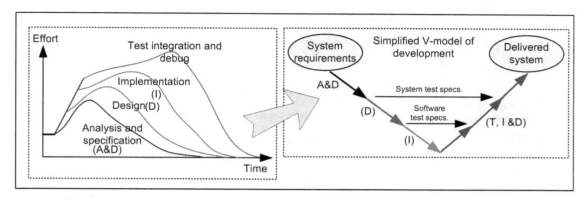

Figure 3.6 Project effort distribution - reality

This is a simplified model; precise details vary from project to project.   But they all exhibit one common feature: the overlapping of phases.   This implies a much higher degree of interaction between stages than that predicted by the simple waterfall model. It also highlights the need for firm, organized project management and formal quality assurance techniques.

Frequently the development sequence is shown using a V-model (above). Although this view is a somewhat simplified one, it does illustrate some important points.   First, it shows the dependency between the various stages in a very clear way.   Second, it shows clearly when you should be generating your system and software test specifications (which also includes system acceptance testing).   In practice it represents what happens during *each* development increment shown in the spiral model of figure 3.8 (see later).

3.1.4 Requirements issues - a practical approach.

The differences between ideal and realistic approaches to requirements analysis and specification should now be pretty clear.   We can now look at a practical, realistic model of the process.   The scenario it applies to is the overall development of the air interceptor fighter aircraft (figure 3.7). Although this is repeating some material, it presents it in a somewhat different way.   Two factors are key to this model:

• A layered process and
• Incremental development.

At the project outset the most important players on the scene are the defence agencies.   Also, from the project point of view, these are the end client(s). Work begins with an analysis of the air defence requirements that the system is required to meet.   And this is probably the *only* stage in which pure analysis is carried out.   Subsequently, analysis and design are carried out as an interlocking pair of operations.   But there are a number of distinct set of A/D operations, each having a 'ceiling' (the input) and a 'floor' (the output).

For the defence staff, the floor of activities is the generation of the statement of requirements (SOR) for the complete system.   These act as the ceiling for the main contractor, whose first task is to analyse the requirements.   Next, sub-system design is performed, using as input the information provided within the SOR.   The floor activity of this work layer is the production of sets of sub-system specifications (one being the navigation and weapons aiming - NAV/WAS - sub-system).   Subsequent

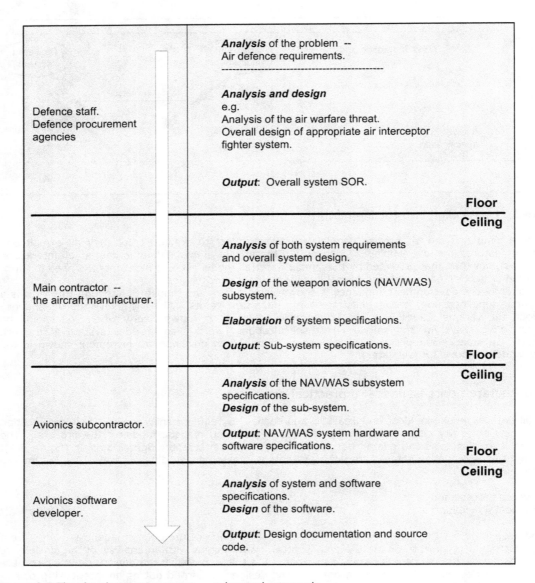

Analysis of the problem --
Air defence requirements.

Analysis and design
e.g.
Analysis of the air warfare threat.
Overall design of appropriate air interceptor
fighter system.

Output: Overall system SOR.

Defence staff.
Defence procurement
agencies

Floor

Ceiling

Analysis of both system requirements
and overall system design.

Design of the weapon avionics (NAV/WAS)
subsystem.

Elaboration of system specifications.

Output: Sub-system specifications.

Main contractor --
the aircraft manufacturer.

Floor

Ceiling

Analysis of the NAV/WAS subsystem
specifications.
Design of the sub-system.

Output: NAV/WAS system hardware and
software specifications.

Avionics subcontractor.

Floor

Ceiling

Analysis of system and software
specifications.
Design of the software.

Output: Design documentation and source
code.

Avionics software
developer.

Figure 3.7 The development process - a layered approach

events are depicted in figure 3.7. For simplicity, only the software development phase is included at
the bottom level.
     It is important to understand that you, as a software engineer, are likely to be involved in the
bottom layer of work. Know your place in the scheme of things. And recognise that the computer is
essentially a component within a complete system. Thus system - not computer - requirements
predominate.

Now let us look how software development itself proceeds in real life. It does not occur in a 'big-bang' fashion. Rather it takes place gradually, as illustrated in figure 3.8, the spiral model. The inputs to (the ceiling of) the design process are the software requirements specifications. Work proceeds by evaluating the specifications and then   developing - in conceptual form -   suitable software structuring.

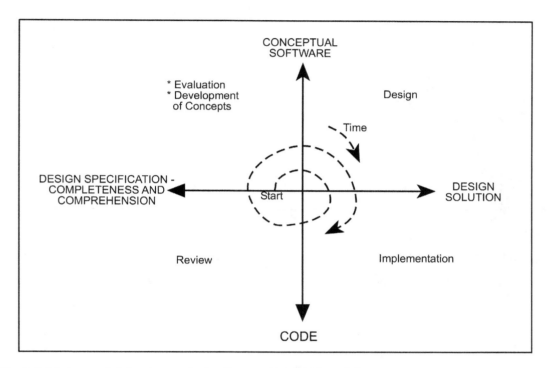

Figure 3.8 Incremental development of software - the spiral model

Next is the design process itself, which translates concepts into design solutions. Following on is the implementation phase, the outcome being source code. This is not the finish, however. Generally issues that come to light during the development lead us to review the design. In turn this leads to a greater understanding of the problem; frequently it also results in changes to the design specification itself. At this stage we retread the path, using our new (or better) knowledge to improve the software product.

The model of figure 3.8 describes the concrete aspects of software development for real-time systems. In the past few companies formalized this process; generally their methods evolved in an *ad hoc* way. Now, though, more rigour is gradually being introduced, reinforced by the use of modern tools and techniques. The rest of this chapter concentrates specifically on the front-end stages of analysis and specification; other aspects are discussed later in the text.

3.2 The importance of the requirements stage.

Why are the front-end stages so important? Because they have a profound effect on overall software error rates and productivity. And these are closely related to system costs.

Let's first consider software errors. There's no need to ask where they occur. The answer, as pointed out in chapter 2, is everywhere. More importantly, what is the distribution of these occurrences? Figure 3.9, based on statistics obtained by Tom DeMarco [DEM78], gives a good general guide.

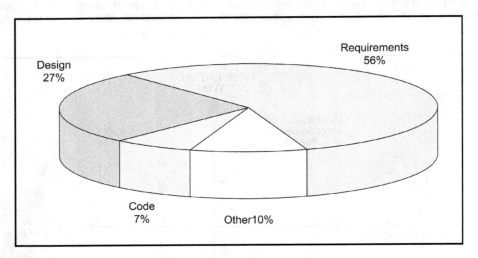

Figure 3.9 Distribution of software errors

   It's not surprising that high error levels occur in the requirements phase. It is, after all, a highly complex procedure to specify fully the requirements of a system. More on this later.
   A second important point is the cost impact of these errors. Figure 3.10 illustrates this, again using the statistics from DeMarco.

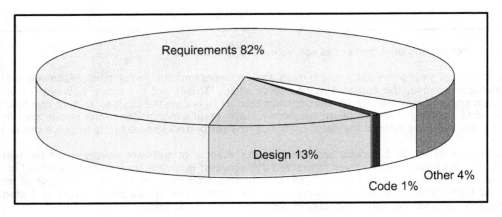

Figure 3.10 Cost of rectifying software errors

   Given that figure 3.9 is correct, this shouldn't be a surprise. Any mistake made at the beginning of a project affects all subsequent phases, a 'ripple-down' effect.   So when requirements errors are discovered at the final stage of development, corrections have to be made throughout the complete design. The resulting corrective costs are extremely high. Mistakes made in later stages have much less impact. In theory there should be no ripple-up effect; in practice, though, this *can* happen. For instance, suppose a major error occurs at the physical design level. It may actually be easier to change the software specification and structure rather than redesign the physical level.

The second issue, costs, is very closely bound up with the first one. Mistakes take time to find and correct. Therefore as the error rate increases the amount of deliverable code per unit time decreases – with consequent cost penalties.

It should now be clear that the requirements stage is the most important aspect of the life cycle process. Unfortunately, many customers and suppliers fail to realize exactly how important it is. Getting this wrong can produce dreadful downstream effects. Most situations are recoverable – at a cost. But there are also well documented cases where whole projects have been ditched as a result of requirements errors. Paradoxically, this stage has the fewest development and support tools within the total software toolset.

3.3 Making mistakes - sources and causes.

3.3.1 A general comment.

Why and how do we make mistakes? Figure 3.11 attempts, in a light-hearted way, to highlight some of the issues involved.

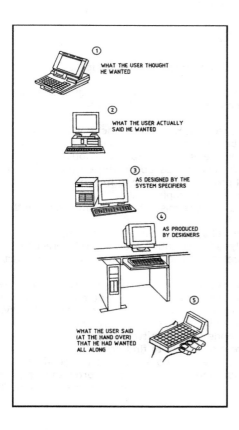

Figure 3.11 Making mistakes

It may be simplistic but it does get to the heart of the matter.   Because it shows that three major factors are at work here:

• How we convert what we think into what we say.
• How we express ourselves.
• How we convert what we see (receive) into thought.

   How do these apply to the requirements stage of a project? Let's first look at the customer-supplier relationship in more detail, as modelled in figure 3.12.

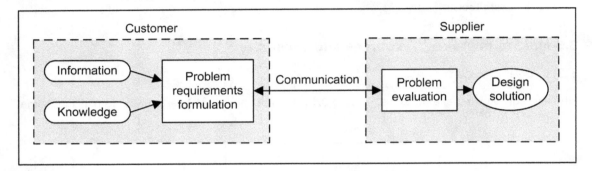

Figure 3.12 Simplistic view of the customer-supplier relationship

   This model also applies to the system designer-software designer relationship. So rules derived to enhance customer-supplier interactions can also be applied later in the software development cycle.

The first step in procuring any new system is to define exactly what is needed. The customer, using his acquired knowledge and available information, formulates a set of requirements.   These are communicated (by whatever means are suitable) to the supplier.   He in turn evaluates these requirements, and produces a design solution based on the evaluation.   This looks simple enough. But then why is it that the delivered product often fails to match up with what was wanted in the first place? The answer, of course, is that it isn't simple at all.
It's important to recognise the source of these mismatch problems because then we can:

• Understand the weaknesses of informal systems (past-current practice).
• Appreciate the use of rigorous analysis/specification tools (current practice).
• Perceive the advantages in using prototyping techniques (current-future practice).

There are four major reasons why mismatch occur (figure 3.13).   First, we don't formulate the requirements properly. Secondly, we don't communicate these requirements correctly. Thirdly, we fail to understand properly these improperly communicated requirements. Finally, because requirements continually change, not all changes may be acted on correctly. How much effect do these errors have, and how significant are they? It depends mainly on two factors: expertise and methods. Experienced people make fewer mistakes and are more likely to find errors in other people's work. Unfortunately this is a process we can't automate; there is no substitute for good people.   What we *can do* is produce tools that help in formulating and analysing problems and communicating ideas. Furthermore, it is essential that these tackle the root cause of errors (figure 3.14), otherwise they're useless.

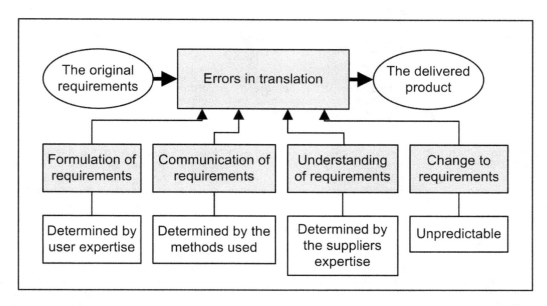

Figure 3.13 Sources of requirements/deliverables mismatch problems

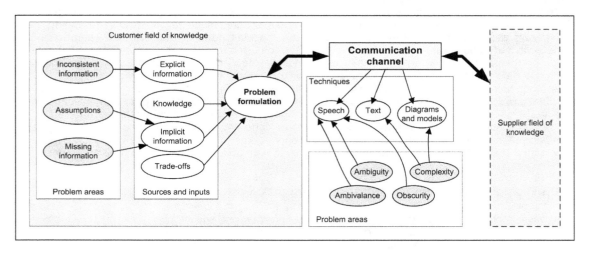

Figure 3.14 Causes of requirements/deliverables mismatch problems

3.3.2 Problems in formulating specifications.

First let's consider what goes on when the customer attempts to put together an SOR. In an ideal situation full information relating to the requirement is explicitly defined. In reality the requirement document is based on explicit information, implicit information and knowledge. Further, in putting together a specification, many conflicting demands are made by involved parties; hence trade-offs must be made. Each aspect has associated problems. And problems are compounded by specifying requirements that appear to be clear and reasonable – but actually are quite imprecise (and sometimes untestable). For instance, what does 'mimic displays shall be clear and uncluttered' mean? How does one define 'clear' and 'uncluttered'?

(a) Explicit information.
This may seem a clear-cut situation. True, but the major problem here is inconsistency of the information supplied. Specification documents are usually weighty items (in both a physical and literary sense). It can be extremely difficult to identify conflicts in such circumstances.

(b) Implicit information.
Implicit information is that which, to the specifier, appears to be present in, or deducible from, the SOR – but isn't. In some instances it is a simple case of missing information. In others, information is omitted or overlooked because assumptions are made concerning the supplier's understanding of the requirements. For instance, the operational temperature range of an equipment might be omitted from its specification. But because the application is an avionic one, say, everybody knows what this requirement is. Really?

(c) Knowledge.
This is a difficult area to describe precisely; there are many facets to it. Problems arise because the customer has a much greater knowledge of the system than the supplier; and much of it is unstated. For instance, there is always some relationship between the system being specified and other systems. The specifier has a good understanding of this, and aims to ensure that system integration is achieved correctly. Unfortunately the supplier is unlikely to have the same knowledge. Hence, during software design, decisions are made which seem perfectly correct for the system being constructed – yet may adversely affect other systems.

There is usually some overlap between this aspect and that of implicit information. The following example, relating to a very large computer-controlled rotating machine, illustrates this point. On initial trials the protection system kept shutting the machine down during start-up operations. It turned out that nobody had bothered to tell the software designers that the machine took a full minute to run up to speed – the assumption was that everybody knew about this. Unfortunately the software engineers didn't, and invoked an underspeed trip far too early in the run-up process.

Another factor, that of balance of judgement, can have significant cost and performance effects on the final product. Consider, for instance, where a particular requirement is extremely difficult to satisfy. The supplier isn't in a position to judge its importance; it's just another target to be met. So the target is achieved – but only with the greatest of difficulty, possibly affecting both software and hardware. Yet the customer may be the only person who knows that the requirement isn't especially important. Thus the specification could well be relaxed, with attendant savings to time and money.

3.3.3 Problems in communicating requirements.

Four basic methods can be used to communicate information: speech, text, pictures and physical models. Models tend to play a much greater role in the later stages of system development, and their importance cannot be underestimated. It's well known that car manufacturers build models of new vehicles – but less well known is that a full-scale wooden mock-up was built of the Swiftsure class nuclear powered hunter-killer submarine. For software systems different, non-physical models, are needed. This topic is discussed further in the section on prototyping.

One view of the communication process is that information is transmitted along a communication channel from sender to receiver. In the ideal world, what is sent is also what is received. But in reality this isn't true; information is corrupted by 'noise' along the way. The major sources of noise are:

• Ambiguity – I don't know what it means.

- Ambivalence – it could mean either this OR that: or both.
- Obscurity – it just isn't clear at all, I'm quite confused.
- Complexity – I hear what you say but I'm now totally confused.

Speech (and here is implied face-to-face contact) is probably the most important and significant communication process. Yet it is the one most prone to noise corruption. It's impossible to eliminate this noise – it is part of human nature. One must accept that there are inherent problems in speech communication; therefore other methods are needed to compensate for them.

Text description is, after speech, the most common method of communicating information. It too suffers from the problems outlined above, but generally these are easier to correct. Unfortunately, as a result of trying to eliminate these deficiencies, textual material becomes extremely complex (have a look at some legal documents). For technical systems we frequently end up with specification documents that are massive, dull and virtually unusable. Some authors of specification documents have an unshakeable belief in their effectiveness – even when experience proves the contrary point.

Pictures (diagrams) are one of the most effective means of communicating information (just think of the amount of money spent on eye-catching television advertisements). Diagrams have two major advantages over other forms of communication. First, they let us express our thoughts easily. Second, they make it much easier (compared with text descriptions) to assimilate information. Engineers have used this as a primary communication tools for centuries; yet for years it was almost entirely neglected by the computer science industry.

The role of diagramming is discussed in much more detail in chapters 6 and 7. Suffice it to say that, as far as specification methods are concerned, diagrams are becoming an important technique. Note that in this context structured text is considered to be a diagram.

Finally, this description has only considered information flow from the customer to the supplier. In practice it is a two-way process – with all the consequent noise corruption effects on return messages.

3.3.4 Problems in understanding requirements.

Even if the specifications delivered by the customer are totally correct, unambiguous, etc., mistakes are still going to be made. First, the supplier interprets the specifications from his point of view (or 'domain'). This is usually very different from that of the customer. Second, difficulties arise as he attempts to convey his response to the customer. He has exactly the same problems as those experienced by the customer when formulating the specification. Is it surprising then that the customer may not quite understand what the supplier is doing, how he's doing it and why he's doing it in a particular way? Therefore it is essential that the supplier uses techniques which make his work meaningful: both to him and to the customer.

3.4 Practical approaches to analysis and specification.

3.4.1 General aspects.

What is the fundamental purpose of the analysis and specification – the requirements – phase? It is to define *what* a proposed system is to do, not *how* it is supposed to do it; 'how' is the function of the design process. However, in practice there isn't always a sharp boundary between requirements and design. And the problem is compounded because some design methods make little distinction between the two. We can see why these overlap by considering the make-up of the requirements work-stage, figure 3.15. The first part of this process is concerned with analysing and recording the *system requirements*. Note this well. Many traditional (i.e. DP) descriptions discuss the analysis of systems, but you can only analyse a system if one already exists.

In the initial run-through, design factors shouldn't affect the outcome of the analysis work. Using the information acquired during the analysis phase the software requirements are now specified. Constraints are usually applied here: programming language, design methods and documentation

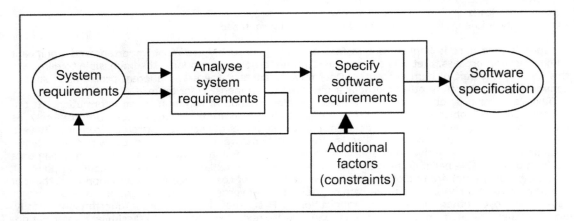

Figure 3.15 The requirements phases – analysis and specification

procedures, for instance. Now this is the point where design aspects do enter the process. There isn't much point in specifying a software requirement if the required system can't be:

• Achieved.
• Completed within the required time scale.
• Done within budget.

Implementation difficulties, actual or anticipated, cause us to review and re-analyse system requirements. As a result the software specifications are, if necessary, changed to a more sensible form. In some cases though, it may be impossible to do this and still meet the original system requirements. Consequently a further review of the SOR must be carried out. Where possible this document should be amended to take implementation factors into account. This is a normal and accepted part of any development process – most problems can be tackled in this way. Occasionally obstacles arise which are impossible to overcome within the given requirement objectives. There are only two courses of action. Either major changes are made to these objectives, or else the whole project must be abandoned.

We've already said that requirements and design may not be easy to separate. But they *are* very distinct parts of the development process. Therefore the software developer should always strive to treat them in this way. The main attributes of the requirements phase are the:

• Basic strategy used.
• Acquisition and presentation of information.
• Information content.
• Choice of method and tool support.

The first question to answer is what the specification document should contain. Sensibly it should provide a good description of the intended system, figure 3.16. This description includes system:

• Function.
• Performance.
• Interfaces.
• Constraints.

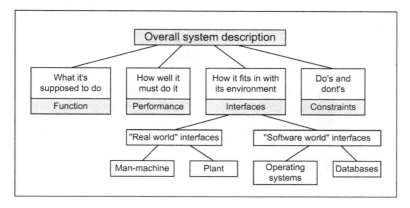

Figure 3.16 Overall system description

Interfaces include those which connect to the physical environment – the 'real world' – and to other software entities.

The description/document must be structured so that it can be understood both by the customer and the supplier. This means, most definitely, that it should not use obscure notation, complex structures or definitions using computer language terms. This latter approach has been advocated by a number of authors. It may be a very useful technique for the architectural design stage – but it cannot be recommended as a way of stating system requirements. We really need methods that are:

• Formal (that is, there are defined rules which must be obeyed).
• Visible (no implicit information).
• Expressive (easy to state what we mean).
• Understandable (making communication simpler).
• Easy to use (an obvious need, yet frequently ignored).

We also need proper tools to support these methods. In structural terms three specific functions should be present in any requirements tool: elicitation, representation and analysis (figure 3.17).

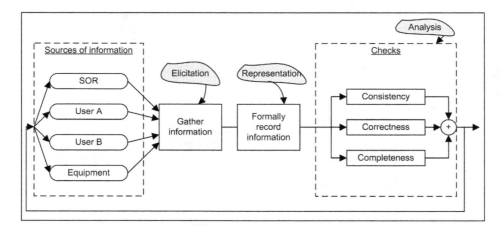

Figure 3.17 Requirements elicitation, representation and analysis

These cover the actions of gathering information, formally recording this information, and then checking it for consistency, conflicts and completeness. Such information is derived from a variety of sources, including users (humans), equipment data and formal documents such as the SOR. It should be appreciated that only the customer can provide this information. In an ideal world these three actions would be performed once, as a set of sequential operations. In practice the process is an ongoing one, with regular overlapping of actions. There are constant iterations through these steps as new data is acquired, ideas refined, and old information modified or discarded.

What's been described so far takes place in all engineering projects. Requirements-handling strategies in engineering are usually quite formalized: but only on a company basis. The techniques are well known and practised, adapted as necessary to suit particular local conditions. Specific prescriptive methods, which can be applied across a variety of applications, are virtually unknown. This hasn't been a problem though, because of the rigour and discipline inherent in engineering projects. Unfortunately, in the past (only the past?), rigour and program development have been mutually exclusive events. To rectify this situation – at least as far as the requirements phases are concerned – a number of methods have been developed. Some have been designed for very specific uses; others intended for general usage.

3.4.2 Tool support and automation.

Defined *methods* are fine. They are the first step in formalizing analysis and specification techniques. Unfortunately there is one problem on which methods themselves make little impact: information complexity. How can we really be sure that, when dealing with complex requirements, information is:

- Consistent (we haven't made mistakes in gathering and recording the data)?
- Correct (there aren't wrong or conflicting requirements laid down within the requirements themselves)?
- Complete (items haven't been omitted)?

It's extremely difficult, time-consuming and tedious to do this manually. Clearly, automated tools are needed. Then the question arises: what can we sensibly automate? Ideas, concepts, meaning: all are beyond automation. We can only work with facts. Now, systems can be described in terms of their internal data, the data flow through them, and actions performed on this data. To a large extent we can automate this description, as shown in figure 3.18.

First we describe individual operations within the system, together with their inputs and outputs. It is then possible to check for consistency between operations, as in figure 3.18a. Assume, for instance, that the requirements specification defines that the output of operation 01 acts as the input to 02. Thus both output1 and input2 represent the same entity. If during the recording process different entities are assigned to these, the error can be quickly identified – provided all information is held in a common store. Thus any automated tool has at its heart a common database.

Many other errors can be picked up in this way. These include:

- Missing inputs; figure 3.18b (an operation, to produce the desired output, needs three inputs; but only two are provided).
- Missing outputs, figure 3.18c (an operation must produce three outputs to satisfy system structure and operation; however, only two are specified in the SOR).
- Dangling outputs, figure 3.18d (specified operations produce outputs which aren't used anywhere).
- Redundant inputs, figure 3.18e (inputs are specified in the SOR, but no operations are performed on these within the system).
- Missing operations, figure 3.18f (inputs are provided, outputs are expected, but no operations are specified in the requirements document).

Constraint effects can also be introduced, figure 3.18g. We can, for instance, define that:

- Operations may be controlled by specific enabling/disabling conditions.

• Selection of operations may be required.
• Repeated activation of operations may be invoked.

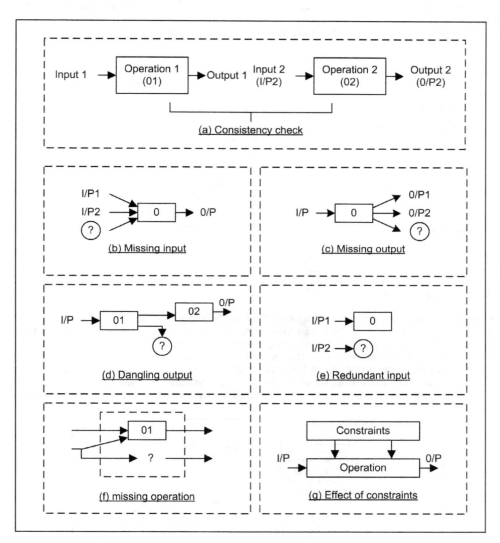

Figure 3.18 Automated checking rules

3.4.3 Viewpoint analysis.

Now what we've said so far is splendid – but its effectiveness depends on how well we can define the set of operations in the first place.   One concept that has been highly effective here is that of viewpoint analysis.

The notion of viewpoints is based on common sense; that is; we all see things from our own point of view.   Consider a system consisting of a propulsion engine driving a ship's propeller via gearing and shafting, figure 3.19. Attached to the engine is a digital control unit, its functions being to modulate engine speed.   To the marine engineer the controller is insignificant when compared with the mechanical systems. Yet the software engineer responsible for the controller programs may have a totally different perception of the situation.   He may regard software as the single most important item in the whole system, electronic hardware being a poor second.   Mechanical systems almost disappear from sight.

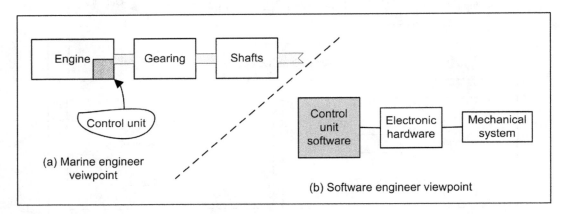

Figure 3.19 Viewpoint concept

The viewpoint analysis concept recognizes that systems cannot be adequately described from a single point of view; many must be taken into account. By setting out a system description as seen from all relevant viewpoints, consistency, correctness and completeness can be monitored.   We can then produce a software specification which is totally consistent, correct and complete – but only in terms of the information recorded in the first place. Be warned: total completeness is another myth.

Now let's see how viewpoint analysis works in practice. Assume that we have been asked to supply a digital controller for the system shown in figure 3.20. How many viewpoints should be taken into

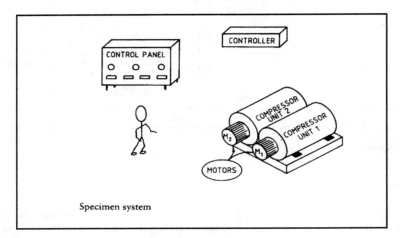

Figure 3.20 Specimen system

account? There isn't a unique answer to this; it really depends on each particular case. One tendency is to think only in terms of inanimate objects; we frequently forget people and their interactions with the system.   For this example we will describe the system as seen from the points of view of the operator and other major system items, figure 3.21.

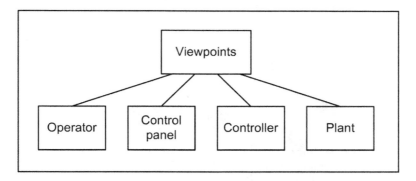

Figure 3.21 Viewpoint diagram for specimen system

Each viewpoint is described in terms of its inputs, actions (processing) and outputs, figure 3.22.

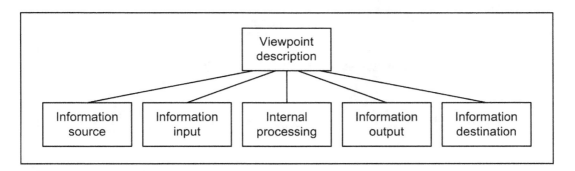

Figure 3.22 Viewpoint contents

The appropriate information is usually recorded in tabular form, precise details depending on the particular analysis method used. In the case of CORE (Controlled Requirements Expression [COR86]), the layout follows the pattern of figure 3.23.

Here part descriptions are given for the operator and control panel viewpoints. The diagram, which is self-explanatory, highlights the important features of viewpoints and viewpoint description diagrams:

• Each viewpoint describes one or more system processing operations.
• Any particular processing operations takes place in one, and only one, viewpoint.
• Inputs and outputs must balance across the full set of diagrams.

There are two aspects of viewpoint analysis that cannot be automated. First, a set of viewpoints has to be established in the first place. Second, *all* relevant information needs to be recorded. It is perfectly possible to have a balance across the set of diagrams and yet have essential data missing.

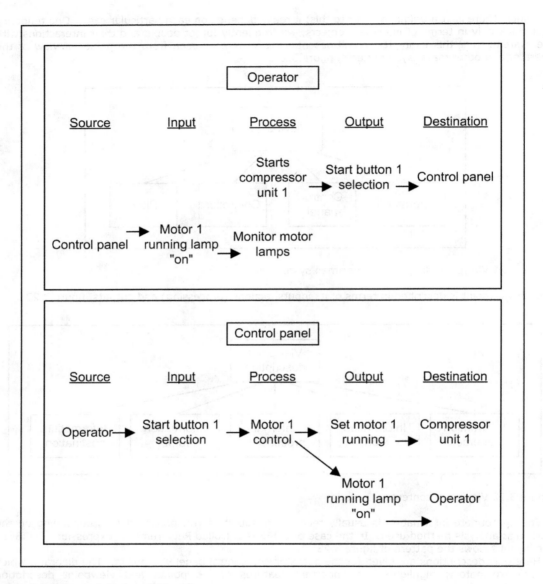

Figure 3.23 Viewpoints description diagram

3.4.4 Viewpoints - analysis versus specification.

Viewpoint analysis is an effective way of extracting, evaluating and collating information. The result should be a comprehensive description of the required system behaviour and its attributes. But two important features still need to be defined: what precisely happens within each process, and how do these relate in time (the system dynamic behaviour). To describe these we need to show three features:

• The data flow through a system.
• Detailed processing of this data.
• When such processing events occur.

One practical technique does this by combining data flow and events in a single description diagram, figure 3.24.

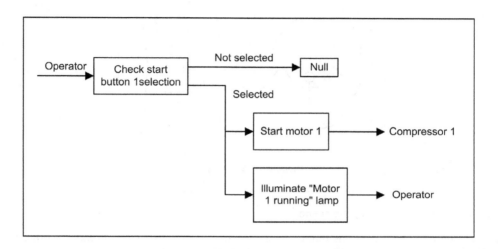

Figure 3.24 Combining data flow and events (control panel viewpoint)

Note that here we aren't really concerned with absolute time, more the sequence of events. Diagrams like these can be formed for each viewpoint, being decomposed as necessary to show more detailed information. By recording this information in the same database as the viewpoint diagrams, consistency is maintained. Moreover, detailed descriptions can be recomposed to eliminate mistakes which may have occurred during decomposition.

3.4.5 Use case analysis.

(a) Fundamentals.
Without a doubt, the analysis methodology of Ivar Jacobson [JAC92] has made an immense impact on the software scene. The technique – called a 'use-case driven approach' – has become very widely used in recent years. It is probably the dominant requirements analysis and specification method in the software world of business systems. Although it isn't so widely applied in the real-time area, its use is spreading rapidly. So what then are the fundamental ideas of use cases? Before answering that, though, there is one other important question to tackle. Exactly what does the method set out to achieve? The answer is a sixfold one. Use case techniques provide us with a way to:

• Analyze clients requirements.
• Organize and present requirements in a way that is useful, meaningful and complete.
• Minimize confusion and misunderstanding between clients and suppliers.
• Validate system-level designs.
• Develop specifications for the software system itself.
• Define the outlines of system acceptance tests (for function, performance and usage).

The underlying ideas are really quite simple (but it usually takes talented people to develop such concepts). They are based on the fact that people are users of systems, figure 3.25 And, in general, system requirements are related to the whats, whens and hows of people/system interactions. *That* is what we set out to define as part of the requirements analysis process.

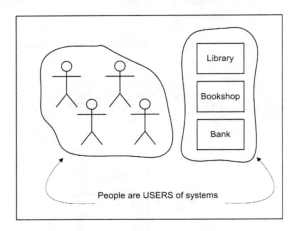

Figure 3.25 Use cases - setting the scene

Of course, the real world contains many people and many systems. First we must establish exactly what is of interest to us, which could be shown as in figure 3.26.

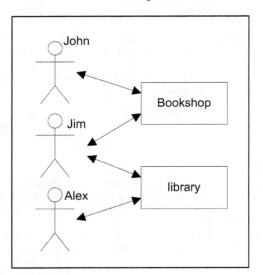

Figure 3.26 Systems and their users

Although this is a step in the right direction, the diagram has one great shortcoming. We have no idea *why* the people use such systems. This leads on to the basics of the use case diagram, figure 3.27.

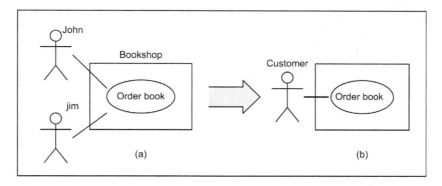

Figure 3.27 The basics of the use case diagram

It shows (figure 3.27a):

- The system of concern is a bookshop.
- There are two users (specifically two individuals).
- The individuals are using the system to order a book (or books). Any illustration of the use of a system is defined to be a 'use case'; hence this example is the use case 'order book'.

From the system's point of view the two users are essentially the same; both are customers. Therefore, rather than focussing on individuals, we try to identify the 'roles' they play in the interaction. In this example both people are 'customers', figure 3.27b.

   At this stage most of the ideas of the use case model has been established. However, it still isn't complete; we have no idea what actually goes on when a customer tries to order a book. Thus the diagram symbol needs to be backed up by a text description, figure 3.28. Here we have the essential components of a use case; a diagram symbol and a text

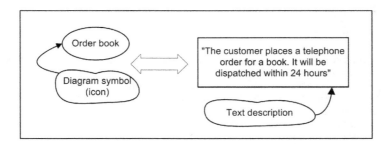

Figure 3.28 The two components of a use case

description of the user/system interaction (there is, in fact, no need to limit yourself to text; anything which imparts information can be used. But more of that later).

   From this it is but a small step to establish the components of the use case model, figure 3.29. This consists of actors, use cases and use case descriptions. Each system will have its own model, with actors depicting users (more correctly, roles performed by users). The reasons why these actors are using the system are shown as a set of use cases within the system boundary.

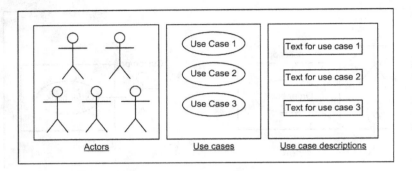

Figure 3.29 The components of the use case model

Supporting these are the use case descriptions. Two simple examples are given in figure 3.30.

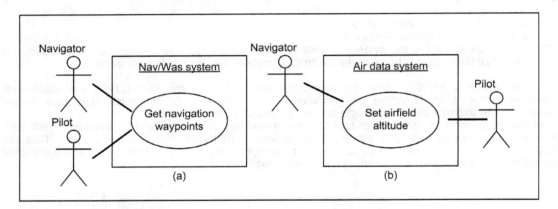

Fig 3.30 Example use case diagrams

Each system is drawn as a rectangular box, with the relevant use cases shown as ellipses inside them. Outside the system boundary are the actors, connected via lines to the use cases. In (a), both the navigator actor and the pilot actor interact with the navigation/weapon aiming (Nav/Was) system in the same way; they use it to find out what the navigation waypoints are. Information flow is a two-way process. In (b), the navigator uses the air data system to set airfield altitude: again a two-way process. However, in this case, the pilot merely receives information from the system; the role played by the actor is thus a 'passive' one.

  Summarizing things to date: the use case diagram shows all users of the system and their reasons for using the system. It should go without saying that all items on the diagram must have useful, relevant and meaningful names. Moreover, we have to be clear exactly where our system boundary lies. In the example given, both systems are within the overall aircraft system (figure 3.31). However, from the perspective of an air traffic controller the pilot and navigator form part of the *aircraft* system.

  Two small asides at this point. First, the term 'use case' is often used to denote two items; the symbol on the use case diagram and the description of the related user/system interaction. In

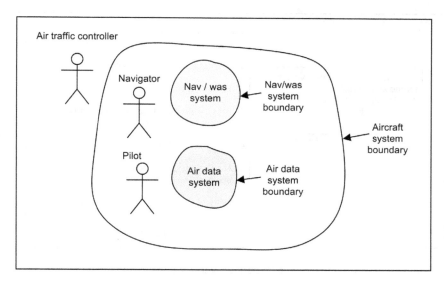

Figure 3.31 System boundaries

practice this isn't a problem; you can usually see which is one is being referred to. Second, there are many definitions of the term itself (Alistair Cockburn states 'I have personally encountered over 18 different definitions of use case, given by different, each expert, teachers and consultants '.   One widely accepted, formalized, description is 'a description of a set of sequences of actions, including variants, that a system performs that yield an observable result of value to an actor'. However, we'll take a more laid-back approach with ' is a way that an actor uses a system to achieve some desired result'. This result or 'goal' should determine the wording used on the use case diagram. If you can't express your goals simply then you don't understand what you're trying to do.

(b) Describing and structuring use cases.

Now let us look into the use case text descriptions in more detail. It is *strongly* recommended that the first attempt should be short, clear and use ordinary language, figure 3.32a.   A structured, formalized version can be used to expand on this at a later stage, figure 3.32b. Trying to do this in the beginning is often a hindrance to clear thinking.

   Observe that the text is enclosed between a START and a FINISH marker. The starting point is pretty self-evident; when the actor begins to use the system. Thus a use case always has a single starting point. This however, is not necessarily true for the finish condition, a point of much confusion. Cockburn's definition is clear and practical: 'a use case is finished when the goal is achieved or abandoned'. That's good enough for me. And this nicely leads into the topic of scenarios, figure 3.33.

   Figure 3.33a is a description of what happens assuming that everything is ok. This is one *scenario* (a particular sequence of actions and interactions) for the use case 'set airfield altitude'. The scenario, identified as 'data within valid range', has a single finish point. But what of the situation where the data entered is not within the pre-defined range?   The interactions that take place in these circumstances are shown in figure 3.33b. Here, if the data is invalid it is rejected and a request made for new data. This is a second, valid sequence of interactions for the use case, a second scenario.

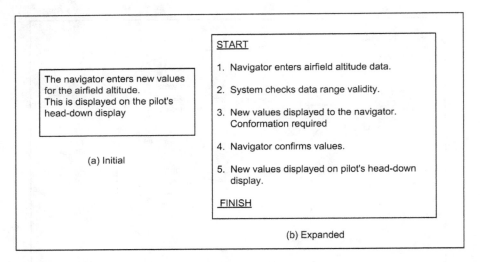

Figure 3.32 Text description - initial and expanded versions

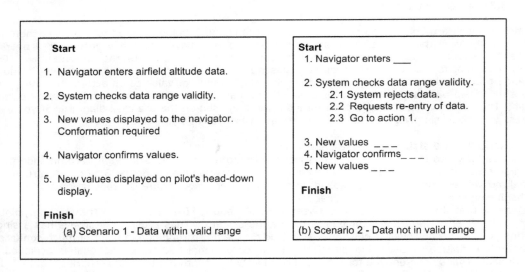

Fig 3.33 Scenarios

    We can simplify our paperwork by combining scenarios as shown in figure 3.34a. Moreover, if it helps, we can use diagrams to show the logic of the scenarios, figure 3.34b. This also brings out that there are two distinct routes through the use case text: therefore two scenarios.
    There are three kinds of scenarios, describing.

- Normal (error-free) use of the system.
- Uses where errors occur but which can be dealt with as part of the interaction process (e.g. entering invalid data).

- Uses where errors occur but which cannot be dealt with as part of the normal processing (exceptions).

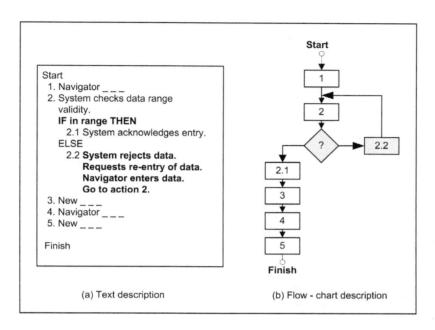

<table>
</table>

(a) Text description   (b) Flow - chart description

Figure 3.34 Combining scenarios

A major failing of analysts is in spending insufficient time and brain-power on the issues of errors and error-handling.   And yet these are, if anything, more important that the normal or 'happy day' scenarios.

   As we combine more and more scenarios, text documents soon become complex, difficult to read, difficult to understand. Hardly a step forward for mankind, as the whole point of use cases is to make things understandable.   One way of simplifying documents is to take a leaf out of programming techniques; use the equivalent of subprograms and subprogram calls (figure 3.35).

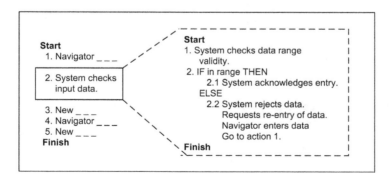

Figure 3.35 Simplifying use case descriptions

Here we aim to write the 'top-level' text as a set of sequential operations; where necessary these can be expanded in a separate text document. In fact, the separate text can be treated as a use case in its own right, figure 3.36.

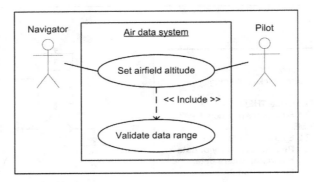

Figure 3.36 Use case diagram for figure 3.35 – the include relationship

The use case 'set airfield altitude' – the *base* use case - is considered to include that of 'validate data range'; this is defined to be an *includes* relationship. We can read the diagram to mean that the base use case *will* use the behaviour of the included use; moreover it will do so at explicit points. One last aspect of the includes relationship; the included use case should always form some part of a base use case. It is not meant to be a use case in its own right. Moreover, the included use case is an integral part of the base one; without this the base use case is incomplete. Observe the notation used and the direction of the arrow.

   Now there are situations where a base use case is complete, as per the 'check alarm status' of figure 3.37.

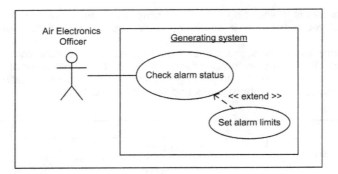

Fig 3.37 The extend relationship

Here the Air Electronics Officer starts the base use case 'check alarm status' to check out the generating system alarms. Most of the time this is the only action that is carried out. However, on certain occasions it may be necessary to (re)set alarm limits. In these circumstances extra functions are performed, defined in the use case 'set alarm limits'. Thus the functionality of the base use case is *extended* by the second one. This is denoted by drawing an arrowed line from the extended class to the base class.

The distinction between includes and extends causes much confusion. One way to resolve this is to ask the question 'if I remove the (included/extended) use case, is the base use case complete?' Another view is that:

- Include use cases collect in one place behaviour which is common to a number of base use cases (figure 3.38a).
- Extend use cases show variations on a theme (figure 3.38b).

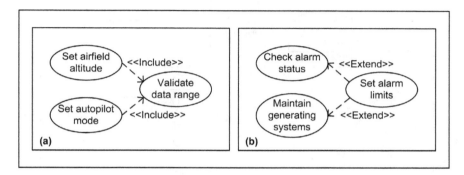

Figure 3.38 Comparing the includes and extends relationships

Unfortunately the distinction between the two isn't always clear-cut. The only advice worth giving is really not to worry too much; do whatever seems right for the problem facing you.

Up to this point we have used actors to represent the roles of people. But frequently systems interact, not only with people, but with other systems, figure 3.39a.

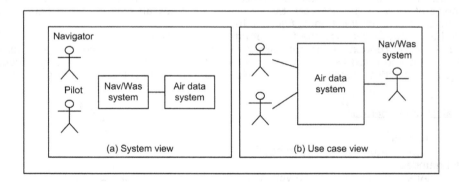

Figure 3.39 External systems as actors

Here the Nav/Was system uses information provided by the air data system. Thus, from the point of view of the air data system, the Nav/Was system is merely another actor, figure 3.39(b).

(c) Preparing for design.
If our brief was to analyze the system requirements and so produce a general set of requirements we would probably stop at this point. But as specifications for software systems, they lack depth and perhaps rigour. More work is needed. In particular we need to specify in detail the flow of information to and from the software system.

The first and obvious statement is that people cannot directly interact with software; user interfaces (hardware) are required (figure 3.40).

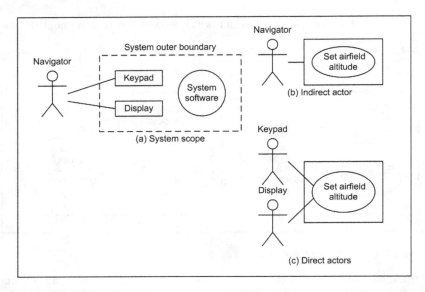

Figure 3.40 System scope, direct and indirect actors

Here we have specified our scope of interest using a system scope diagram, figure 3.40a, or something similar. Including the interface devices (i.e. keypad, display) is a most important. Now, from the point of view of the software the navigator becomes an *indirect* actor, figure 3.40b; the devices themselves are the *direct* ones, figure 3.40c.

What we have done is changed the focus of attention from the system to the software. In effect figure (c) defines the context of the software within the system. It is imperative that all interface signals are defined and listed as part of this process. Relevant parameters should be noted, initially from a system perspective. Later these can be elaborated to include electronic and software features, viz:

Signal: Lye temperature.

Initial definition:
        Temperature range 0 to 70°C.
Interim update:
        Analogue signal, 0 to 10 volts dc.   0 volts ≡ 0°C, 10 volts ≡ 100°C.
Later update:
        Input on: ADC board.
        Channel: 4.
        Digitisation: 8 bits.
        Format: straight binary.
        Memory address: 5000(h) (absolute)

Existing use case descriptions may, if desired, be updated to take the changes into account. However, a very effective way forward is to show such actor-system interactions in graphical form as per figure 3.41.

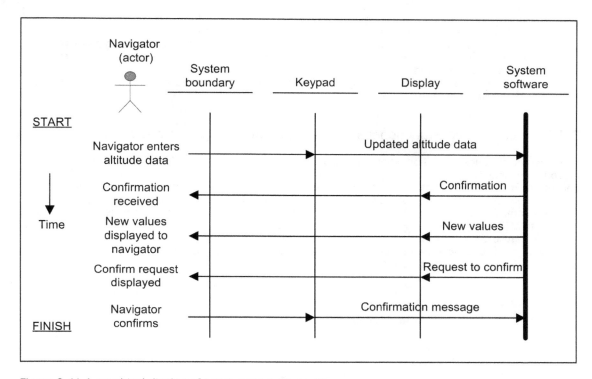

Figure 3.41 A graphical display of actor-system interaction

Cross-refer this to figure 3.40a. You will see that all items in this diagram are repeated on figure 3.41. Each one has its own time line or trace, where time runs from top to bottom of the diagram. Messages going between the different items are shown as horizontal lines, arrows denoting direction. You will also see that the system boundary has been placed on the diagram.
    You will only understand the value of this diagram when you use it in a real design. It is one of the major bridging pieces between high level (system) and software level design. In effect it guarantees that we at least start software design from the right place. Furthermore, you will find it to be of immense value when carrying out design traceability exercises.

(d) Some final points.
Just where do you start when faced with having to do high-level analysis/design of a new system (from a use case perspective, that is)? Just how do you go about developing the use case model? Generally, real-time systems have fewer actors (in the people sense) than business or IT systems. Thus identification of users should be a first priority. So define the system boundary so that only users and external systems are shown as actors. Now proceed to identify the way in which these use the system under consideration. Much information will be contained in the system SORs, for example:

- 'The system will produce a graphical display of plant parameters when requested to do so' - a particular operational requirement.
- 'The active suspension system will provide hard, firm and soft rides in response to driver input commands' - a mission requirement.
- 'The line operator must have facilities to override the automatic control system' - a specific reference to a user (people).

With business systems it may be feasible to proceed into software design before fully completing the use case model. A regularly quoted figure in OO literature is to aim for an initial completion figure of 80% – but there appears to be no evidence to back this up. For real-time (and especially embedded) systems doing this is akin to digging a hole into which you will later fall. Always complete your use case model before going forward to hardware and software design (or if you don't, make sure the omissions are justified *and* red-lined).

And finally, use cases are not the holy grail of software; they are just one more weapon in the armoury of analysis and design tools.

3.4.6 Functional, non-functional and development requirements specifications.

So far we have concentrated on what is required of a system. Now let us look specifically at the issue of software specification. Our objective during the specification phase is to produce a definitive document that states what the system is required to do. Fundamentally each requirements specification document consists of three parts: functional, non-functional and development requirements, figure 3.42. This model of the software requirements specification is based on that defined in STARTS [STA87]. Functional requirements specifications relate to system behaviour as shown in figure 3.43. They describe system operation from three perspectives: what systems do, when they do it, and how they respond to deviations of normal behaviour. Note that they should not define *how* these requirements are to be satisfied.

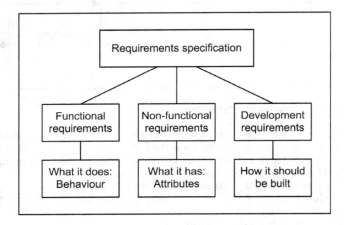

Figure 3.42 Software specification features

Observe that data input to the system, output from the system and that contained within the system itself forms part of the specification model.

The 'when' aspect expresses the dynamic behaviour of systems, both in terms of system events and real time. Events may be time dependent; but here the important point is their relationship to each other. For instance, it should not be possible to launch a missile until its hatch cover is removed. Time may be absolute, being defined in terms of the normal calendar time clock. Alternatively it may be a relative value, as in 'the low oil pressure alarm is to be inhibited for 40 seconds after the start switch is pressed'. It's also important that, when specifying dynamic behaviour, we distinguish between parallel actions and sequential ones. This can have a profound effect on resulting design decisions.

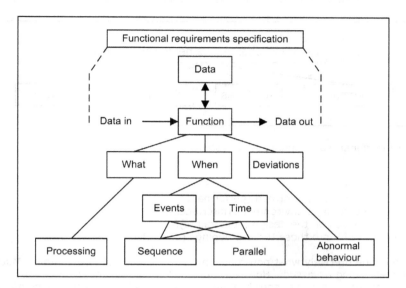

Figure 3.43 Aspects of functional requirements specifications

All real-time systems must be designed to cope with abnormal conditions to ensure safe operation. Where possible all significant deviations should be defined, together with appropriate exception-handling responses.   The information and diagrams produced previously form the basis for the software requirements specification document.   These identify the various functions, the data flows, processing of data, dependencies and deviant behaviour. The major working diagrams are those that combine system data and events; viewpoint descriptions are less useful. These diagrams need to be augmented by text specifications to provide a full description of the function. There isn't a particular prescriptive format for these documents; only guidelines can be given. The following listing (figure 3.44) is a very simplified high-level description of part of a flight control system.

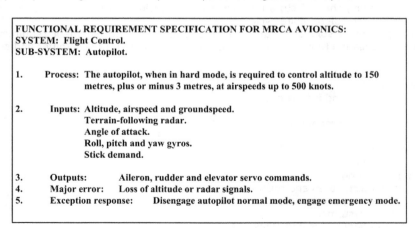

Figure 3.44 Specimen functional requirements specification

Non-functional system requirements specifications are shown in figure 3.45.

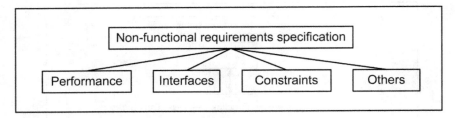

Figure 3.45 Non-functional requirements specification

These define:

• How well a function should be performed (performance).
• How the system connects to its environment (interfaces).
• What limitations are placed on the design (constraints).
• Anything which doesn't fit into these three groupings (others).

It's impossible to define precisely what non-functional specifications should contain. Much depends on the particular system being assessed. However, guidance can be given. As an example, consider the system described by the functional specification of figure 3.44. Its corresponding non-functional specification on the following page (figure 3.46.). This, of course, is a highly simplified version; the real one would occupy many pages of text.

It can be seen here that there is overlap between sections. For instance, use of the VRTX executive is listed both as an interface requirement and as a design constraint. But this is necessary because it applies to both areas of design. Furthermore, it's not always easy to decide which category items fit into. The temperature range requirement is listed here as an 'other' constraint; but it could equally well be viewed as a design constraint.

Functional specifications are highly visible parts of any development. Therefore, no matter what analysis and specification technique is used, it's normally fairly easy to identify these factors. Non-functional specifications are equally important. Unfortunately, when using informal techniques, they can disappear in the detail,. To minimize this problem – and that's all we can ever hope for – methods must be used which bring these factors formally into the design process. They then remain visible throughout the rest of the software life cycle.

The third component of software requirements specifications, development requirements, varies considerably from application to application. In the simplest situation the customer and supplier agree on:

• What is to be supplied.
• When it is to be supplied and installed.

At the other extreme requirements cover:

• The extent of supply.
• Delivery and installation.
• Formal acceptance testing.
• Project management structures and techniques.
• Formal progress reporting procedures.
• Configuration control systems.
• Design methods, methodologies and plans.
• Quality assurance.
• Reliability aspects.

• Legal, contractual and certification aspects.

One generalization can be made. As projects get larger the number of system requirements needing formal consideration increases. Even if the customer hasn't demanded such formality the supplier should impose it. Because without strict project management, formal rules, defined reporting procedures, proper recording techniques and configuration control, chaos is always likely to break out.

NON-FUNCTIONAL REQUIREMENT SPECIFICATION FOR MRCA AVIONICS:

SYSTEM: Flight Control.   **SUB-SYSTEM:** Autopilot.

1.   PERFORMANCE:
Computation: The control algorithm is of the form
$Ka[(1+ST_1) (1+ST_2)]/[(1+ST_3)(1+ST_4)]$
Computation time: This must be achieved in 5 milliseconds.
Computation accuracy: Calculations must be accurate to within 0.01%.
Control loop update rates: 100 per second.
Variation on loop sampling time: 1 millisecond from sample to sample.
Response to loss of altitude signal: 100 microseconds maximum.
Redundancy: Quad redundant processor system.
System fault handling: Majority voting on processor outputs.
     Mean Time Between Failures (MTBF) per control channel: 5000 hours.
     Reliability per control channel: 99.98%.
     Mean Time To Repair (MTTR) per control channel: 1 hour.
     Storage capacity: 1 MByte.

2.   INTERFACES.
2.1   Interfaces – MMI.
The pilots will be able to select hard, medium or soft rides via a touch screen facility on the head down display.
2.2   Interfaces – Aircraft.
(Analogue input signals: These are derived from the following sources:
Altitude, airspeed and groundspeed.
Terrain-following radar.
Angle of attack.
Roll, pitch and yaw gyros.
Stick demand.
     All are digitised using a 12 bit analogue to digital converter having a
conversion time of 10 microseconds.
(Analogue output signals: These are fed to the following items:
Aileron, rudder and elevator servo controllers.
     A 12 bit digital to analogue converter is used on the output of the controller.
(Avionics data bus: All state information is to be fed out onto the aircraft Mil-Std 1553 data bus.
2.3   Interfaces – Software.
The application software will be designed to interface to the VRTX32 real time executive.

3.   DESIGN CONSTRAINTS.
Programming language: Ada.
Operating system: VRTX32.
Avionic's data bus communication protocols: Mil-Std 1553b.
Processor type: Motorola PC604.
Maximum memory capacity (including expansion capability): 500 Kbytes.
Spare processor performance capacity on delivery: 50% min.
Documentation: JSP188.

4.   OTHER CONSTRAINTS.
Maximum size: Half ATR case size.
Maximum weight: 10 lb.
Temperature range: -55 to +125 degrees centigrade.
Servicing policy: Line replaceable unit.
Test: Built in test to identify faults to unit level.

Figure 3.46 Specimen non-functional requirements specification

3.5 Communication aspects – the role of prototyping.

3.5.1 Prototyping – an introduction.

In engineering a prototype is a pre-production version of a manufactured product such as a component, sub-assembly, system, etc. The purpose of building a prototype is to prove design and manufacturing aspects as early as possible – before resources are committed to full-scale production. A number of questions are evaluated during prototyping, including:

- Is the product actually feasible? In other words, are problems present which are fundamentally impossible to overcome?
- Are there unforeseen high-risk technical and cost aspects?
- Are the design and build correct? That is, has the correct product been built (validation), and has the product been built correctly (verification)?
- Can it be built in a manufacturing environment (as opposed to the hand-crafting methods of the prototyping phase)?
- Can it be built for the right price?

Once this phase is completed manufacture can commence with a very high level of confidence in the final product (even then success isn't guaranteed).

Normally prototypes are built to full scale. In some cases though, scaled down versions are cheaper and easier to produce. For instance, a three-eighths scale remotely controlled F15 aircraft research vehicle was used to evaluate digital flight control systems.   But no matter which method is used, prototyping is carried out for one basic reason: to answer the questions set out above.   Once this is done the prototype is usually consigned to the scrap-heap; it has served its purpose.

3.5.2 Software prototyping.

Prototyping of real software systems is, at this time, still in its infancy (perhaps its omission from the software design cycle says more about the attitudes of software practitioners than pages of words). Fortunately, though, software engineers are now beginning to understand that prototyping can bring real benefits to professional designs.   Put in a nutshell, it helps us to produce the right jobs, on time, and within budget. It can be applied in a number of different ways – and at different times – in the software life cycle, figure 3.47. Please note that the terminology used for prototyping is not consistent across the software community.

(a) Exploratory prototyping.
This is used as a tool in the development of the SOR to a point where it is acceptable to both parties. A particular version of this is animation prototyping. This involves the use of animated graphics to enhance communication between the customer and the supplier.

(b) Solution prototyping.
Here the system software requirements are prototyped, typically using commercial visual software tools. Frequently these prototyping tools produce executable code.

(c) Investigative prototyping.
This enables the designer to evaluate alternative software solutions at the design stage. Again, visual software tools may be used for this work.

(d) Verification prototyping.
This method is used to evaluate source code produced by using formal specification methods.

(e) Evolutionary prototyping.

This describes the use of working prototypes to evaluate the effects of modifications and upgrades.

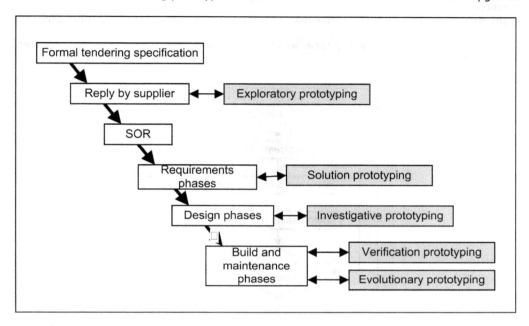

figure 3.47 Prototyping within the software life cycle

A number of points need to be made here concerning definitions, usage and prototype facilities.

First, definitions. The definitions given here are not necessary generally accepted. This is especially true of evolutionary prototyping. For many workers, true evolutionary prototyping spans the whole life cycle.

Second, usage of the prototyping methods is not simple and clear-cut. For instance, investigative prototyping can be (and frequently is) implemented using tools designed for solution prototyping.

Third, prototype facilities vary considerably. At one extreme are models designed for use in very specific parts of the software life cycle – and destined to be thrown away after use. At the other end of the scale are general-purpose models from which actual production systems emerge.

This chapter is concerned with the 'front-end' section of the software development cycle, up to the start of the design phases. Two aspects of prototyping are relevant to this area: exploratory and solution methods. The following sections discuss these in more detail.

3.5.3 Requirements prototyping.

In this section the combination of exploratory and solution prototyping is, for brevity, defined as 'requirements prototyping'. There is, in fact, another reason for grouping them together. Basically they attempt to solve the same problems.

Central to requirements prototyping is the use of models ('prototypes') to demonstrate the essential features of the proposed system. Equally important is the provision of tools for constructing and manipulating these models. Requirements prototypes serve a number of purposes, the primary ones being to:

• Act as a reference point for supplier-customer communication.
• Allow both parties to increase their understanding of the proposed system.

- Allow both parties to appreciate properly the content and implications of the requirements documents.
- Highlight important qualities such as dynamic behaviour, response times, exception handling, etc.

Figure 3.48 describes the prototyping cycle as applied either to the tendering or the requirements phases – or both.

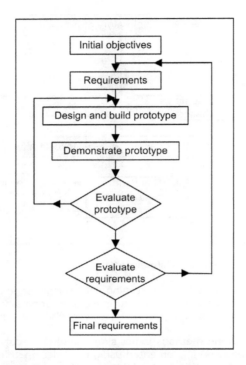

Figure 3.48 The prototyping cycle for requirements extraction

   From some initial objectives a set of requirements is formed, expressed in a preliminary defining document.   This, together with verbal and other sources of information, form guidelines for the construction of a prototype.   Once the prototype is built it is demonstrated and evaluated, being modified until it satisfies the initial specification.   At this point the requirements themselves can be evaluated using the prototype facilities.   Problems found here normally result in changes to the requirements until they are acceptable to both parties.   The outcome is a definitive requirements specification.   In the first instance this forms the SOR; later it acts as the basis for the software specification (in practice, of course, events don't take place quite so neatly).
   What are the limitations of prototypes?   In other words, how do they differ from the final (production) version of the system? This isn't an easy question to answer. There aren't at the present time, clear, defined and agreed guidelines.   Prototypes vary from simple static text type models through to those that are virtually full simulations. As a general rule prototypes should behave like the real system but with reduced functionality. Differences occur because prototypes:

- May be required to illustrate only part of the final system.
- Might require the use of computer resources that aren't available in the target system (e.g. the model itself may require 500kByte of RAM space to run in, yet the target system may only have 128kByte available).

• Do not aim – or may be unable – to produce real-time responses.
• May not be powerful enough to demonstrate all operational functions.

All prototyping methods should be economical, fast and adaptable, for the reasons given below.

(a) Economical.
Requirements prototyping is used right at the front end of the software development cycle. One possible conclusion of the analysis phase is that the proposed system is unattainable. Now, whether the project is abandoned at this stage or pursued in a modified form, the first lot of work is a write-off. Therefore costs must be kept to a minimum. This also implies a short time scale.

(b) Fast.
Answers need to produced quickly, especially prior to and during the tendering phases of the project.

(c) Adaptable.
Development of prototypes is a continual – and not a once through – process. Thus it is essential that the model can be modified easily and quickly.
   Unless these targets are attained three problems may be encountered:

• Slowness in responding to customer enquiries and requirements. This leads to a lack of confidence by the customer in the supplier's abilities.
• Inflexible models.   The consequence is that substantial effort is needed to modify and upgrade prototypes as time goes by.
• Excessive effort in developing prototypes in the first place. Prototyping is *not* an alternative to design.

Methods designed to satisfy the aims outlined above are categorized as 'rapid prototyping' – the process of building and evaluating quickly a set of prototypes.

3.5.4 Practical rapid prototyping of system requirements.

Rapid prototyping has its origins in the development of interactive information systems. From this, three major factors were identified: the user interface, the modelling environment and an output support system, figure 3.49.

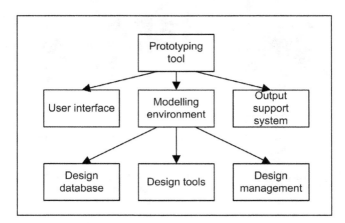

Figure 3.49 Elements of a prototyping tool

Such work showed that effective tools are needed if prototyping is to be an economical proposition. Without these it takes as much effort to develop a prototype as the production system itself. This perception lead to the development of computer aided rapid prototyping, also called *fast prototyping*. Central to this are a software design database, design tools specific to the prototyping method, and an overall design management sub-system. The function of the user interface is self-explanatory, but output support system features are tool specific. The output system is primarily concerned with demonstrating prototype operation and attributes. At its simplest level it produces fixed static descriptions in text form.   At the other extreme it provides dynamic interaction features, representation of requirements in programming language form and debugging facilities.

Requirements prototyping in real-time systems has two distinct aspects. The first describes user interaction with display systems – interactive information handling (IIH). The second relates to the interaction of a system with its external environment.

Interactive information handling is associated with human-computer interactions (HCI), usually involving screen displays. Here 'screen' prototyping is used to elicit user feedback on the 'feel' of the interface before its design is finalized. An example of this, figure 3.50, is a mock-up of a proposed avionics cockpit instrument layout

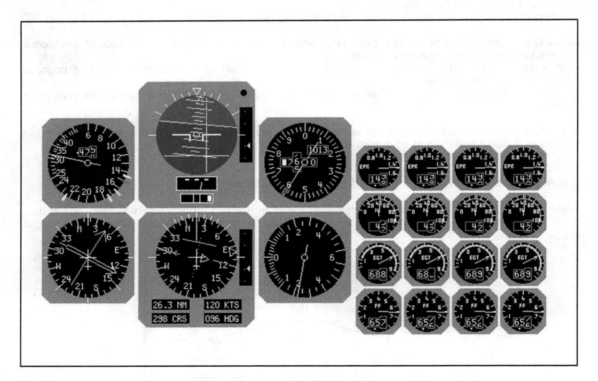

Figure 3.50 Screen prototype   -   proposed avionics cockpit instrument layout (courtesy of Professor D.J.Allerton, University of Sheffield)

HCI operations rarely involve complex information processing or logic functions, the primary concern being the presentation of information. The purpose of screen prototyping is to ensure that operator responses are efficient, correct and timely. IIH in real-time systems is broadly similar to that in batch and on-line systems. These have features which are common to all applications, and which recur with great regularity. This includes menu formats, report generation and screen painters.

The same cannot be said for system-environment interactions. Tools designed to prototype these functions must support very diverse activities. At the present time this is a rapidly growing area of work. Experience has shown that mimicking system actions (*animation prototyping*) is a powerful and meaningful way demonstrating system behaviour. Moreover, with such tools it is possible to add interactive animation facilities to basic screen prototypes.

3.5.5 Animation prototyping - concepts and application.

First, some definitions. Animation prototyping is 'the visualization and demonstration of *intended* system behaviour'. Central to this is that behavioural aspects are *pre-defined*. Simulation, by contrast, is 'a prediction and demonstration of *actual* system behaviour'; behaviour is normally *computed* as the simulator runs.

The application of animation prototyping to real-time systems can be illustrated using the nitrogen plant of figure 3.51.

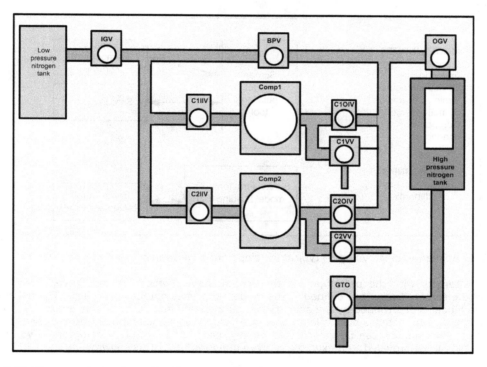

figure 3.51 Nitrogen plant schematic diagram

This represents a chemical plant, designed to take in gas at atmospheric pressure and compress it into liquid form. This liquid is deposited, at high pressure, into a storage vessel. Two compressors are used, connected in parallel. A variety of valves are fitted which, together with the compressors, provide control of plant operation. It is required to equip this system with a processor-based controller having appropriate human-machine interfaces. Let us look at how animation prototyping can be applied here.

First, it is essential to clearly understand the nature of prototyping run-time and development environment (figures 3.52 and 3.53).

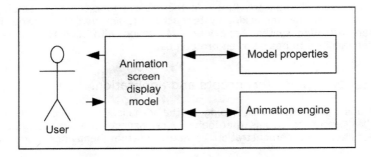

Figure 3.52 Animation prototyping - typical run-time environment

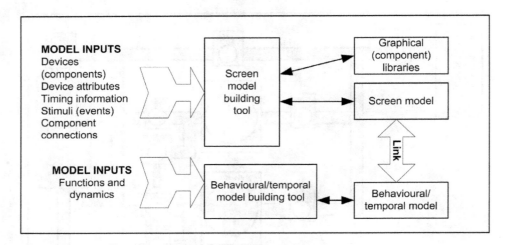

Figure 3.53 Animation prototyping - typical development environment

The user interacts with the prototype via the screen model (which can also accept user inputs). Details of the screen display are defined in the model properties database (or file). The behaviour of the screen model is determined by the animation engine, taking into account time and/or user inputs.
   Usually the screen model is built using a graphics-based model building tool.(most modern tools are PC-based). Such models can be constructed rapidly, easily and cheaply if comprehensive graphical component library is provided. An example is given in figure 3.54. This shows:

• Figure 3.54a: a selected icon – a toggle switch – from the predefined library of components. It is
   customised by editing its associated property dialog box.
• Figure 3.54b: the customised icon, together with the completed property dialog box details.

However, in engineering, many symbols, icons, etc. are domain-specific; hence it is essential that the user has facilities to create these as and when required.
   Associated with the screen model is the behavioural/temporal model, figure 3.53. This is usually built as a separate item and then linked up with the screen model. Both functional and dynamic information is provided to the model as it is built. A variety of methods can be used to build this model, figure 3.55. This is usually based on information supplied by the customer.

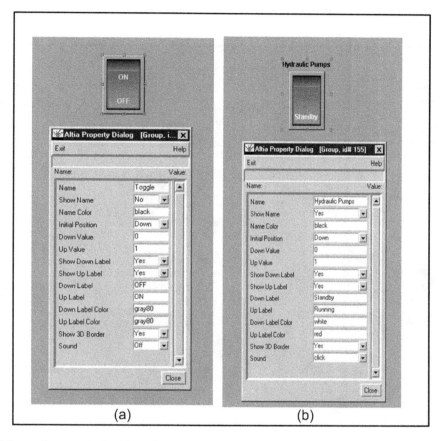

Figure 3.54 Example steps in building the screen model

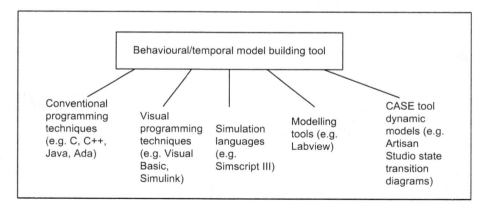

Figure 3.55 Methods for developing the behavioural/temporal model

An example animated screen model is that of the nitrogen plant, figure 3.56.

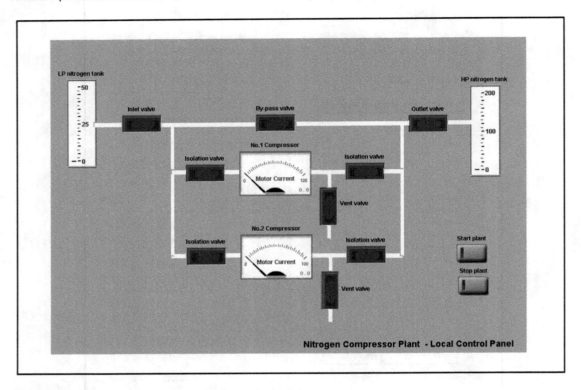

Figure 3.56 Nitrogen plant - animated screen model

This serves two purposes. First, it shows the intended functionality and layout of plant local control panel. Second, because it is animated, it can be used to verify the ease of use, clarity of display and correctness of behaviour of the interface.   Without a doubt the technique is a powerful one for resolving HCI requirements in real-time systems.

   Screen prototyping, as a method of describing interactions between the plant and its environment, is quite limited.   Instead, animating plant operation itself is highly effective as a learning and communication tool, figure 3.57.   Given here are particular frames from the animation, showing power-up, normal running and fail-safe conditions.   Attached to each frame is the corresponding section from the SOR.   In the initial stage of analysis each component is described in 'black box' terms; little internal detail is provided.   Even so the model allows the user to step through various sequences and to interact with the display. As development progresses the model can be elaborated and refined.   In particular, time constraints, component performance factors and safety features can be included.   Thus the prototype is developed in an evolutionary manner, ultimately approaching the performance of a simulator.

   Just to recap: rapid prototyping is an effective and realistic requirements analysis method, but to be commercially practical three criteria must be satisfied.   First, models must be produced quickly – ranging from a few days to a few weeks. Second, the model should represent the problem in terms of the customer's viewpoint. Third, both the customer and the supplier must be allowed to interact with the model.

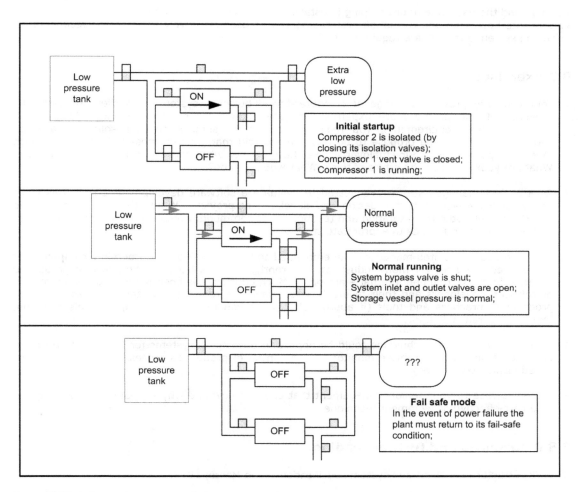

Figure 3.57 Animated operation of the nitrogen plant

3.6 Review.

On completing this chapter you should now:

- Be able to explain the realistic development of software in real-time systems.
- Appreciate how important it is to properly and fully establish the true requirements of systems before plunging into design.
- Recognize the problems associated with formulating, communicating and understanding requirements.
- See why tool support is important for developing and maintaining analysis and specification documents.
- Understand the basics of viewpoint and use case analysis and appreciate that these are complementary, not conflicting, techniques.

• Understand the basic role of prototyping in establishing system requirements.
• Appreciate how rapid and animation prototyping can be used effectively as front-end techniques in defining system and software requirements.

3.7 Exercises.

1. Your company provides a range of computer-based business systems.   A client requests the provision of one of the more expensive implementations for his application.   However, on evaluating their requirements, you realize that a much simpler, cheaper solution would be satisfactory.   When you propose to do this you are told that your business is to make as much money as possible for your employer – give the customer what was asked for in the first place. What are your views on the ethics of this? What would you do?

2. As a project manager, you are requested to evaluate a software development plan.   This gives details of a two-year software design and development project.   Within this time frame, three months are allocated to integration and testing. What comments would you make concerning this; justify them with reference to appropriate statistics?

3. You have been appointed manager of an embedded software development group in a company that makes diesel engines for many industries.   Currently, relations between the software group and clients – both external and internal – are poor. Much criticism has been made of the 'remoteness' of software developers and their failure to understand the real needs of the business.   List the procedures, practices and tools (if appropriate) which you might use to improve this situation. Explain your reasoning.

4. Explain how use case techniques could be applied in developing systems for factory control room operation (this involves remote monitoring and control of production processes, using computer-based display techniques).

5. Present a case to your senior management that explains how and why animation prototyping can be a cost-effective development technique.

3.8 References and further reading.

[DEM78] Structured analysis and system specification, T. De Marco, 1978.

[FAR75] Reliable computer software - what it is and how to get it, project report, Defense Systems Management School, Fort Belvoir, Virginia, Nov. 1975.

[STA87] The STARTS guide - a guide to methods and software tools for the construction of large real-time systems, NCC Publications, 1987.

Controlled Requirements Expression (CORE), Systems Designers plc, Hampshire, UK, 1986.

Embedded Graphics and Data Models – New approaches in the development of graphical user interfaces, Klaus Gerstendörfer , Robert Schachner and Peter Schuller, https://www.xisys.de/download/archives/EmbeddedGraphics-Innovations_002.pdf.

Mastering the Requirements Process: Getting Requirements Right, Suzanne Robertson and James Robertson, 2012

Object-Oriented Software Engineering: A Use-Case Driven Approach, I.Jacobson et al, Addison-Wesley, 1992.

Rapid Control Prototyping, National Instruments, http://www.ni.com/rcp/

Rapid Prototyping for Embedded Control Systems, MathWorks, https://uk.mathworks.com/solutions/rapid-prototyping.html

Requirements Engineering - A good practice guide, I.Sommerville and P.Sawyer, 1997.

Software Engineering, 10th Edition, Ian Sommerville 2015.

The Unified Modelling Language User Guide, G.Booch, J.Rumbaugh and I.Jacobson, 1998.

Writing Effective Use Cases, Alistair Cockburn, 2000

For an interesting demonstration of animation techniques see http://opcweb.com/.
From Open Automation Software, https://openautomationsoftware.com/

END OF CHAPTER

Chapter 4

Software and program design concepts

The effects produced by poor software – covered in chapter 2 – can't be dismissed lightly. Equipment damage, personal injury and deaths have resulted from mistakes in software.   Even where such disasters are avoided software liabilities can financially cripple a company. Three factors are usually at work here: late delivery of the software, overrun on budget and massive installation/maintenance efforts. Therefore the primary goal of any software team is to eliminate the possibility of such events. To do this it must deliver dependable software, on time, within cost. These 'high-level' objectives can be attained only by using professional design methods. Such methods enable designers to achieve specific 'low-level' targets for quality code production. These features, already discussed in chapter 2, include:

- Formal and rigorous design methods.
- Properly documented software.
- Understandable designs.
- Robust and stable software.
- Maintainable programs.
- Portable and re-usable software.

These are the goals of the software engineer. How well they are achieved depends considerably on both the tools and techniques used in the design process. Here we limit ourselves to techniques, the purpose of the chapter being to:

- Outline fundamental design strategies and design factors incorporated within these strategies.
- Describe how and why modular design is essential for the production of good software.
- Show the influence of structured programming on software design.
- Describe modern design methodologies, including functionally structured, object-oriented and data flow methods.

Later work (in Volume 2) extends this by showing how such methods are used to produce working design documents. These aspects are also described in the context of specific design methodologies.

4.1 Design fundamentals.

4.1.1 The design and development process – an introduction.

Design and development is the process of turning ideas (the specification) into reality (the product), figure 4.1. There are a number of distinct stages in this operation; each one can be analysed and described as a separate item. Here we'll concentrate on that identified as 'design'.   But remember, in producing the product, they are highly interactive. The idea that design is a once-through activity, never to be repeated, belongs to the world of science fiction. Consequently any useful design method must be able to handle change easily, simply and efficiently.

   The purpose of this section is to describe the design process in general conceptual terms. However, many people find that abstract descriptions of processes aren't especially helpful. So the approach used here takes a particular (fictional) auto-engineering design problems and shows alternative ways of solving it.   It then generalizes from these specific ideas and methods to the more abstract design concepts.

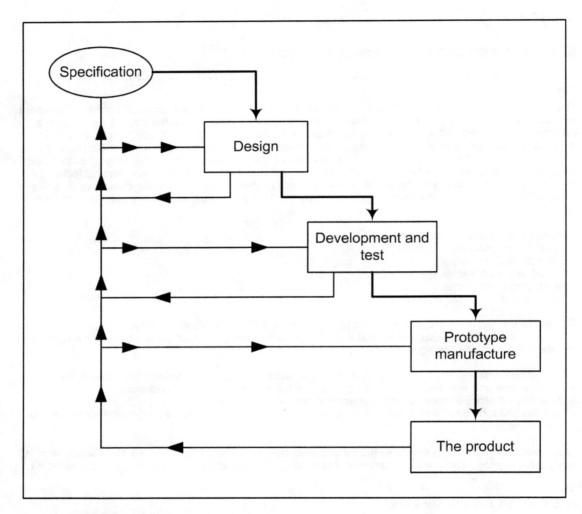

Figure 4.1 The design and development process

Assume that the objective is to design a vehicle power-train system. The fuel source is diesel, the final drive method being two road wheels. From this simplified specification the designer organizes his ideas, in the first case expressing the solution in very general terms.   As with most forms of engineering this involves the use of diagrams (figure 4.2). Here the design specification is translated into a number of feasible alternatives. The expanded descriptions are more detailed and refined, but still operate at the conceptual level. Now the designer can move – in stages – to the general design level (figure 4.3).

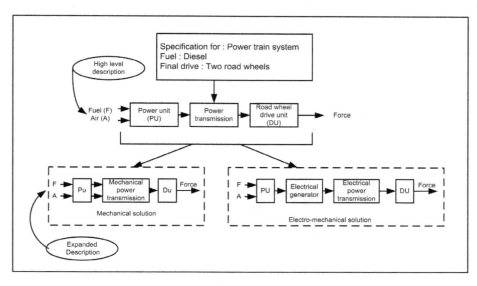

Figure 4.2 Specification translation – high-level description

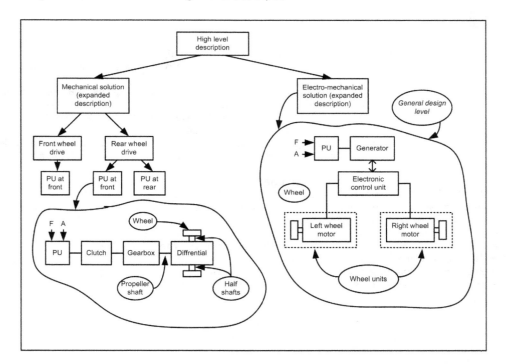

Figure 4.3 Translation to the general design level

At this stage the 'best' solution is identified, and work proceeds into the detailed design phase (figure 4.4).

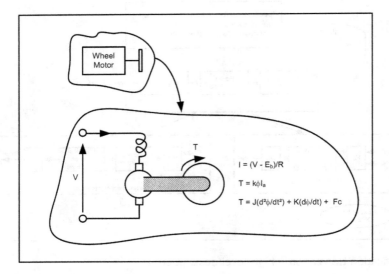

Wheel
Motor

$I = (V - E_b)/R$

$T = k\phi I_a$

$T = J(d^2\phi/dt^2) + K(d\phi/dt) + Fc$

Figure 4.4 Detailed design level

This approach should sound reasonable and logical. Good. But you may then well ask 'what's so special about this? Isn't it what we'd expect to happen?'. Yes, but because the approach is 'sensible' we tend not to see the profound design concepts inhere in the method. Let's look at it again, stage by stage.

First, there is translation from a specification to a conceptual solution. This is a creative activity which cannot be taught; it must be learned. Here there is no substitute for experience and knowledge. Moreover, at even at this very abstract stage, the designer is guided by his knowledge of what is practicable. So, note point one: creativity and knowledge.

The second stage, expanding the basic ideas, is one that involves both design creativity and design technique. Expansion takes place in a controlled, organized and logical manner. Note point two: method and organization.

Observe here that two solutions have been generated (many others are possible). This highlights the fact that there isn't a unique answer to each problem. A good designer will try first to identify realistic alternatives and then assess their qualities. Here, for instance, the assessment factors involve cost, performance, technology level, manufacturing aspects, etc. Point three: identification and evaluation of design options.

It may seem surprising that it is easier to assess information when dealing with an abstract model. But what this does is allow us to ignore detail and concentrate on the big picture (the really important view). Point four: postponement of detailed design decisions for as long as possible.

When the descriptive model is expanded into something fairly specific the following factors can be tackled:

• Identification of functions and partitioning by subsystems.
• Identification of interfaces between subsystems.
• Evaluation of subsystem interaction.
• Identification of work-loading and allocation.
• Assessment of manpower requirements.

Point five: general design evaluation.

At this stage the basic feasibility of the project has been assured. Detailed design calculations can be carried out knowing, at least, that the right problem is being tackled. Point six: solve the right problem.

The process described here is one of working from a very general top-level view of the problem to a specific design solution. This approach is usually called 'top-down'. However, no real design proceeds in this way. The designer always guides the work towards feasible solutions (often unconsciously). That is, he uses knowledge relating to the bottom end of the design process, a 'bottom-up' method. Added to this is a further complicating factor. Frequently the designer identifies high-risk areas early on in the design exercise (in the example here for instance, the use of electrical power transmission may raise special technical difficulties). Such problems are likely to be tackled early (and in some detail), a 'middle-out' design approach.

   Gathering all these facts, recommendations and ideas together enables us to define the rules of workable design techniques:

- Use method and organization in the design process.
- First define the problem solution in general concepts.
- Identify and evaluate all <u>sensible</u> design options.
- Postpone detailed design decisions for as long as possible.
- Identify system functions.
- Partition the overall system into manageable subsystems.
- Identify interfaces between subsystems.
- Evaluate subsystem interaction.
- Solve the right problem.
- Base the design method on a top-down approach augmented by bottom-up and middle-out actions.
- Always review and, where necessary, re-do designs (iterate).
- Be prepared to throw away awkward, complex or redundant design parts (no matter how attached to them you become).

By using these rules we've introduced order and logic into system design, that is, structure. Now, you'll see the words 'structured design' in every textbook on software engineering. Some computer scientists actually believe that this general methodology was invented by the software community. In fact all good engineering design is structured; the Egyptians practised it thousands of years ago when they built the Pyramids.

4.1.2 Fundamental design strategies.

A number of design methods are currently used by the software community. Therefore, to explain the concepts and principles involved, let us look at the problem outlined below.

   The overall task in question is the design of a vehicle anti-skid braking system. Its purpose is to eliminate vehicle skidding by preventing lock-up of the wheels. The software-based control system measures the speed of each wheel, calculates acceleration/deceleration values, and, using this data, detects the onset of wheel lock-up. Should lock-up occur then command signals back-off the braking effect. Speed sensors and brake actuators (hydraulic servo units) are fitted as appropriate.

   Figure 4.5 shows two possible system design solutions to this problem. The reasons for showing these are to reinforce several important points:

- Software engineers do not design embedded *systems*.
- The purpose of the software is to make the system work correctly (in other words, to carry out very specific functions).
- How the software is designed is up to the software engineer, but it *must* provide the required functionality.
- A good understanding of system structure and operation is needed in order to produce a dependable software design.

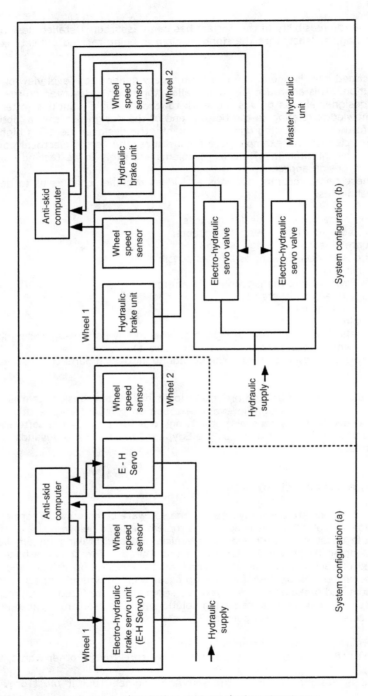

Figure 4.5 Anti-skid braking system - alternative system design structures

Currently three distinct methodologies are used for software design:

• Functional structuring.
• Object structuring.
• Data flow structuring.

In reality there is a fourth approach, defined by Tom DeMarco as the 'Mugwump School' .   It is practised by 'people who believe design is for cissies and that the structure of the system should be whatever occurs to the coder while seated at the terminal'.   This has no place in a professional environment; yet all too often real-time software is designed in this way.

(NB: functional and data flow structuring are often considered to be synonymous.   Although they have much in common they are *not* the same).

First consider describing the system and its design using a functionally-structured method (figure 4.6).   Here the system structure is expressed in terms of the functional interaction of the different parts. In this case four functions are defined:

• Measure wheel speed.
• Store measured data.
• Calculate vehicle conditions.
• Output commands to brake units.

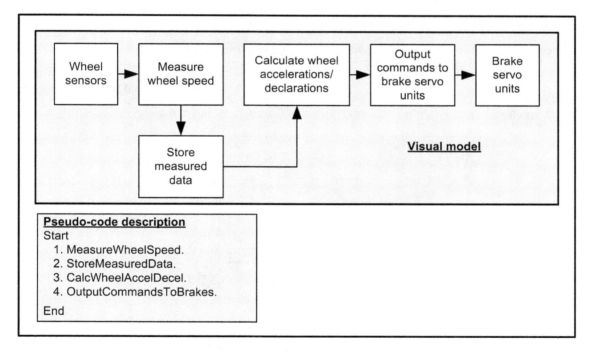

Figure 4.6 Functional view of the anti-skid system

Using this functional description we could implement the system shown in figure 4.5a. Equally well we could adopt the method of figure 4.5b.   In contrast, the object-structured method describes the system as a collection of objects (figure 4.7), not functions.

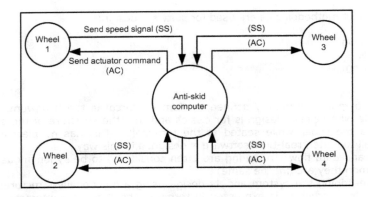

Figure 4.7 Object-structured view of the anti-skid system

Communication between objects is carried out using messages, the ones shown here being 'Send speed signal' and 'Send actuator command'.   Object internal actions aren't shown (at this level) in order to hide the 'how' from the 'what'. By using this technique objects can be treated as separate but co-operating entities.   This profoundly changes how we view the problem and institute design solutions. Remember that when using a functional approach, speed measurement, computation and actuator control are all linked together.   But with object structuring they are quite clearly decoupled. Moreover, each object has clearly defined responsibilities, viz:

• Wheel 1: Measure wheel speed, store wheel 1 data, generate speed signal.
• Anti-skid computer: Calculate acceleration/deceleration commands for all wheel servos.

These may not seem especially significant – until we change the system.   Suppose now that each wheel is to be monitored for tyre pressure, this being linked into a diagnostic computer. Changing the object-structured design to reflect this modification is fairly simple, figure 4.8.

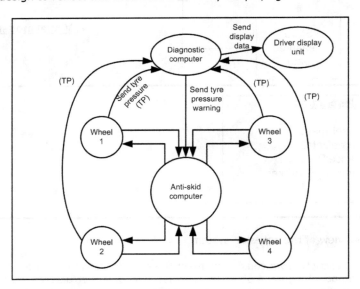

Figure 4.8 Modified object-structured diagram

By contrast the corresponding functionally-structured design would require a major re-build. However, this example isn't meant to imply that object structuring is better or easier than functional structuring. It's just a different way of looking at the same problem.

The final method is that of data flow structuring, figure 4.9. It is based on the following concepts:

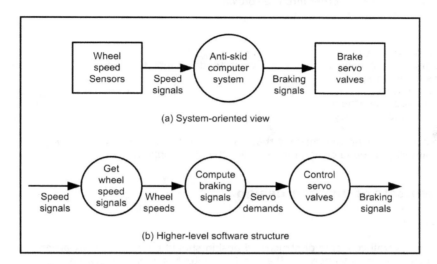

Figure 4.9 Data flow view of the anti-skid braking system

- The software is initially treated as a single component part of the overall system (figure 4.9a).
- Emphasis is placed on establishing the requirements, features and qualities of the overall system (and not merely the software).
- The software is formed as a set of communicating software machines, each having clearly defined functions and responsibilities, figure 4.9b.

There is one essential difference between this technique and an OO approach. Here the model is based on a materials flow one, the 'material' being the data that flows between the machines (or 'processes'). By contrast OO methods assume a client/server relationship between objects.

More will be said later concerning this topic when software design processes are described.

Each method described above illustrates one specific way of tackling a design and development problem. But these aren't mutually exclusive; using one doesn't preclude use of the others (shrieks of horror from the OO purists). Each provides a different view of the problem. In practice many solutions use a combination of the methods, picking them as appropriate. Some design methodologies are composites of these, which, at first, can be quite confusing.

4.1.3 How to generate abysmal software – the good kludge guide.

There are at least three ways to develop software: unplanned, apparently planned and properly designed. The first is practised by those who don't believe in software design. But, surprisingly, this is also true of the second group. Only it doesn't seem like it at the time. Such people produce plans; and don't use them at the coding stage. Documentation produced for the software is often done <u>after</u> coding. It may look impressive; whether it really describes what the code does is another matter.

Lee Harrisberger, in his book *Engineermanship, a Philosophy of Design,* describes the production of a 'kludge'. In essence this is a product that, no matter what you do, is always going to be a mess. Producing code without designing the software in the first place results in a kludge. For those who consider design rules to be an infringement on their creativity and individuality, the following good kludge guide is offered. Moreover the rest of the chapter can be skipped.

- Don't plan.
- Don't introduce structure or order into the software.
- Begin coding straight away.
- Be clever.
- Be obscure.
- Don't use standard methods – invent new ones.
- Insist that the source code listing is sufficient to document the software – and use cryptic and meaningless comments.
- Never revise the design.
- Make the software unportable.
- Sacrifice all to code efficiency.

The real reason for giving this guide is that it neatly and concisely highlights why so much software is abysmal. Simply put, good design methods are the direct opposite of these.

4.2 The elements of modular design.

4.2.1 Introduction.

At this stage the overall concepts of structured design should be clear (if they aren't, go back and re-read earlier sections). We can now put them in the context of specific software design methodologies. But before doing so the more important elements and building blocks of the design process need to be explained. Some of these we've already met within the framework of general design procedures. Now their functions as software design elements are examined.

4.2.2 Modules and modularization.

It can be seen that a basic feature of 'good' design is the partitioning of systems into smaller chunks. The primary reason is to reduce the total problem into one of manageable proportions (the 'head full of information' limit). In software terms this process is call 'modularization', the elements resulting from this being 'modules'. It is a basic requirement that modules should be fairly simple, thus enabling us to:

- Understand their purpose and structure.
- Verify and validate their correctness.
- Appreciate their interaction with other modules.
- Assess their effect on the overall software structure and operation.

But precisely what is a module? Many definitions are possible; here it is considered to be 'a software unit which has a well-defined function and well-defined interfaces to other program elements'. Clearly, a module can be defined using functional, object or data flow structuring. How it's implemented is – at this stage – not important. Before doing that, the designer must answer one major question: precisely how should a system be modularized?

There isn't a unique solution to this; much depends on the particular application. Even then, significantly different approaches can be used. Consider, for instance, writing software to implement the anti-skid braking and tyre-pressure monitoring systems. One solution is shown in figure 4.10 (for simplicity only two wheels are automated). Note the similarity between this and figure 4.6. This reinforces the fact that software design is just one stream within the total range of design techniques.

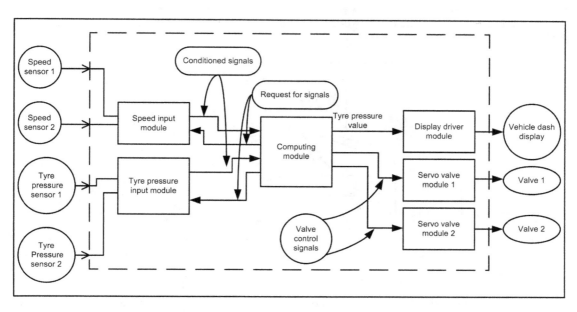

Figure 4.10 Modularization – solution 1

An alternative solution is that of figure 4.11.

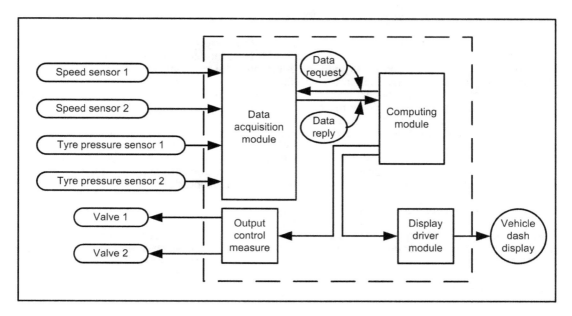

Figure 4.11 Modularization – solution 2

This might be the one which maps the software onto the hardware in a more logical manner.   Then again, it might not. It depends on the decisions that were made when designing the modules (figure 4.12).

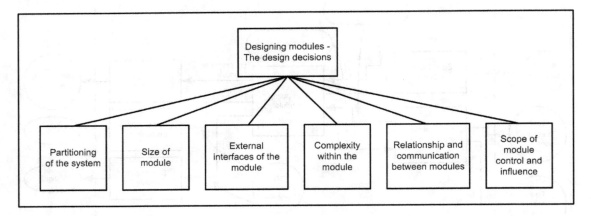

Figure 4.12 Modules – design decisions

These determine the resulting module structure, organization and performance.   But how can we decide whether the modularization we've arrived at is a good one or not?   The answer (in part, at least) lies in the properties of modules known as coupling and cohesion.

4.2.3 Coupling – a measure of module independence.

Modules cannot exist in isolation. Each one is designed to perform part of the total system function; therefore they must communicate with each other. Now, experience has shown that the amount of interaction between modules has a significant effect on software quality.   Where modules are well defined, having clear functions and simple interfaces, levels of interaction are low.   In other words, modules are relatively independent.   Such designs are usually easy to understand; they are also reliable and maintainable when put into service.   Moreover, the software exhibits a high degree of stability; changes within a single module don't 'ripple through' the program.

   In aiming for low interaction we need to distinguish between information volume and information complexity.   Transferring a large amount of data between modules may be a fairly simple task – if we're dealing with simple data types.   For instance, moving an array of 500 elements is both straightforward and easy to comprehend.   Yet a module which transfers five different data items may be much more difficult to understand – because it has a complex interface, as in:

WriteReal (Integrate(Square,a,b,Simpson,Intervals), 15);

where Integrate and Square are both function procedures.   Consequently, reducing information *complexity* is a primary design aim.   But this isn't the only factor which affects module interaction. Information *type and communication* methods also strongly influence system behaviour.   Thus when evaluating the degree of module independence we need to take all three into account.   This is done using a software measure called 'coupling'. Module coupling occurs in a number of ways, as follows:

- Content coupling.
- Common coupling.
- Stamp coupling.

• Data coupling by reference.
• Data coupling by value.

These are discussed in detail later.
   When modules communicate, the information content may take various forms, figure 4.13.

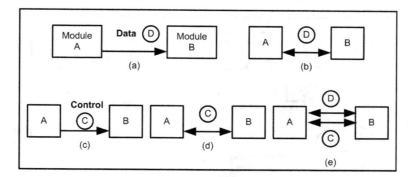

Figure 4.13 Communication between modules

In (a), module A sends data to B, just about the simplest contact method (typified by the conditioned speed signals of figure 4.10). Naturally enough data transfer can be a two-way process, (b). Modules also need to be able to control actions within other modules, leading to the use of control signals, figure 4.13(c) ('flags', 'control couples'). Again looking at figure 4.10, the 'request for signal' can be regarded as a control couple. This increases the interaction between modules; what happens in one depends on decisions made in the other. Control coupling can also be a two-way affair, (d), while the most general case involves two-way data and control couples, (e).
   Note that no assumptions have been made about the relationship between modules. They may, for instance, have equal standing in the system. Alternatively there may be a hierarchical structure, involving calling and called modules (figure 4.14).

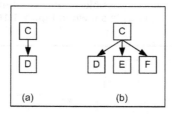

Figure 4.14 Hierarchical module structure

   Two simple examples are shown here. In the first, C invokes D to perform some task; in the second, C first invokes D, then E, and finally F. These invoked modules are activated only by command of the calling module. Operations like these can be implemented quite easily in software, especially when using procedurized high-level languages. However, when modules have the same rank their activation is quite different; fundamentally it is a system (usually an operating system) function. Be warned: much published work on structured design implicitly assumes that modular designs are always hierarchical.
   Many early texts on this topic were written from the DP point of view. In such designs control couples can be minimized. But for embedded software they are a natural and commonplace requirement, being essential for event signalling. So although they increase the coupling between

modules, they can't be dispensed with. The rule is, use them with care and thought. And, with hierarchical modularization, control flags should only be transferred at a single level. If they pass through a number of levels there is a marked increase in coupling between modules.

Now let's turn to *communication connection* methods, using the output control module of figure 4.11 as an example. There are two quite distinct methods for transferring information into the module (figure 4.15).

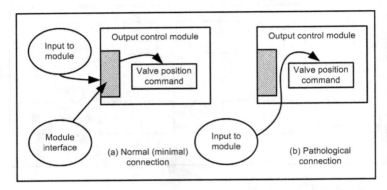

Figure 4.15 Module connection methods

Using the 'normal' (sometimes called 'minimal') method, all information transfer is done via a controlled interface. Assume, for instance, that the computing module wishes to update the valve position command. Information is transferred into the output control module via its interface; setting up the command value is performed by code within the module. This gives secure, reliable and testable module operation. However, if the valve position command information can be loaded directly from outside the module, these benefits are lost. This is called a 'pathological' connection (yes, I know it's a crazy word but that's computer science for you).

Information complexity and type are highly visible items; hence they are readily controlled. By contrast, module *connection* methods can be quite difficult to manage. There are many ways (deliberately or accidentally) to increase coupling between modules through poor choice of connectivity.   Let's begin with the worst possible situation, commonly met in assembly language programming. This, called 'content coupling', is shown in figure 4.16.

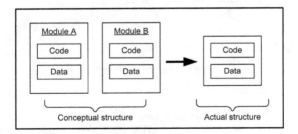

Figure 4.16 Content coupling

Our concept is one of separate modules, each having their own code and data areas. In reality all items can be accessed from anywhere within the program because there isn't a mechanism to prevent this (it depends entirely on the discipline and professionalism of the programmer). Therefore module A can, at any time, make a pathological connection into B (and vice versa). But there is a more subtle (and very undesirable) feature here. Because the code written for A is visible in B, it can be used by

B. So, thinks the programmer, if there are identical functions in A and B, why write the code twice? Do it once only and use it in both modules.   The result?   A saving on memory space (usually insignificant) --and instant tight coupling. Code sharing should *never* be done unless there are very good reasons for it (discussed later under 'functional decomposition').

  Improvements can be made by limiting the amount of code and data that can be accessed globally (figure 4.17).

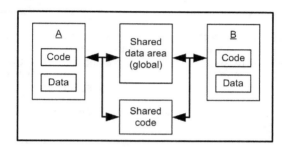

Figure 4.17 Common resource sharing (common coupling)

Here each module has its own private code and data areas. A global data area is used for the sharing of common information, while some code is available for general use. This structure is frequently met in high-level languages, particularly the older ones such as Coral66. Modules are built using program segments; this serves to keep code and data private.   Shared resources are normally provided via some form of 'common' attribute of the language.

  Limiting resource sharing significantly improves (that is, loosens or weakens) coupling between modules.   It is, though, intrinsically unsafe.   All global data areas are accessible by all modules; therefore they can also be modified by all modules. Better coupling is attained by defining a specific data structure for holding shared data, then passing pointers to this structure between modules (figure 4.18).

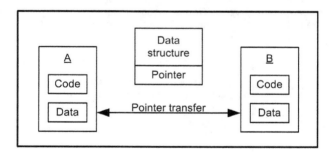

Figure 4.18 Data structure coupling (stamp coupling)

For this to work properly both modules must know how the data area is structured.   Moreover, the information within each module must be consistent.

  Data structure coupling (called 'stamp coupling') is useful for handling file information. Larger real-time systems frequently use comprehensive file storage systems, including duplicated on-line data bases.   However, mass storage is rarely incorporated in small embedded systems.   Here stamp coupling is most likely to be used for the design of real-time executives or operating systems.

In all real-time designs a primary concern is the handling of program data, this being located in normal RAM store. To transfer such information between modules we can use either direct or indirect data coupling. With direct transfer, figure 4.19, the sending module passes the *value* of the data to the receiving module.

This is a highly secure method – data values can be modified by only one module at a time, the current holder. In many instances transmitted items are copies of the originals. As these originals are held in the sending module the recipient cannot change their state.   There may not seem any particular advantage in this – until the receiving module corrupts the data. At least then we can 'roll-back' the program to the point where the data was good, a technique sometimes used in critical systems.

It isn't possible to use direct data transfer for all applications, two particular commonplace examples illustrating this.   Consider first where the data includes relatively large arrays of floating point numbers, each one occupying 8 bytes of RAM space. Making copies of these structures would soon exhaust the data store space of a normal embedded computer. Another situation also negates the use of the direct transfer method.   This occurs when the receiver module isn't able to directly pass data back to the original sender – a regular requirement when using hierarchical structuring. To cope with these situations the *address* of the data (not the data itself) is passed between modules (figure 4.20).

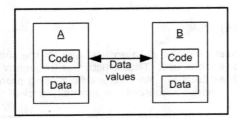

Figure 4.19 Data coupling – by value

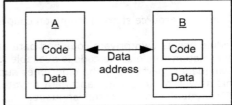

Figure 4.20 Data coupling - by reference

Thus the receiving module accesses the data using the address information – access by reference.

Coupling by reference is much more secure than stamp coupling. This security is enhanced by using modern languages which ensure consistency of data structures amongst program modules.   It is, though, less secure than coupling by value (for obvious reasons). Taking all factors into account we can draw up a table (table 4.1) that shows their influence on module coupling.

System parameter	Factors producing high coupling (poor)	Factors producing low coupling (good)
Information complexity	Complicated/obscure information	Simple/clear information
Information type	Control	Data
Module connection method	Pathological connection	Data by reference
Coupling technique	Control, common or stamp coupling	Data by value

Table 4.1 Factors affecting module coupling

In conclusion, the basic aim of the designer is to produce program modules that are as independent as possible – achieved by having low coupling.

4.2.4 Cohesion – a measure of module binding.

An ideal module has a single entry and a single exit point (figure 4.21a).

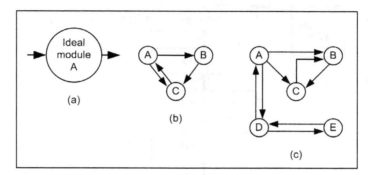

Figure 4.21 Module interconnection complexity

One way to achieve this simple structure is to keep module function and operation very simple. Now, any complete system is made up of a number of modules, interconnected to perform the required function (figure 4.21b). So far, so good - for a very small design. But adding even a few more modules (figure 4.21c) makes the connecting link structure fairly complex. As a result it becomes difficult to understand system functions and operations. Link complexity can be reduced when the modular structure is hierarchical - but it still remains difficult to grasp system details.

Here is a classic two-way pull situation. Improving factor 1 (module simplicity) degrades factor 2 (system complexity). Is there an easy answer to this problem? Unfortunately, no. The 'right' balance between the number of modules in a system and the size/function of these modules is subjective.

We can reduce system complexity by grouping elementary operations together, these becoming the *elements* of a single module (figure 4.22).

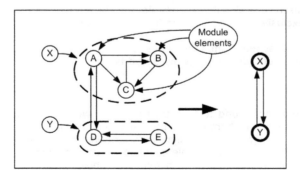

Figure 4.22 Complexity reduction

Where elements of a module are very closely related, most module activity is internal. Elements don't need, or want, to 'talk' to other modules. Consequently such designs have low module coupling. The parameter which defines how strongly elements are interelated is called 'cohesion' (the 'glue' factor). High cohesion results from strong relationships. This not only leads to good designs; it also produces maintainable software.

It's one thing to say that a high glue factor is desirable; it's quite another thing to implement it. What the designer needs when modularizing a system is some *measure* of cohesion.   One such measure was proposed by Yourdon and Constantine, the seven-level model of figure 4.23.

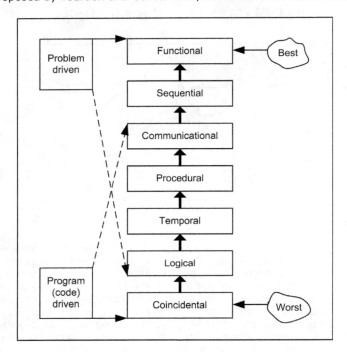

Figure 4.23 The seven-level cohesion model

In reality this is not a discrete scale; it's impossible to draw a clear line between levels.   Moreover, these aren't mutually exclusive qualities.   For instance, a module may have both sequential and temporal cohesion.

Cohesion can be approached from two points of view, the problem (system) or the solution (program). The results are quite different, as discussed below.

(a) Coincidental cohesion.

If the elements of a module are found to be unrelated, then we have zero cohesion. Such modules usually come about because 'somewhere had to be found for the code'. There are, though, underlying reasons for this: inferior design, weak design co-ordination or pressure to produce operational software. It can be difficult to minimize module coupling in such designs.

Another common reason for ending up with minimal cohesion is demonstrated by the flowchart problem of figure 4.24.

During program design the programmer realizes that instruction sequence B occurs twice.   To improve code efficiency he produces a module for B, the individual statements forming the elements of this module.   In practice, this method is simple to apply during the initial design stage.   Later though, when modifications are made, difficulties arise. It may be, for instance, that the left path B has to be changed, but not the right one. The result? We'll probably have to create an extra (new) module, thus disturbing the original structure of the system.

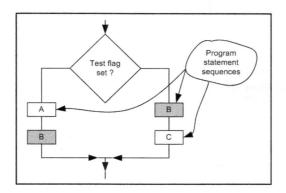

Figure 4.24 A problem of cohesion

(b) Logical cohesion.
Let's assume that our programmer is writing code for the anti-skid braking system (shown earlier in figure 4.11). Further assume that a new system requirement calls for each input signal to be filtered. Ergo, he forms a 'filter' module to perform this function. Into this he inserts the code for each channel filter (the elements), these being related by their logical functioning (logical cohesion).

Now, the code could be written so that each time the module is activated all input signals are filtered.   But this might not be necessary (or desirable); some inputs may need servicing more frequently than others.   The solution is to process selected signals only, by using a general module activating call accompanied by a selector tag.   The tag identifies which inputs are to be filtered. Furthermore, it is commonplace to use a single body of code to perform the program function. Unfortunately, the result is that it then becomes difficult to modify any individual filter function without affecting the others.

These problems are inherent in modules which house logically related elements.   The reason is simple; such modules do not carry out a single function only. 'Filter' isn't a single action. It is, in fact, a collection of separate functions grouped together for our convenience.

In the example here the makeup of the 'filter' module was driven by system requirements. Quite frequently such designs make good sense in embedded systems. The resulting modules often exhibit much better cohesion than groupings derived from program code functions.   However, when used without care it promotes tight coupling, leading especially to maintenance problems.

(c) Temporal (time) cohesion.
When elements of a module are related by time then we have 'temporal cohesion', i.e. time is the glue.   A frequently quoted example is that of an initialization routine to set up the hardware of a processor system.   All such set-up operations have to take place within a particular period of time. Therefore it makes good sense to group these together in one module – then execute them all at once. But, once again, care and common sense must be used in the program design. When temporal grouping is used, unrelated parts of the system may be located within the resulting module. This, like logical grouping, may well lead to maintenance problems.

(d) Procedural cohesion.
Module elements have procedural cohesion when each one is part of a well-defined operation – the procedure. All elements of a procedure *must* be present if it's to perform its desired function.

Therefore the binding of elements is good. Procedural cohesion usually results in low coupling – but then again it may not. It hinges very much on how the procedure was devised in the first place. Where, for instance, it performs a clearly defined mathematical operation (say computing the sine of an angle), cohesion and coupling are good. But frequently procedures are used to implement sub-tasks of larger tasks. The resulting module coupling depends very much on the initial partitioning of the overall system.

(e) Communicational cohesion.

A module has communicational cohesion when its elements act on common data. The actions performed on the data generate the connecting links between the elements, typical instances being shown in figure 4.25.

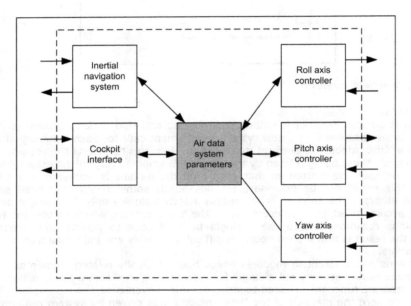

Figure 4.25 Communicational cohesion

(f) Sequential cohesion.

Here the elements are organized as a sequence of operations, figure 4.26. Observe that the output

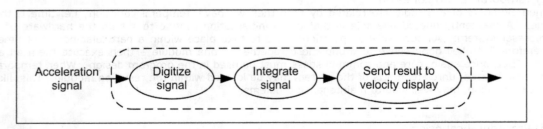

Figure 4.26 Sequential cohesion

from one element acts as the input to the next one. Sequential structures can be formed starting from the code point of view (a flowchart approach). But much better function groupings occur when designs are tackled from a system point of view. Any module designed in this way may contain only one function. On the other hand it may hold either part of a particular function or a number of related functions., It fits in naturally with the data flow approach to designing software structures.

(g) Functional cohesion.

In general terms a functional module is one that performs a single function. Such structures have the highest level of cohesion because all elements are essential to the operation of the module; none is redundant.

   Thus the concept of functional binding seems clear enough – until we try to define it. One definition could be that, for functional cohesion, each element in the module is an essential part of that module. From an abstract point of view this excludes all other forms of cohesion.   Therefore each element must perform a single function. Is this recursive, I ask myself? Yourdon and Constantine give a precise but negative form of definition. That is, 'functional cohesion is whatever is not sequential, communicational, ….etc.'. Even they admit this isn't very helpful, by saying that 'any truly adequate definition of function is a structural defect in the theory through which camels and Mack trucks could readily pass'. And, when taking a system point of view, designers often disagree on what makes up a single function.

   There's no doubt that good modular designs have high module cohesiveness. And high-strength modules have far fewer faults than low-strength ones. How then does a designer arrive at a 'good' final structure? One approach is to produce an initial design, assess it using the rules given above, refine it, re-assess it – and so on. But it's stretching imagination (and credibility) to think that, in a commercial environment, such practices exist. Moreover, it isn't a case of using a simple design template for cohesion; many modules exhibit a number of cohesion qualities. For instance, a plant sequence controller may have a performance specification that reads (in part):

```
At time  =  T + 10
          Shut Nitrogen and Hydrogen valves
          Open vent valve
          Run purge motor
```

Thus the items are time related. The cohesion is quite strong because all activities must be done in this particular time slot. At the same time there is a strong functional relationship between these operations – from a system point of view. This module has an extremely high glue strength.

   Sensibly, then, the only workable design methods are those that inherently produce high cohesiveness. Can we define such methods? The answer lies in figure 4.23. Observe: module structures derived from the system (problem) point of view have the highest glue factor. In other words, if we start in the right way, we'll end up with the right results.

4.2.5 Size and complexity.

What is the ideal size for a module? One general – but not very helpful – rule can be laid down: don't make it too large. As a result, the amount of information given at any one time is limited. This enables the reader to see the module code as a whole, making it easier for him to absorb and understand it. Smaller modules usually have very clearly defined (and usually simple) functions. Unfortunately, when using small modules, it then becomes difficult to absorb the overall functioning of the system. So, ultimately, the minimum size of a module is determined by our ability to digest information. One figure frequently quoted is to limit program size to between 30 and 50 executable statement. The number of lines of source code corresponding to this depends on the programming language and environment. But, using a high-level language, one would expect to see a listing of (roughly) between 60 and 100 lines. This equates to two pages of source code per program module.

Using the number of statements as a guide to module size is really only a rough and ready guide. A second factor is the complexity of the language constructs used in the module. Compare, for instance, a program consisting of only sequential statements with one using highly nested combinations of iteration and selection operations. Obviously it's going to take much more mental effort to understand the second one – even if both have the same print-out length. Much work has been done to develop models of software complexity – software metrics. A number of different rules have been developed.

One technique is based on counting the number of operators and operands in the program code. Furthermore, it takes into account the number of distinct items as well as the totals. Program complexity is deduced from a count value computed using these values. This method gives a better guide than a simple count of instructions; more complex instructions give a higher count value.

A second method uses a count of the number of independent paths through a program as a measure of complexity (McCabe's cyclomatic number). This approach has its roots in graph theory. Extensions to this work have been done taking data (program variable) references into account.

It seems, however, that any pronouncement on module size is likely to be challenged. Moreover, a distinction must be made between library (service) modules and application modules (discussed later). But personal experience has shown that limiting module size to only a few pages of print-out is a good rule. It seems to produce little benefit in the initial design stage; error rates are relatively unaffected. The difference shows later on, though. Such code is quickly comprehensible, making updating and modification work a relatively easy task (especially if you didn't write the code in the first place). Limiting size has another advantage. It becomes much easier to perform static analysis of the code during the software test phase.

This topic – that of software metrics – is covered in more detail in Volume 2.

4.2.6 Some general comments on modules.

(a) Why modularize programs?

- The 'divide and conquer' approach produces programs that are easy to manage, understand and test.
- Program development can be done on an incremental basis ('a bit at a time').
- Errors are easier to track down and correct.
- Modifications are usually localized, so maintaining high program stability.
- Portability can be increased by burying machine-specific features within designated modules. Thus, when moving to other target systems, only these modules need changing.
- Libraries of useful functions can be built up (especially true of complex maths functions), so leading to software re-use.
- It is easier to attack the problems of slow code and memory inefficiency when using modular construction (the 'code optimization' requirement).
- In a large system, development times can be pruned by using a team of designers working in parallel. Although various work-sharing methods could be used, allocating work on a module basis has two particular advantages. First, it enables programmers to work independently; second, it simplifies integration of the resulting code.

(b) What are the ideal characteristics of 'good' modules?

- Each module has a clearly defined task.
- There is a one-to-one relationship between system function and module function – functional cohesion.
- There isn't a need to see the internals of a module to understand its function.

- Modules can be combined to form 'super' modules – without regard to their internal implementation details.
- It is possible to test a module in isolation from other modules.
- Module functional connections are defined by their functional relationships with other modules.
- Module control connections are defined by their code. Each module should have a single program entry point and a corresponding single exit point (though see 'exceptions').
- Data connections are made with the lowest form of coupling – parameter-passing mechanisms.

(c) What are the disadvantages of modularization?

- Much greater effort has to be put in at the initial design stages.
- Much greater project management is required (even if, in a small job, it's self-management).
- Much more time is spent designing (as opposed to coding). Thus productivity, measured in a very narrow way over a limited part of the job, decreases.
- Program run times usually lengthen.
- More memory is required (most noticeably RAM).

4.3 Program control structures – the influence of structured programming.

4.3.1 Introductory comments.

The first real step away from undisciplined program methods was made in the late 60's by a group of academics. Their proposals, summarized as *Structured Programming (SP)*, were typified in a 1969 article by Edsgar Dijkstra. SP is a methodology used for translating module descriptions and specifications into program source code. Its primary objective is to reduce software complexity, so:

- Reducing the number of mistakes made in the first place.
- Reducing the time and effort taken to correct such mistakes.
- Improving overall reliability, correctness and safety.

As defined by Wirth SP 'is the formulation of programs as hierarchical, nested structures of statements and objects of computation'. Over the years its original ideas were modified. Nowadays we generally consider the basic rules of SP to be that:

- Programs are designed in a top-down manner.
- Programs are constructed as hierarchical modules.
- The program control structures are limited.
- Program correctness can be proved.

Until recently, structured design and structured programming were regarded as being synonymous. However, this link has been weakened as design structures may now be either functional, object or data flow oriented. Nonetheless, in all cases, the rules concerning control structures and program correctness still apply. These are the items which go right to the heart of good programming.

4.3.2 Fundamental control structures.

Is it possible to define a minimum set of program control structures from which *any* program can be built? And why should we want to do this in the first place?

Much of the heat generated by arguments concerning the first question results from ignorance of the reasons behind the second one. The primary reason for restricting control structures is so that we can prove that programs are correct.   Consider, for example, the program operations described in figure 4.27.

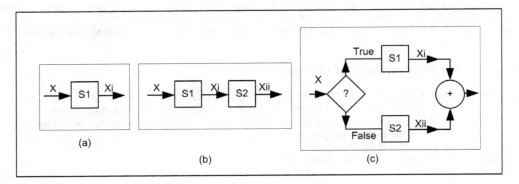

(a)

(b)   (c)

Figure 4.27 Simple transformation actions

In 4.27a the variable X is operated on by the program statement S1 to give Xi. Now, provided we can define the range of values taken on by X (called a pre-condition), then we can define those of Xi (post-condition).   This can be considered to be an elementary step; we're dealing with a single statement that produces a single transformation. For figure 4.27a, suppose that:

```
TRANSFORMATION S1:        Xi  :=  X/2;
PRE-CONDITION:            0 ≤ Xi ≤ 10
Then POST-CONDITION is    0 ≤ Xi ≤ 5
```

If the statement S1 (as actually implemented in code) generates a result that violates this assertion, then clearly the program is incorrect.

Figure 4.27b is again quite straightforward, as is 4.27c (although proving its correctness is rather more difficult). But what about the case of figure 4.28? Here the effects produced by individual

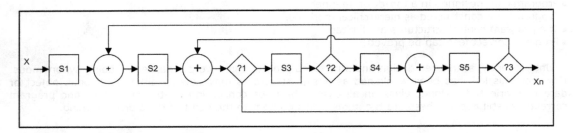

Figure 4.28 Complex transformation action

statements are easy to check out.   Unfortunately, as their interaction is quite complex, this isn't a great deal of help. It can be seen that the current output depends on:

• The current input and
• Previous inputs.

In other words, the transformation has memory. In this case trying to prove the relationship between X and Xn is a fairly daunting task. Yet flow structures like these can easily be generated, especially when programming at a low level (such as assembly language operation). Frankly, with such designs, it is highly unlikely that their correctness is ever verified because:

• They're too complex to analyse in the time available.
• It would cost too much to prove it.
• Programmers just wouldn't do it because of the tedium of the job.
•

   The groundwork in tackling this problem was done by G. Jacopini and further refined by others, notably Wirth, Dijkstra and Hoare. Jacopini showed that only three basic flow control structures were needed to form any program: sequence, selection and iteration (figure 4.29).

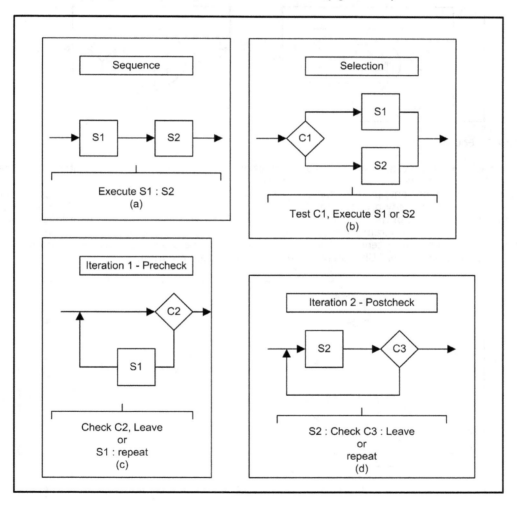

Figure 4.29 Basic control structures of structured programming

Note that the two iteration structures can always be implemented using either the pre-check or post-check operation; thus only one is needed (figure 4.30).

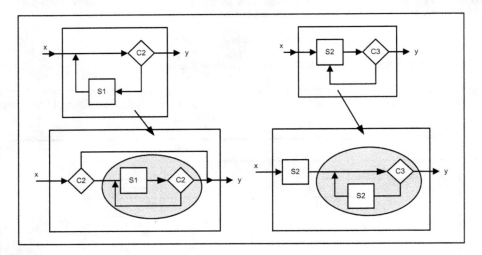

Figure 4.30 Equivalence of iteration structures

These basic forms were later augmented by variations on the multiple select operation, the 'Else-If' and the 'Switch Case' statements (see later, vol. 2).

A second (very important) point is that each structure has one entry point and one exit point. From these simple beginnings any program can be built up. Moreover, when using such building blocks, the program always consists of the basic control structures (figure 4.31) – no matter what level it's looked at. Therefore, given a program formed like this, we can first prove the correctness of the individual building blocks. Then, by extending this to larger groupings, the proving process encompasses larger and larger program sections. Ultimately it takes in the complete program.

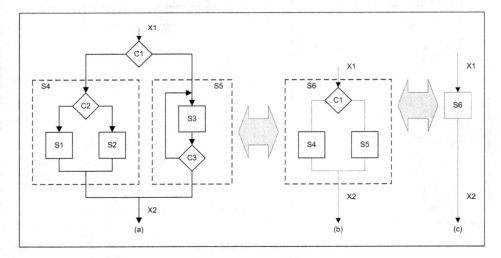

Figure 4.31 Composition of a structured program

In informal (non-mathematical) terms, program correctness is checked as follows:

(a) Sequential operation.

- Are all statements listed in correct order?
- Are these executed *once* only?
- Are sequence groups executed from a single entry to a single exit point?
- Do the statements represent the solution to this problem?
- Does the order of execution produce the required result?

(b) Iteration operation.

- Are the controlled statements executed at least once (post-check)?
- Can control pass through the operation without ever executing the controlled statements (pre-check)?
- Is iteration guaranteed to finish (that is, are the loop termination conditions correct)?
- Is the correct number of iterations carried out?
- Is the control variable altered within the loop itself?
- What is the state of program variables on exit from an iteration?

(c) Selection operation.

- Are all alternative courses of action explicitly taken into account (including answers that don't fit the question)?
- Are the alternative statements constructed using the basic structures of SP?
- Have the questions relating to sequential operations (and, where appropriate, iteration) been considered?

That's fine. But, you may well argue, few programmers are actually ever going to carry out a correctness check on their code. It's enough effort to produce it in the first place. Does this diminish the value of the control structures of structured programming? The answer, emphatically, is no. Programs built using these rules are much more likely to be reliable, robust and trustworthy.

Modern high-level languages directly support these aims, in many cases building in extra controls. For instance, several languages prevent statements within a loop changing the loop control variable. Consequently, when good design practices are combined with high-level language programming, the result should be quality software.

4.3.3 Uncontrolled branching of control – the great GOTO debate.

Most languages enable a programmer to branch without constraint using a 'go to' statement (the destination being either a line number or label). In assembly-level programming this is done using a 'jump' instruction. As this construct is not allowed in SP it became a controversial issue, fuelled by Dijkstra's famous letter 'Go To statement considered harmful'. More heat than light was generated in the resulting arguments, most combatants losing sight of the underlying arguments behind this conclusion.

Is the GOTO statement by itself a problem? No, of course not. When used with care and attention, particularly when confined by conditional expressions, there aren't any particular difficulties. The problems come about because of the 'creative' aspects of GOTO programming. Consider the program fragment shown in figure 4.32.

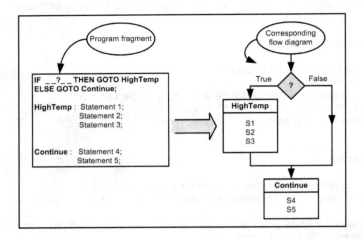

Figure 4.32 Well-controlled use of the GOTO statement

Here the resulting control flow is perfectly well controlled and structured, even though the GOTO is used. Now look at that in figure 4.33. In this the use of the GOTOs is controlled – but not very well.

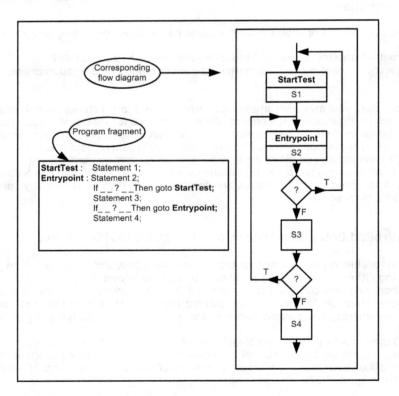

Figure 4.33 Poorly-controlled GOTO statements

The result is a complex interactive control flow structure – produced from only a few lines of code. What then is the likely outcome if program jumps are made without any form of control?

It is clear that the GOTO statement provides a means for writing poor, unprovable programs. What Dijkstra observed was that where the GOTO was used extensively, programs were complex – and difficult to verify. Generally, good programs contained few GOTOs (note, though, that the absence of GOTOs doesn't necessarily mean that a program is a good one).

Is it possible to eliminate the GOTO statement (or its equivalent) from real-time programming? In theory it is possible to write any program without having unconditional transfers of control. But this involves a time (and complexity) overhead which may cause problems for time-critical applications. For example, suppose that during program execution an exception occurs which requires prompt attention. Further, the only way to handle this is to branch instantly to the exception handler. But that requires an unconditional transfer of control. So in reality, we can't throw away the GOTO or its equivalent; but it should be used *only* in very exceptional conditions.

4.4 Functionally structured software designs.

4.4.1 Background.

Software structures can be derived in many ways, each one having its supporters and critics. But how does one make sense of the various claims and counter-claims? Well, the real test of any method is to see how well it works in practice. Judged against this, techniques based on functional structuring of programs rate highly.

'Functional structuring' is here used as a general characteristic (generic) term, covering a number of design methodologies. It belongs firmly in the Yourdon-Constantine-Myers-Meiler-Ward-Mellor-DeMarco school of design, its premise being that a program takes it shape from the functions carried out by the system. The overall design approach is based on many of the ideas and concepts discussed earlier in this chapter. However, it is very important that you recognise the method is essentially *program* (and not system) oriented. Please read this last sentence again!

We start by defining system functions, figure 4.34. Then, from these, the modular structure of the program is devised using a set of 'transform' rules. These use a top-down, stepwise refinement

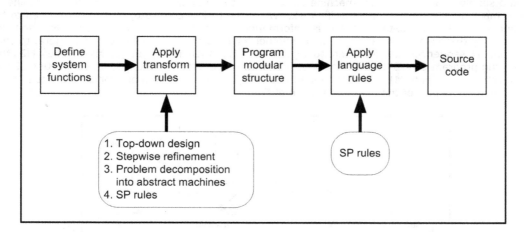

Figure 4.34 Functional structured design

decomposition method, resulting in a set of abstract machines. Structured programming is an inherent (and sometimes implicit) part of this process. Once the program structure has been obtained the program source code can be written. And once again the rules of SP are applied, in this case to the flow control constructs.

System functions can be defined using one of two methods. In the first designers use an 'informal' style, based on their own experiences. Alternatively they may choose to use a prescribed technique. Functions, for instance, may be described in terms of system data flow, data transformations, and connections between transformations (see later for detail). Here, though, we aren't particularly concerned with how we derive system functions. The important point is how we devise program structures to implement these functions.

4.4.2 Problem decomposition using abstract machines.

Programs devised using functional structuring are based on the concept of abstract machines organized in layers (figure 4.35).

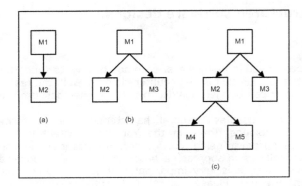

Figure 4.35 The layered abstract machine concept

Taking a simple view, an abstract machine corresponds to a module. In (a), computing machine M1 invokes machine M2 to perform a specific task. When the task is complete, control is returned to M1, together with relevant data and status information.   In (b), M1 invokes both M2 and M3. Unfortunately there isn't any indication as to whether M2 runs before M3 or vice versa. Here, to avoid confusion, all sequences run from left to right (thus, M2, then M3).   In (c) M1 invokes M2, thus transferring program control to this machine. M2 in turn activates M4 and M5; on completion of their tasks it returns control to M1, which then starts up M3. This is shown in more concrete terms in figure 4.36 when used as part of the anti-skid system of figure 4.5.

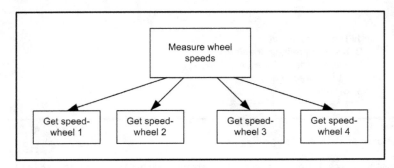

Figure 4.36 Abstract machines – task level

When using abstract ('virtual') machines it is important to focus on the service they provide, not *how* they do it. Ideally it is best to completely ignore the 'how' until fine details have to be worked out. This may seem a pretty abstract point, removed from the reality of program design. If so, look at how we regularly use abstract machines at the program level- without even realizing it (figure 4.37).

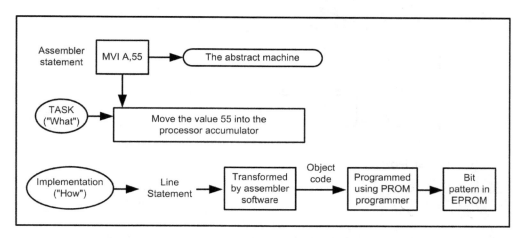

Figure 4.37 Abstract machines – program level

Here a line statement in assembly language can be considered to be an abstract machine. We invoke it to perform a particular task, completely ignoring how it's translated into object code or how it works at the processor level. Moreover, we assume that the operation always works correctly when the code is installed in the target computer. If this isn't an example of abstract operations, what is?

The process of building up the complete program structure is one of hierarchical decomposition, figure 4.38. Note that in this example both M2 and M3 invoke the same machine (module), M5.

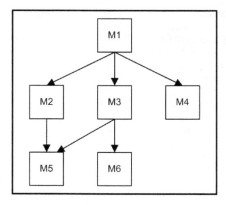

Figure 4.38 Hierarchical decomposition – general form

In other words, a low-level module is shared by a number of higher-level ones. Now this is undesirable as it can lead to complex and unforeseen interaction between modules. Ideally, hierarchical decomposition should result in a pure tree structure, figure 4.39.

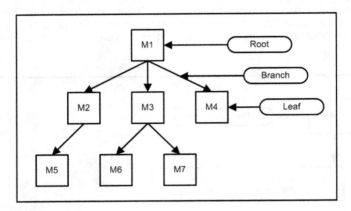

Figure 4.39 Hierarchical decomposition – pure tree structure

In this case a module at any level can be invoked directly by only one higher-level module; sharing is banned.   Thus higher-level modules have sole control over the modules they call.   Further, the branches of the tree are fully decoupled from each other (data coupling is needed to achieve this). The final result is a highly controllable, visible and stable structure.

A tree structure, taken to its logical conclusion, results in each and every module having its own code. This *could* be done but it would be very inefficient (and perhaps costly). Because, within all computer systems there are 'building brick' functions that are used repeatedly (e.g. standard maths functions, communication protocols, real-world interfacing, etc.).   The idea of writing separate code every time we use one of these functions is unrealistic. The sensible way to implement them is to use standard procedures (subroutines), calling them as required in the program.

Now this presents us with the need to handle a second form of problem decomposition, based around the building bricks. Traditionally it has been called 'functional decomposition' (which is confusing); for convenience the term 'service decomposition' is used here.   When such decomposition is used the pure tree structure degenerates into the more general hierarchical structure. Therefore it is vital that modules designed as program building bricks must be fully tested and totally predictable in operation. Where appropriate, formal correctness testing should be carried out.   Once this is done such service modules may be used as single objects ('primitives') in the program structure.   But even so the programmer must always be aware of the effects of service decomposition.   Sloppy use of this destroys the inbuilt qualities of functionally decomposed programs.   Hence the design and use of service modules must be rigorously controlled. Where possible they should be placed in a library, with access to the source code being a privileged operation.

When designing any system we need to identify the main program first and then (later) the service sub-programs.   The main program is designed as described earlier, but *must* have a pure tree structure.   Service sub-programs are produced to carry out common tasks defined by service modules. Modules within the main program may invoke service modules, but these service modules don't appear explicitly in the structure. Also, they can be invoked by modules *at any level* in the pure tree structure of the main program.

4.4.3 Example implementation.

Let's tackle the task of implementing the anti-skid braking system of figure 4.5. There isn't a unique answer to this (or any other) problem; one possible solution is shown in figure 4.40.   For simplicity only part of the design is given.   This is pretty well self-explanatory, the partitioning used leading automatically to low coupling and high cohesion. Many diagramming methods are available to describe program structures obtained using hierarchical decomposition; these shouldn't be confused with the underlying principles of the method.

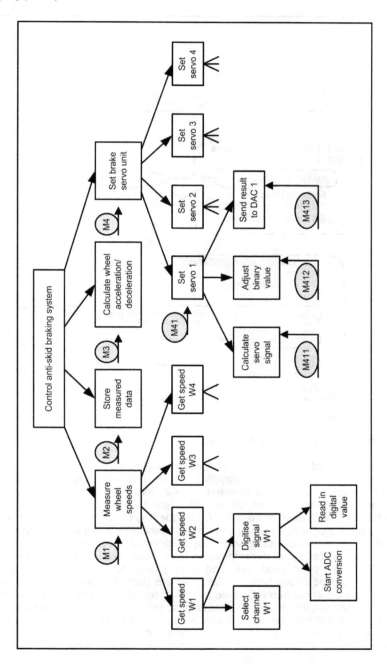

Figure 4.40 Functional structure of the anti-skid braking system (part)

From this information the program source code can be produced, typified (in part) by that in figure 4.41. Observe that at the highest level – machines M1 to M4 –

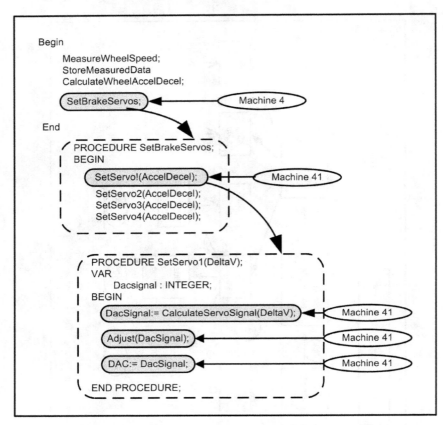

Figure 4.41 Program structure for figure 4.40 (part)

simplicity is the keynote. Each machine is implemented using a parameterless procedure. At the next level down the procedures become more complex.   Note also that the 'SetServo1' machine (M41) communicates with the ones below it via parameters. Consequently machines M411, M412, and M413 use only local parameters in their computation. Also, it's impossible for them to communicate with each other; they haven't the means to do this. Consequently, these modules affect only a very small, localized part of the total program; they are said to have localized scope of reference.

Tree structuring of designs makes it especially easy to develop programs in an incremental way. For instance, assume that hierarchical decomposition has been carried out on the braking system problem.   figure 4.40 has been produced, and coding now begins.   Using incremental methods, machines M1 to M4 would be coded first – a fairly simple (but not trivial) action. Now the modules stemming from M1 can be implemented, while all other second level modules are coded as dummy stubs. Frequently these contain simple text messages, printing up 'module not yet implemented' or something similar. Once the first set of modules is coded and working, the next set can be tackled, then the next set, and so on until programming is finished. In my experience this is the quickest, easiest and least frustrating way to develop reliable software. But it really does require coupling and cohesion to be right for it to work effectively.

4.5 Object-oriented design.

4.5.1 An introduction.

It has already been shown in section 4.1 that designs may be structured as sets of interconnected objects. In the example given (figure 4.7) the computing objects were clearly linked with physical items. Generally, though, objects don't have such a clear-cut relationship. Mostly they are abstract items which represent computing processes within the system. In formal terms an object, as far as object-oriented design (OOD) is concerned, may be defined as:

'A software machine which has a number of defined operational states and a defined means to access and change these states'.

A change of state is achieved by passing a message into an object, as shown conceptually in figure 4.42a. So, in simple terms, an object-structured program executes as a set of interacting machines (figure 4.42b), communicating using messages. These objects, acting together, determine the function and behaviour of the overall software system.

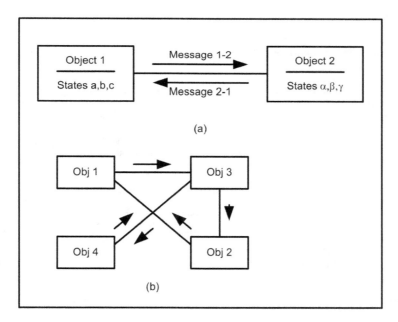

Figure 4.42 Fundamental concept of object-oriented design

A more complete definition would point out that objects usually contain data and operations (discussed later). However, the definition used here emphasises the key features of OOD from a system perspective (as opposed to a program viewpoint).

At this point it is timely to ask 'why use an OO approach to software design?'. Because, for many real-world applications, software objects map quite naturally onto system models. Moreover, in such systems many events occur simultaneously (concurrently). This concurrency can be shown simply and clearly using OOD. In contrast, functional structuring is geared towards a sequential view of life. One consequence of this is that we find ourselves redefining our problem to suit the design method (it is worth repeating that the computer is merely one component in the overall system. It and its

processing activities form part of a totally integrated activity. Some software techniques give the impression that the important actions take place only within the computer, the outside world being a minor irritating side-issue).
There are a number of major steps involved in producing an OO design, as follows:

• Identify the objects and their features.
• Identify the relationships between objects.
• Define the communication (messaging) between objects.
• Define the interface of each object.
• Implement the objects.

These points are discussed in the following sections.

4.5.2 Object-oriented design – the identification process.

From a program point of view an object must have specific qualities. It should, for instance, be:

• Able to represent system functions properly.
• Easy to build.
• Simple to integrate into the overall system.
• Amenable to testing and debugging as a separate unit.
• Straightforward to maintain.

This looks very much like the specification for a module. In fact, at the source code level, a module and its equivalent object may be virtually identical (this, to some extent, depends on the programming language). Therefore the ideas of cohesion, coupling, abstraction and data hiding all apply.
How does one go about identifying and implementing objects? Well, consider again the system requirements of the anti-skid braking system. What would an OO design look like here? One possible solution is shown in figure 4.43.

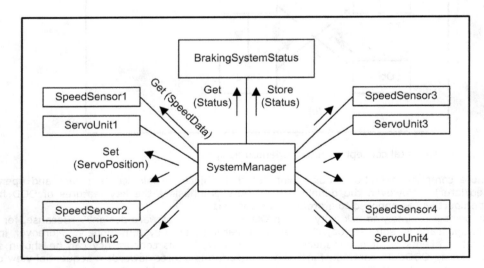

Figure 4.43 Object-oriented design of the anti-skid braking system (1).

This has been derived by first clearly defining the problem structure and then mapping objects onto this. It can be seen that three mappings have been used:

- Object to physical device (*SpeedSensor*, *ServoUnit*).
- Object to abstract device (the data store *BrakingSystemStatus*).
- Object to system function (*SystemManager*).

Observe that the message names imply a client/server (client/provider) relationship between the SystemManager and the other objects. In fact, for many OO design techniques, all relationships are based on this client/server model   It is an essential (but usually implicit) feature of the design process.   Unfortunately this doesn't always fit in well with many real-time applications, especially embedded systems. More of this later.

An alternative OOD solution is shown in figure 4.44.

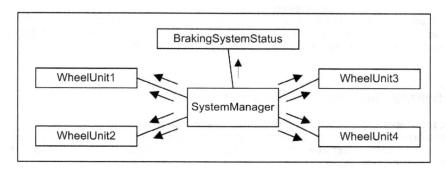

Figure 4.44 Object-oriented design of the anti-skid braking system (2).

Here each wheel unit objects encapsulates the features of both a speed sensor and a servo unit. In fact, this provides us with a way of implementing top-down design and problem decomposition, the 'parent/child' structure (figure 4.45).

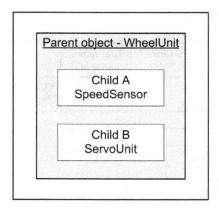

Figure 4.45 Object structuring – parent/child organization

This, in OO terms, is a form of 'aggregation'. In broad terms, aggregation describes a situation where an object has a number of component parts. For example, a multi-function printer object consists (or contains) a printer object, a scanner object and a fax object.

The design diagrams need to be augmented by text definitions of the objects and their essential features (in practice this is likely to be done in an incremental fashion; see the section on class, responsibility and collaboration (CRC) techniques). To illustrate this there follows an outline definition of the SpeedSensor object:

Object: SpeedSensor.
Function: Provide wheel speed data in binary form.
Operation performed: Sample speed transducer.
Operation demanded: Provide speed data.
Data held: Wheel speed.

The 'operation performed' can be viewed as a response to a system requirement.   In contrast, 'operation demanded' is a response to a message from some other object.   At this level of design there must be correspondence between the two operations.   After all, it doesn't make sense to perform something that isn't needed.   And obviously, one can't demand an operation that doesn't exist.

4.5.3 Relationships and communication between objects.

The first (identification) stage of design defines the broad relationships of the objects and the messages sent between them. The second stage firms up on these items, specifying them precisely and totally. It also identifies passive, active and interrupt-driven objects (see following text), together with exception-handling issues.
Assume a client object demands an action by another object (figure 4.46), transfers control to this object, and the demand is then immediately serviced.

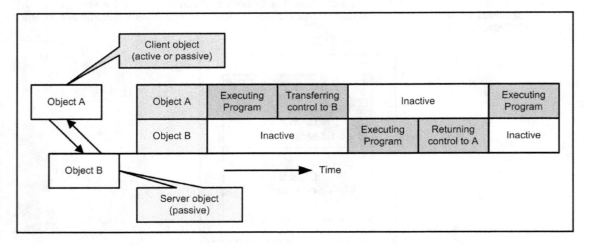

Figure 4.46 Passive object behaviour

On completion of the demanded action, control is returned to the calling object.   In this case the receiving object is said to be a 'passive' one. Note that with a passive object structure one, and only one, object is 'alive' at any one time.

By contrast, 'active' objects may be working simultaneously, figure 4.47.

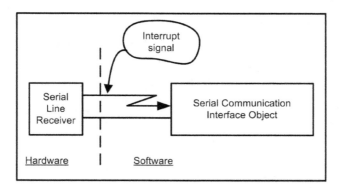

Figure 4.47 Active object behaviour

With such arrangements the receiving object may or may not react instantly; it depends on its current situation.
Interrupt-driven objects should be shown so that they stand out from normal objects (figure 4.48).

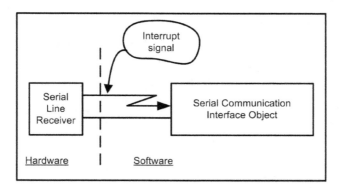

Figure 4.48 Interrupt-driven object

In all cases the reasons for generating such interrupts should be made clear. It may be necessary to use *ad-hoc* notation to illustrate these points; some modelling languages do not support such features. Generally, if the receiving object cannot perform its task, it should raise an exception signal.
Conceptually, an interrupt-driven object is an active one.
Communication between objects is, as pointed out earlier, implemented by messages. Such messages consists of either data and/or commands (in this context the operations *Read(Data)* and *Store(Data)* are essentially data-transfer messages). Where passive objects are used, there is an

inbuilt hierarchy in the structure. Moreover, communication takes place using a call/return protocol. Active objects, though, are regarded as independent items operating as concurrent communicating processes.

At a system level the difference between active and passive objects may not seem significant. They are, in fact, profoundly different. When designs use active objects they need the support of a real-time operating system (RTOS).   By contrast, passive objects can be built using standard code structures, viz:

• With OO languages, the class.
• With non-OO languages, subprograms (functions, procedures) having associated (bound) data items.

A second important point concerns system and software performance, i.e. responsiveness and throughput. Software designers, when using OO techniques, tend to produce designs that consist of many objects. This may well result in implementations that work correctly; unfortunately they may also work very slowly. The reason is simple; as the number of active objects increases, the operating system (OS) overheads also rise.

One way to reduce the OS loading problem is to use passive objects wherever possible.   Two workable approaches are:

• Top-down: decompose each major (active) object into a set of subordinate passive objects.
• Bottom-up: group sets of objects together into single active super-objects.

In practice both top-down and bottom-up methods are likely to be used.

4.5.4 Object interfaces.

One of the primary aims in object-oriented design is to hide as much information as possible. It's a variant on the 'need to know' principle; what you don't know about can't hurt you. We do this by separating an object into two parts: the visible and hidden sections, figure 4.49.

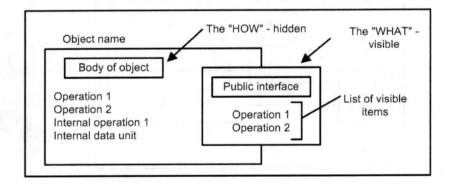

Figure 4.49 Global view of an object

The visible section (the interface) describes essentially the services it provides. In the outside world of software only the interface details can be seen. The body itself implements the required functions of the object. How these are achieved is hidden within the body, being of no concern to the user. In fact, it is imperative that internal operations and data cannot be accessed directly by external objects. As shown here, for example, the object contains three operations and one unit of internal data. Operations 1 and 2 are made available for use by other objects (*clients*) as they are listed in the interface section. Hence they are considered to be public items. By contrast, the internal operation and the data unit remain hidden – they are private to the object.

Modern mainstream diagramming methods don't usually show interface or implementation aspects on the *object* diagram (e.g. figure 4.42b). These aspects will be discussed shortly.

4.5.5 Object oriented design – implementation-related issues.

Up to this point most of our discussion has related to system-level analysis and design aspects. In particular it has focussed on how we can generate – by toil, sweat, rigour, persistence and creativity – a successful OO design. However, the issues covered here are much more related to implementation factors, such as:

• How to produce effective and efficient code-level designs.
• How to describe in diagram form the source code structures and relationships of OO designs.

In the next section we'll look at how to:

• Incorporate software reuse techniques in our work, supported by appropriate diagramming methods.
• Implement software so that it can readily adapt - in a dynamic way - to changing run-time demands.

Earlier the concept of the abstract software machine was introduced, see figure 4.40. Part of this figure is reproduced in figure 4.50, which concentrates on the machine 'Set Brake Servo Unit'.

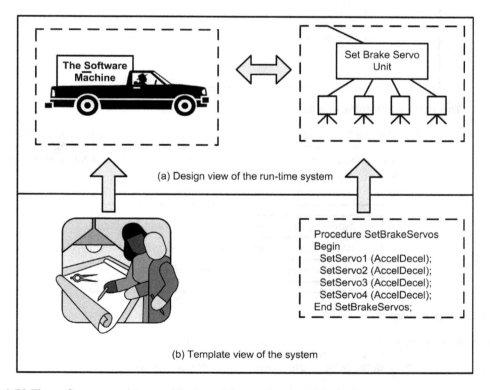

Figure 4.50 The software machine and its template - structured techniques

To explain a fundamental point, take the very simple analogy between a software application and an automobile system, figure 4.50a. If a software machine is considered to be equivalent to an actual vehicle, then its declaration code is equivalent to vehicle manufacturing plans. Thus the source code (here a procedure declaration) acts as the plan or template for the machine, figure 4.50b. Putting this another way, *the work done by a software system is actually performed by software machines, but the machine features themselves are defined by their 'template' code.*

An object can also be viewed as a software machine, though clearly it differs from the structured model. *The* major difference is that the object encapsulates both operations and data; further, its operations are bound to its data. With this in mind, the OO equivalent of figure 4.50 is shown in figure 4.51. Here the software template from which objects are created is called the *class*.

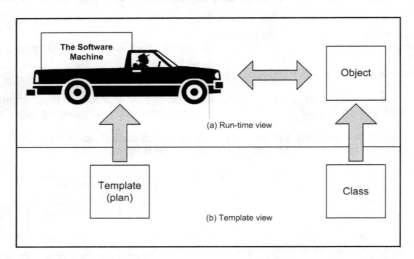

Figure 4.51 The software machine and its template - OO techniques

Note this most carefully (imprint it on your brain – it will help you deal with the dross regularly found in OO articles). Thus the class (essentially a source-code declaration) defines the form, content and behaviour of objects. The 'default' symbol used for a class is given in figure 4.52, a rectangular box having three compartments.

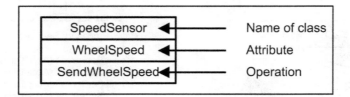

Figure 4.52 Class symbol

The name of the class is shown in the first (upper) section. Its attributes (qualities) are listed in the middle section, whilst its *visible* operations appear in the bottom section. Note that at the program level, attributes become data items; operations are implemented by subprograms (procedures or functions).

From a diagramming point of view, how do we represent classes and their related objects?   One standard notation is that given in figure 4.53.

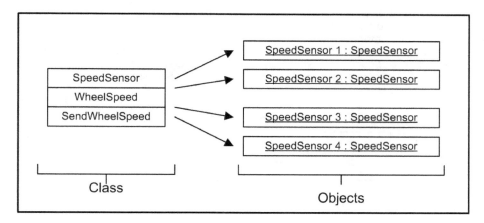

Figure 4.53 Class and object notation

Here each object is represented by a rectangle, being identified as follows:

```
ObjectName : ClassName
```

Two important points are illustrated here.   First, class attributes (i.e. WheelSpeed) and operations (SendWheelSpeed) are not included in the object figure.   Second, you cannot deduce from a class diagram how many objects will be created (this has extremely important consequences, as you will see later).

Using the newly-introduced notation, let us update the OO design (originally shown in figure 4.43) to that given in figure 4.54.

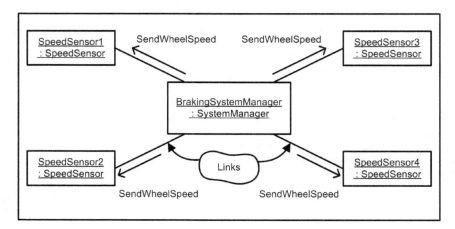

Figure 4.54 Updated OOD of the anti-skid braking system - PART.

The object notation is self-explanatory, following the syntax defined in figure 4.53. Note, however, some new terminology; the connections between objects are defined to be 'links'. Note also that message names have been redefined to relate more clearly to the provided operations of the objects. Thus what we have in front of us is a design description of the actual object structure of the software system – the 'things' that, by working together, produce the required functionality of the software system. This diagram is commonly called an *object communication* diagram.

   We saw a moment ago in figure 4.53, for a single class, how the class and object diagrams relate. But what of the situation of figure 4.43, which contains objects belonging to three classes? How do we show the template for this in class diagram form? The answer is given in figure 4.55. This, it can be seen, shows both the classes

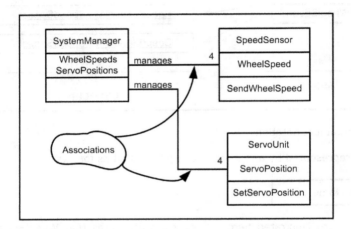

Figure 4.55 Class diagram (simplified) of the anti-skid braking system (1)

and their inter-relationships.   In this case the relationships are deemed to be 'associations'; the naming used ('manages') denotes the nature of the relationship between the objects.

   The specific nature (i.e. syntax and semantics) of class diagrams will be covered later. For the moment the following interpretation of figure 4.55 is sufficient:

If we create one *SystemManager* object, then we must also create four *SpeedSensor* and four *ServoUnit* objects.
The *SystemManager* object is the client in a client/server relationship.
The *SystemManager* object manages the other objects. It does this by sending messages to these objects. However, no information is provided as to the nature of the messages.

The object communication diagram allows us to show the messaging between objects. From figure 4.56 it is clear that a *SpeedSensor* object would expect an incoming message invoking the operation *SendWheelSpeed* (if possible, the naming of the message should be identical to that of the operation). The implementation of the operation is called a 'method'. However, we cannot deduce anything concerning outgoing messages generated by *SpeedSensor* objects.

   Next for consideration is the translation of the class diagram into code. The example given here (figure 4.57) is loosely based on a Java implementation. It is not intended to act as a language tutorial; rather it sets out to illustrate general principles (an Ada code example would look significantly different but would still conceptually be the same). Figure 4.57a is the class diagram, whilst 4.57b shows the basic code template relating to this. Figure 4.57c is a fuller form, which includes the declaration of the attribute *WheelSpeed* and the method *SendWheelSpeed*. Note that the attribute is hidden from the outside world by being declared to be private. In contrast, the method is made available to external bodies as it is denoted to be public.

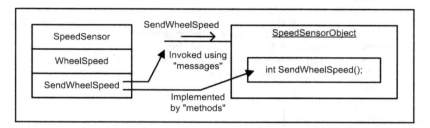

Figure 4.56 Concept - methods and messages

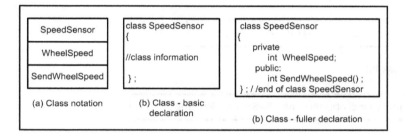

Figure 4.57 The class - diagram to code

Let us now see how the class diagram of figure 4.55 might be translated to code. For the present we'll concentrate on defining the classes as shown in figure 4.58.

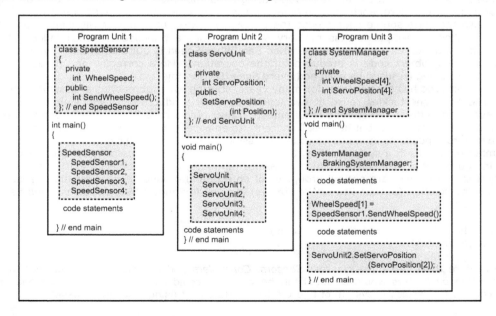

Figure 4.58 OO class design - key program-level details

For demonstration purposes, each class has been placed in separate program unit. These may be compiled separately. Within the individual units, objects of each class are created as and when required. For simplicity we will ignore the mechanisms by which objects in the different program units communicate (a most important topic, discussed in later chapters).

    Two important points are illustrated here. First, all data items (e.g. *WheelSpeed*, *ServoPosition*, etc.) are localised to, and hidden within, the program units; there are no global items. Second, message passing is accomplished by a client making a call to a supplier (server), as in program unit (package) 'SystemManager':

```
SpeedSensor1.SendWheelSpeed ();
```

and

```
ServoUnit2.SetServoPosition (ServoPosition[2]);
```

The general syntax is:

```
ServerObjectName.OperationProvidedByServer (Parameters);
```

4.5.6 Reuse and run-time flexibility issues.

Reuse of software applies to two areas of work: design and implementation. Take the case of program unit 1 of figure 4.58. Here, each time an object of class SpeedSensor is declared (i.e. created) we, in effect, reuse the class source code (reuse the template). Now, each object will contain an integer data item called WheelSpeed; thus memory storage must be provided for each individual item. However, the situation concerning the operation SendWheelSpeed is quite different. When the class code is compiled, object code is produced for the operation. More correctly, one piece of code is generated, this being (re)used by each and every *SpeedSensor* object.

    Reuse of this type has been with us for many years, starting with subroutines at assembly language level. The technique tackles reuse at two levels: designer productivity (fewer source code items, hence less design effort) and storage requirements (fewer object code items, hence reduced memory needs). Both are important, but here we'll concentrate on aspects relating to design productivity.

    Our aim is to produce as little source code as possible. One way to achieve this goal is to minimize the number of classes in a system. How, though, can we do this? Let us consider the object design shown in figure 4.59a. We *could* produce a class (a template) for each object. Much more sensible, though, is to see if there are natural groupings of objects and produce a class for each group. One such grouping solution (a 'classification' of objects) is given in figure 4.59b, decisions being based on commonality of:

• Function and behaviour (related to operations)
• Qualities (attributes).

As shown here there are three classes: *Sensors*, *Controllers* and *Actuators*. In a perfect world all objects within *each* class would be identical; hence these could be produced from just one unit of source code. As a result the system of figure 4.59 could be built using just three classes.

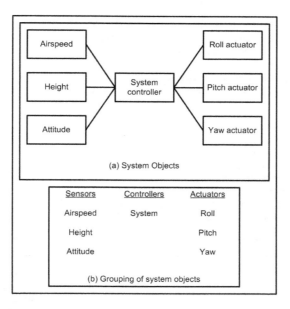

Figure 4.59 Classifying items

Unfortunately, reality is rarely so obliging. It is likely that the initial classification exercise will collect together objects that are similar *but not identical*. In our example the various sensors are (it turns out) really quite different at the detailed level. Thus a single class cannot act as the template for all objects that naturally belong to that class. It might, at this point, seem that we are back to square one, needing a class for each object. However, object-oriented programming offers us a way out of the problem: the use of inheritance. Central to this as a design technique is the concept of class structuring, figure 4.60.

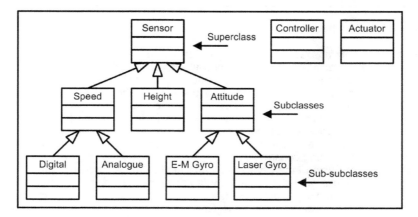

Figure 4.60 Class structuring - subclasses and superclasses

We have made a design decision that the actuator objects can be built from a single template: one class only is needed. As there is just one controller object, classification is not an issue. However, the sensor aspects lead to a different form of class structure, one involving subclasses and superclasses. These, it can be seen, are organized in a hierarchical manner.   At the top there is the superclass *Sensor*, class.   Below this are the three subclasses *Speed*, *Height* and *Attitude* which in turn have a number of subclasses.

The superclass Sensor gives the most abstract definition (in terms of attributes and/or operations) of a sensor object.   A subclass adds detail to the superclass definition which is specific to that individual subclass.   However, it also automatically acquires the properties of its parents, this being known as inheritance.   Thus, moving down the hierarchy, classes become progressively more specialized. But now for a most important point. *What we have here is essentially a class-cataloguing exercise; we aren't decomposing objects*. Thus a Laser Gyro class is a specialized form of an Attitude class; in turn this is a specialized form of a *Sensor* class.

Note: some terminology. A superclass is also known as a parent or base class, while a subclass is often called an extended or derived class.

Producing such inheritance diagrams may be intellectually stimulating; but how does it help to raise software productivity? This is where the inheritance features of OO languages come in to play. Let us see what they can do for us by looking at the example of figure 4.61.

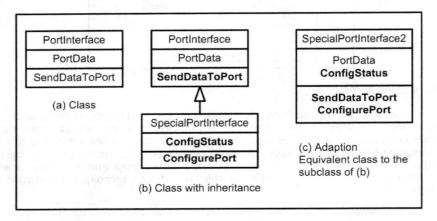

Figure 4.61 Inheritance - what it does

First we define a class *PortInterface*, figure 4.61a.   It has an attribute *PortData* and an operation *SendDataToPort*. We later decide to produce a specialized version of this, *SpecialPortInterface*, figure 4.61b. This adds another attribute, *ConfigStatus*, and another operation, *ConfigurePort*. As a result of inheritance, *SpecialPortInterface* is equivalent to the class of figure 4.61c, *SpecialPortInterface2*. However, there is a significant difference between the two *from a source code point of view*. Without inheritance we would have to produce two separate classes. As each one has to be complete in its own right, there will be duplication of source code.   But with inheritance, there is no need to reproduce the superclass material in the subclass. It is automatically inherited (and thus reused) by applying appropriate programming constructs.

The benefits obtained by using inheritance are quite limited in designs structured *à la* figure 4.61. However, if we now take figure 4.62 the reuse benefits are more obvious. Another factor to take into account is how changes made to the parent class(es) affect the design.   Such changes are, in fact, automatically propagated on code recompilation to their subclasses.   This can profoundly improve productivity *vis-à-vis* maintenance efforts, software configuration control and program version control. But a word of warning concerning inheritance. You don't inherit only the good things; you also get the dross. Please; use inheritance carefully.

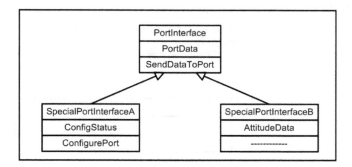

Figure 4.62 Inheritance - example 2

Now let us look at a second major use of inheritance, the provision and control of interfaces. Take the example of figure 4.63, where the superclass has been marked as being 'abstract'.

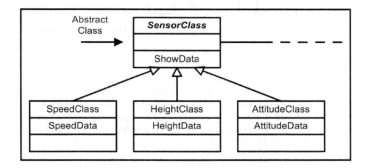

Figure 4.63 The use of an abstract class

This means that we never intend to build *SensorClass* objects. Our aim is to create objects of the subclass type: *SpeedClass*, *HeightClass* and *AttitudeClass* (hence these are termed 'concrete' classes, object creation also known as *instantiation*). At first sight it may seem that the base class is used merely to define the root point in the inheritance structure (actually a commonplace application of abstract classes). In fact *the* key aspect here is the operation *ShowData*, which is inherited by all subclasses.   The result is that all objects generated using this template end up with identical interfaces.   This approach, in effect, provides for reuse of the interface.   Hence, should we add a *TemperatureClass* subclass, then its objects would also present the same *ShowData* interface.

What are the benefits of having a standard, consistent interface? Twofold. First, interfaces usually become simpler and cleaner, making overall object testing simpler.   Second, integration testing also becomes more straightforward as a result of the consistency and clarity of interfaces.

We could achieve the same aims without using an inheritance structure. So why use inheritance? Well, there are two particular advantages. To start with, it guarantees that as new subclasses are added their interfaces will, by default, be correct. The inheritance process takes care of that. Another way of looking at it is that policing of the interface standard is enforced automatically; it doesn't require manual checking (although never underestimate the creativity of programmers).

The second advantage is quite different, one related to flexibility issues. It gives us a simple yet powerful way of leaving decisions concerning code execution to *run-time*. To understand what happens, and to see the advantages of the approach, take the following example, figure 4.64.   The scenario is that we wish:

- To provide a consistent interface for all objects – the operation *ShowData*.
- To call on this operation as and when required.
- To allow, when required, the program run-time conditions to select which *ShowData* operation should be called.

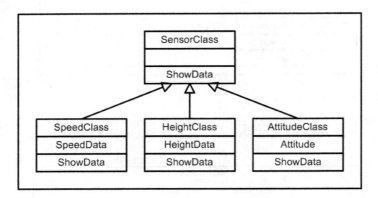

Figure 4.64 Overriding operations

Unfortunately, it turns out that the detailed actions within *ShowData* vary from subclass to subclass. Thus each one must have its own version of the operation.   What we then need is a way of making a 'general' *ShowData* call and have the correct operation invoked.   This is known as *polymorphism*.
    The first step is to denote on the class diagram that each subclass has a *ShowData* operation.   This indicates that the operation in the superclass is to be replaced (overridden) by that in the subclass. Suppose we have the following part declaration:

```
SpeedClass     TrueAirspeed;
HeightClass    RadarAltimeter;
AttitudeClass  AngleOfAttack;
```

Then the following message/operation relationships would be true:

MESSAGE	RESULTING OPERATION
TrueAirspeed.ShowData();	ShowData (from SpeedClass)
AngleOfAttack.ShowData();	ShowData (from AttitudeClass)
RadarAltimeter.ShowData();	ShowData (from HeightClass)

Such statements would be placed in the program source code; as such the choice of ShowData operations are made at compile time. Here we have a case of *static polymorphism*.
    Although this is very useful in simplifying source code, it doesn't meet the requirement of point (c) above.   It is here, however, that the power of OO languages excel.   We can use a source code statement like

```
SomeObject.ShowData();
```

and have the run-time software work out which particular operation should be called (this is called *dynamic polymorphism*).   Precise details are language-dependent but the general principles are as follows:

- Because of the way *SomeObject* is declared, the compiler knows that the actual object called at run-time is undefined.
- However, it also knows that it will belong to one of the following: *SpeedClass*, *HeightClass* or *AttitudeClass*.
- At some stage of program execution, SomeObject is replaced by the actual object identifier.

Thus, when the statement *SomeObject.ShowData();* is reached, the run-time code works out which specific operation should be invoked (typically using a look-up table technique).

Two points to note here:

- There is a run-time time overhead incurred in deciding which method to invoke and
- It is impossible to statically verify the code.

4.5.7 Composite objects - aggregation.

Up to now we have seen the object or class as a single entity. It is possible, though, for an object to consist of various parts. The concept is shown in figure 4.65a.

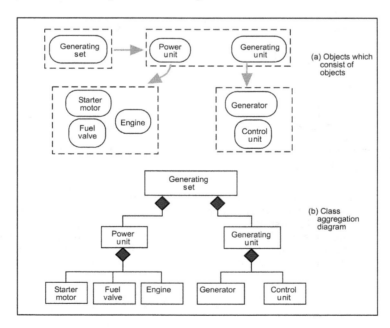

Figure 4.65 Object aggregation

This, from a high-level view, contains one object only: the *Generating Set*. In fact the generating set consists of two major components, a *Power Unit* and a *Generating Unit*. Each of these in turn is made up of further components. Thus the generating set is said to be an *aggregate* object; it is a combination of its parts.

Now let us look at this from a class point of view. The naming used in fig 4.65a is generic; i.e. *Generating set*, not *Generating set serial no. 3568*. Thus it is clear that we can also define aggregation relationships at the class level, as shown in fig 4.65b. Here the diamond symbol is used to denote aggregation (compare with the use of an arrow for inheritance). If we use this as the template for our <u>object</u> diagram, then the top-level object *Generating Set* is defined to be a parent. The contained objects *Power Unit* and *Generating Unit* are children of this parent. They in turn act as parents to their child objects.

4.5.8 Devising the object model – a responsibility-based technique.

The core components of an OO design are shown in figure 4.66.

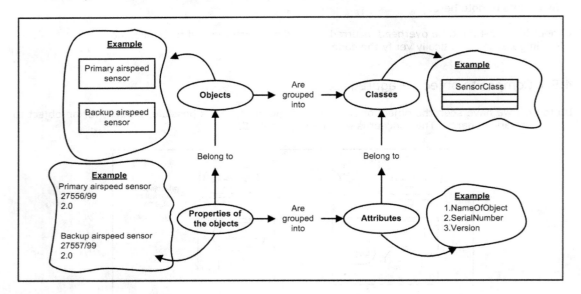

Figure 4.66 Core components of OO designs

As part of the design process, all items, together with their inter-relationships, have to be identified and defined. But faced with a blank sheet of paper, where does one start? The answer, according to 'classical' OO techniques, is to first develop the class model, placing great emphasis on class attributes. Such approaches are based on information modelling techniques, having their roots in database systems and the like. However, the majority of real-time systems are not data-driven; the central issue is that of system dynamic behaviour. In short, it relates to:

- What a system does.
- How it does it.
- Why it does it.
- When it does it.

Even real-time systems that contain large amounts of data (e.g. machinery monitoring, command and control, etc.) are shaped primarily by their dynamics and functionality. More generally, all real-time designs are heavily influenced by two factors: reaction to events in the outside world and dynamic processing within the software.

Clearly, successful design techniques must naturally fit in with this view of systems. But how can we – without experience – gauge the usefulness of different design methods? To answer this, let us pose a different, apparently unrelated, question. What actually does the work in a software system? The answer, obvious in hindsight, is 'the software machines' (objects), acting both individually and collectively. In other words, the dynamic and functional behaviour of a software system is determined by the *object* structure. Not, you will note, the class structure. Thus a successful design method must start from this point of view. And that is exactly the route proposed by responsibility-driven methods. Their root concepts can be simply and easily outlined using a non-computer example, figure 4.67.

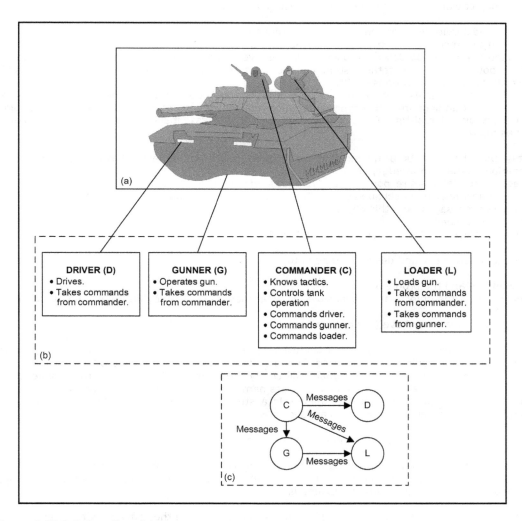

Figure 4.67 Collaborating objects

Here we have a main battle tank and its crew: driver, gunner, loader and commander (the objects). Each object has a specific job to carry out. However, for the tank to function properly, all need to work together in a defined, organized manner. Now, suppose we had to:

• Produce a job description for the crew members and
• Show the collaboration structure of the crew as a whole.

The (simplified) results might be something like that shown in figures 4.67b and c.

Let us return to the job specifications, specifically for the commander. Looking at these in more detail, it can be seen that they are based on three factors:

• What the object knows – information or knowledge (vehicle control, battle tactics).
• What the object does – service (controls tank operation).
• Who the object works with – collaboration (driver, gunner, loader).

Knowledge and service will, for convenience, be grouped together as responsibilities.

Implicit in this model is that the objects collaborate by sending messages to each other. Note also; such collaborations can be described using a client-server model, where any object can be a client, a server or both. Thus the total system can be described in terms of objects (and/or classes), responsibilities and collaborations – CRC.

The CRC method has its roots in the teaching of object-oriented techniques, being devised by Kent Beck and Ward Cunningham. However, experience has shown it to be very effective for developing the initial designs of real-time OO systems. As such it is a essentially a front-end method, being applied as follows:

• Identify potential objects using existing information (e.g. requirements documents, operational information, domain knowledge, etc.).
• For each object define its responsibilities (its knowledge and the service it provides).
• For each object specify its collaborators. These are defined to be other objects that send messages to or receive messages from this object
• Repeat until satisfied.
• Classify the objects to form an appropriate set of classes.

However, to produce a sound design, you need to:

• Clearly understand the problem to be solved.
• Emphasize what the objects are responsible for, what they do, when they do it and what information they exchange.
• De-emphasize what they have (their attributes).

A minor aside at this point. If you feel confused by the use of the term CRC when mostly we've discussed objects, I wouldn't be surprised (a much better name for the method would be ORC). Perhaps the words of Beck and Cunningham will clarify the matter: 'We settled on three dimensions which identify the role of an _object_ in a design: class name, responsibilities and collaborators'.

Developing a design using CRC techniques is a step-by-step process, gradually building up a complete solution. In general it proceeds as follows:

Step 1: Make a preliminary list of potential, suitable objects.

Step 2: Use a single physical card to represent each object, its layout being similar to that shown in figure 4.68a. Each card is identified with the class (object) name; on it is listed the responsibilities and collaborators, as in figure 4.68b for example.

Step 3: List the major operational scenarios of the system into which the software is to be embedded (use cases are especially helpful here). For each one specify:

- What causes the scenario to start.
- When the scenario finishes.
- Precisely what happens between these two points.

Step 4: Form a small team to develop the design. Give each person a card (or cards; it will depend on the number of objects and the size of the team).

Step 5: Pick one of the operational scenarios and 'walk' your way through it, bringing in the objects as required. During this the team members play the roles of the objects, seeking to establish:

- What their responsibilities are.
- Who they collaborate with.
- What messages they pass to each other.
- If the design actually works.
- If more objects are needed.
- If any of the existing objects are redundant.

As responsibilities and collaborations emerge from the role playing, note these on the appropriate cards. When (if) new responsibilities are identified, these can be allocated to the existing objects. Alternatively, new objects can be created to deal with them. During the exercise, if objects become complex, consider splitting them into a number of simpler objects.

Step 6: Repeat step 5 for all other scenarios until the design is satisfactory.

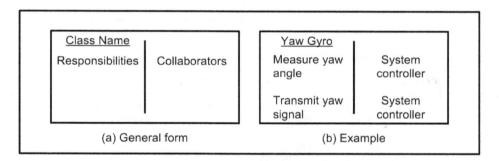

Figure 4.68 CRC cards – Structure and content

   The results of applying steps 1 and 2 to the system described in figure 4.59 is shown in figure 4.69. Steps 3 to 6 can now be applied in an iterative way to bring the high-level design to completion.

4.6 Structured design and functional flow modelling.

4.6.1 Software design and structured charts – limitations.

Visualize the situation where you have been appointed software manager of the anti-skid braking system project. You have never worked on this project or even have any previous knowledge of the design. So, on day one, you set out to get an in-depth knowledge of the system and its software. Assume that the project documentation held by the software team consists of:

- A structure chart(s) as per figure 4.40 and
- Source code modules for the application, at varying stages of completion.

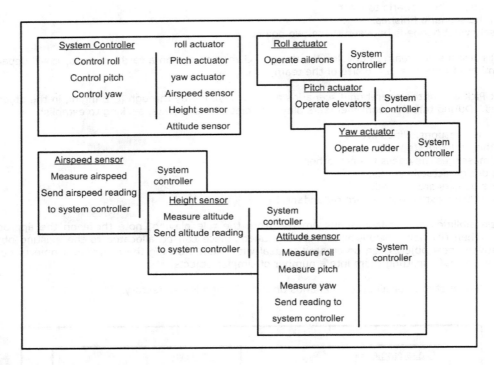

Figure 4.69 CRC cards for the system of figure 4.59

The question is, how helpful is this material, especially the structure chart? Well, it would certainly give you a very clear guide as to how the software should be structured. Moreover, it would allow you to do a code walk-through to check compliance of the code (the implementation) with its design specification (the structure chart). But there are many things that you *can't* deduce from the current information, such as:

• Precisely what each processing function sets out to achieve.
• What specific data is used when calculating wheel accelerations and decelerations.
• What the qualities (attributes and attribute values) of the input and output signals are as seen in the real world.
• Co-ordination and timing aspects of the system.

You may even have some questions of your own to add to these.
   The lesson here is clear. The structure chart, as a means of specifying software structures, is an excellent technique. Unfortunately it says little concerning the system-related features of the design. In the scenario outlined above you would have to go further afield for the relevant system documentation. Now suppose that your searches throw up a diagram similar to figure 4.10, together with fully descriptive text support information. How useful would this be to you? Very much so, I suggest.
   Why then don't we have diagrams like this specifically aimed at supporting software development? The short answer is, we do: the Functional Flow Diagram (FFD). Briefly, the FFD and its related text:

• Enable us to graphically depict the required software processing from a system perspective.
• Provide extensive information concerning processing, signals, interfaces, etc.

- Act as a design specification for the generation of related structure charts.
- Allow us to develop designs in a top-down modularized fashion.

One widely used variant of the FFD is that of the Real-time Data Flow Diagram (DFD), developed by Paul Ward and Stephen Mellor in the early 1980's. The FFD technique described here is similar to that of Ward and Mellor but with some important differences (see later). Also, the notation used is such that diagrams can be produced by general-purpose drawing packages; it isn't necessary to use a CASE tool.

4.6.2 The materials flow model of software processing.

The underlying processing model of the FFD is that of materials flow, a well-established technique in the world of engineering and science. Using appropriate diagramming methods, it allows us to model the function, structure and operation of real systems. It has been effectively employed to describe many and varied engineering systems; these include manufacturing and production operations, control applications, digital electronic devices, etc..

A simple example of a production line operated by robots (figure 4.70) demonstrates the fundamental ideas.

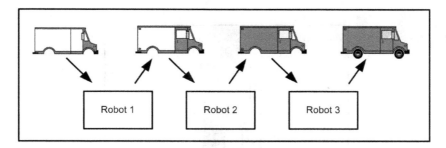

Figure 4.70 A simple example of a materials flow model

This is a very simplistic view of a vehicle assembly line, where the robots perform a variety of welding and assembly operations. A basic body shell enters the production line (left) and moves down the line, eventually emerging ready for final testing. At each individual stage it is worked on by a robot that carries out a set of predefined actions. As you can see, the overall operation is clear and easy to understand. But more importantly, it contains the key elements of functional flow design methods, viz.:

- Each robot is completely independent. It knows exactly what to do and how to do it. Arrival of a vehicle on the line provides the stimulus to begin operations.
- The robots are entirely concurrent in operation.
- Provided that material (the vehicles) is available on the production line, all robots may be working simultaneously (and may possibly work at different rates).
- Without synchronization of activities material may be produced faster than it can be accepted (or vice-versa). In such cases methods are needed to either prevent or else handle a build-up of material on the line.
- In the more general case some synchronization of the robots may be required, say, for example, on line start-up.

In computer systems we find similar structures in pipelined multiprocessor designs, each processor being equivalent to a robot. For example, in a tactical shipborne weapons system, the incoming material could be a sonar signal. As this passes through the system, figure 4.71, it is 'worked-on' by the various processors, e.g. processor ('robot') 1 for front-end signal processing, processor 2 for spectral analysis, processor 3 for threat-analysis, etc.

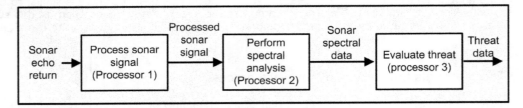

Figure 4.71 Simple FFD example – multiprocessor support

   The FFD model is also an effective way to show the structure and operation of multitasking designs. And, of course, it isn't just limited to the simple linear production line situation; more complex interactions can be dealt with.
   Now let us turn to a materials flow situation where we have only one 'robot' capable of doing work, figure 4.72.

Figure 4.72 Materials flow model – single work resource example.

Here, for example, the objective is to turn the input raw material (a bar of steel) into an art deco product. We can represent the processing involved using a FFD, as shown in figure 4.73.

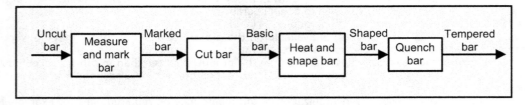

Figure 4.73 FFD example (part) - single work resource.

There is one very important aspect relating to the processing that, unfortunately, cannot be deduced from the diagram.   And that is?   One, and only one, process can be active at any one time.   In computer terms this is similar to carrying out a set of actions within a single sequential program. Our operator mimics the action of the processor itself.

Observe how alike figures 4.73 and 4.71 are, yet the underlying computer mechanisms are entirely different. Thus the FFD can show the abstract (ideal) software structure of a system without concern for implementation details.

At this point you should have a good understanding of the fundamentals of FFD techniques. Hence we can now proceed to look at functional flow design principles in more depth.

4.6.3. Software design using functional flow design techniques.

Fundamental to functional flow design techniques are the basic ideas of:

- Top-down design.
- Hierarchical structuring.
- Stepwise refinement.

The highest-level design diagram – the 'context' diagram, figure 4.74 - is totally system-oriented. What it does is show the complete system in its simplest form: a set of external items connected to a software 'black box'. It contains:

- A single processing unit (a software machine) representing the complete software system.
- The external items which this software interfaces to.
- Data and/or signal flows into and out of the software.

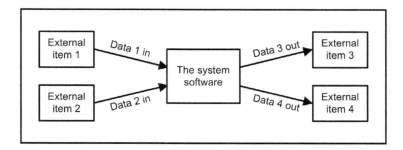

Figure 4.74 FFD design – the context diagram.

The result of applying these ideas to the anti-skid braking system of figure 4.5 is shown in figure 4.75.

A context diagram serves a number of purposes, but the crucial points are *implicit*, not explicit. First, it makes us focus on system, not software, aspects of the design. Second, it emphasizes that in embedded applications, the computer is just one component part of a complete system.

We can now begin to develop the software design for the system defined in the context diagram. This is done by using a FFD to define the functions to be carried out by the software. The process, called 'levelling', results in a diagram – the *first-level FFD* - having the form of figure 4.76.   Each block represents a piece of software processing carried out by a software machine, a 'software robot' if you will (note that in data flow terminology these are called 'data transformations').   However, it is strongly recommended you treat these blocks as clearly identifiable software machines; further, this approach should carried forward into the implementation stage.

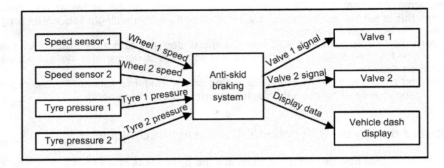

Figure 4.75 Context diagram – anti-skid braking system

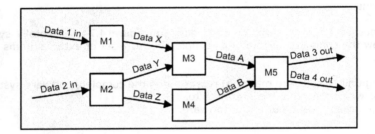

Figure 4.76 First-level FFD – general form

For the anti-skid braking system, the levelled form of the software machine of the context diagram ('Anti-skid braking system') is shown in figure 4.77.

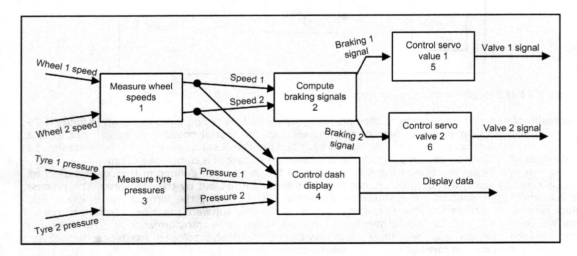

Figure 4.77 First-level FFD – anti-skid braking system

The diagram should be self-explanatory, otherwise there is something lacking in our appreciation of the design objectives. Some points to note:

- The number of software machines (SM), and their functions, are determined by the designer.
- Their names are assigned by the designer.
- External entities aren't usually shown at this level (though this is a convention and doesn't need to be adhered to rigidly.   However, some CASE tools automatically include entities on lower level diagrams).
- All external data/signal flows on both diagrams are totally consistent – they are said to *balance*.

The FFD figure 4.76 is said to be the 'child' of the context diagram.   Not surprisingly, the context diagram is considered to be the 'parent' of the first-level FFD.

If desired, we can level each individual SM to show its function in more detail. For example, the SM 'Compute braking signals' may be elaborated as shown in figure 4.78.

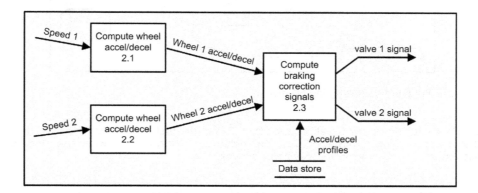

Figure 4.78 Second-level FFD – levelled form of the SM 'Compute braking signals'

This is the child of figure 4.77; thus figure 4.77 is its parent. As before, the diagrams must balance. From a conceptual point of view, each SM in the child diagram should also be viewed as a software machine. The build technique should match this view of the software.

A new symbol has appeared on this diagram, that for a data store. It is denoted by a pair of parallel lines, similar to that used on electrical diagrams for capacitance. It can be seen that in this case it:

- Holds acceleration and deceleration profiles for the vehicle.
- Is used as a read-only store

More generally stores are read/write structures.

In graphical terms the result of applying a functional flow design techniques to a problem is a multi-level diagram showing, in layered form (figure 4.79), the:

- Function of the software, as a set of software machines.
- Interactions of these SMs.
- Data/signal flows, both external and internal, of the software system.

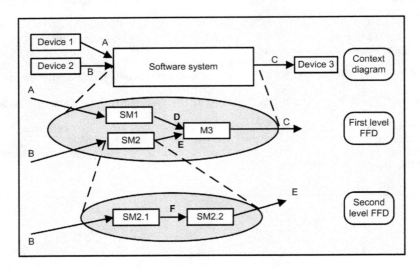

Figure 4.79 Levelling and balancing in FFD design

If we wished we could level any (or all) of the other SMs of the first-level FFD. This may, if desired, be repeated at the second level, third level, etc. There comes a point, though, when the work done by an SM is relatively simple; hence further levelling achieves little.

4.6.4. Organizing the execution sequence of the software machines.

The functional flow diagrams, as they stand, show exactly what processing is to be carried out. Unfortunately they don't explain *when* or *why* the individual software machines are executed. This comes about because the ideal FFD model assumes that an SM:

- Is responsible for controlling its operations, independent of the state of the other SMs.
- Can execute once the correct input data is present.
- Can run simultaneously (concurrently) with all other SMs.

For this to work in practice each SM would need its own computer. However, at this stage we are not going to consider designing software for concurrent systems; we will limit ourselves to uni-processor systems. In such cases one, and only one, SM can be active at any one time. And that brings us back to the questions of when and why.

   Can we deduce this information from the current FFD? Well, in part we can. For example, in figure 4.77 it seems logical that SM1 must operate before SM2; in turn SM3 must run before SM4 is activated. But we have no idea whether SM1 is run before or after SM3, SM2 before SM4, and so on. So, in situations where the SM execution sequence *must* be correct, it needs to be defined explicitly and clearly. In other words the SMs are executed in accordance with some set of rules, specified in an associated document, figure 4.80.

   As shown the specification is defined using structured English, similar in form to that of a program design language (PDL).   Sensibly, as long as the specification is clear, precise, unambiguous and testable, any suitable technique can be used.   A more complex specification is given in figure 4.81 Even so, its logic can be clearly understood. Later we will look how state machines can be employed in this role, especially for specifying more complex behaviours.

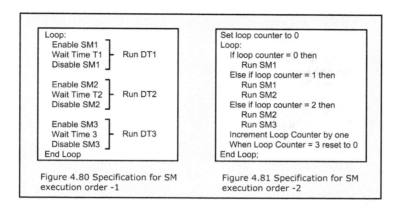

Figure 4.80 Specification for SM execution order -1

Figure 4.81 Specification for SM execution order -2

4.6.5 Functional flow design using graphical techniques.

With this approach, designers use interactive graphics to produce a design based on a block-diagram style approach. This, of course, is fundamentally a materials flow model of the software process. There is no defined standard notation or process; features are vendor-specific. However, the fundamentals are pretty similar in most tools, although detail and implementation aspects may be quite different. It is up to the software developer to decide which tool best suits the needs of the project (see for example SCADE, Simulink and LabVIEW). Figure 4.82 below is an example of a data flow diagrams produced using the National Instruments LabVIEW tool.

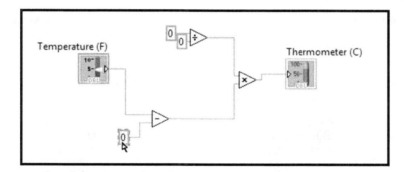

Figure 4.82 Example graphical design model - LabVIEW dataflow diagram

To reiterate; the ideas underlying the conceptual model development are based on functional flow techniques. Nevertheless, differences show when it comes to designing and implementing this conceptual model.

From a *design* perspective the differences between the conceptual and practical models are twofold:

• The diagramming syntax (icons).
• The design process.

From an *implementation* aspect, the differences are quite radical in nature.   Tool facilities often include:

- True automatic run-time embedded code generation.
- Support for a (specified) range of hardware boards, instruments, etc.
- Provision of an operating system.
- Debugging development tools.

What these tools offer is essentially a real-time integrated development environment (IDE); see later work for further details..
   It takes experience to fully appreciate the features of these graphical design and programming environments.

4.7 Design patterns.

4.7.1 Introduction and basic concepts.

Patterns have been with us for quite some time now, starting essentially with the Model-View-Controller (MVC) one of Smalltalk76.   However, it wasn't until OO languages (in particular C++ and Java) were more widely used that the topic became a 'hot' one. The reason for this was all to do with just one factor: code reusability.   OO techniques, in particular class structuring aspects (association, inheritance, aggregation and polymorphism), gave designers powerful ways to describe and implement patterns.   Before looking into this in detail, however, we first need to answer three important questions:

(a) What are patterns?
(b) Why do we use them?
(c) How do we implement them?

Let us start with the first question; what exactly is a pattern?   It turns out that there isn't a single definition; mainstream dictionaries give many alternatives.   However, the key factor is that these depend very much on where and how the pattern is (or is to be) used. So, for our work, we'll define a pattern to be:

(a) A pictorial way to describe the appearance or structure of things and/or
(b) A pictorial plan to act as a guide for doing or producing something.

These points are illustrated in the 'pictures' of figure 4.83.   Figure (a) is self-explanatory, something that might be produced by a fashion designer to describe the outcome of a knitting project.   The purpose of figure (b) is to define what <u>should</u> happen during receipt of a phone call. Lastly, figure (c), specifies the required appearance of a UI used within an industrial system.
   The role of design patterns in the development process is shown in figure 4.84. It can be seen that the design patterns features are dictated by the requirements of the system being developed.   The result is a pictorial description of *what* is to be produced, this acting as a specification for the build process. We wouldn't, though, normally specify *how* it is to be built.
   Moving on to the second question: just why do we use patterns?

- It reduces the amount of design effort. We don't have to start from basics, just pick up an 'off the shelf' design. This translates directly into cost savings.
- It should result in greater reliability of the product, being based on proven methods. This translates indirectly to cost savings; we are much less likely to spend time and money dealing with failures of

the finished item. And this goes hand-in-glove with the intangible cost benefits of having a reputation for good products.

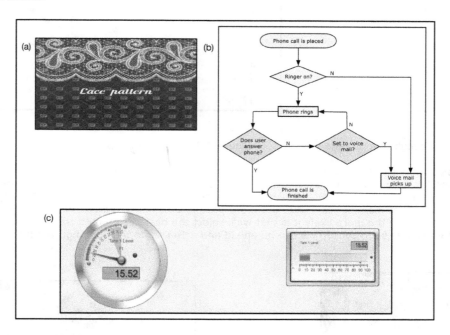

Figure 4.83 Examples of patterns

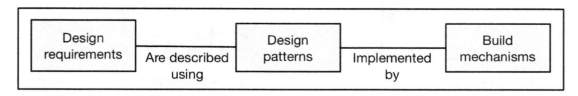

Figure 4.84 The role of design patterns in the development process

And, if you think about it, all this hinges on the reuse of tried and tested techniques.

We can get a deeper insight into this topic by looking at a common-place real world project: tiling in the home. Let us suppose that you need to have some tiling done in your house. You contact your local friendly tiler and present him with your design requirement: 'tile me a floor'. You'd also like to get some idea what the end result will look like. This can be done very simply by consulting a book of standard tiling patterns, as for example those of figures 4.85 and 4.86. Each pattern, from an implementation point of view, has pros and cons; it's up to you to decide which best meets your needs.

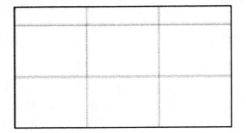

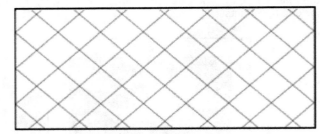

Figure 4.85 Straight tile pattern   Figure 4.86 Diagonal tile pattern

For example, from the build point of view the straight pattern is the simplest one.   Thus it's no surprise that it is very widely used, especially by novice tilers. In contrast, implementing the diagonal pattern is much more challenging. Yet it has a number of features that make it worth using, such as making a small room look bigger. Thus the more precise a design requirement is (e.g. 'it should be easy to tile the floor') the more likely it is that we'll select the best design pattern.

Once a pattern has been chosen we can go ahead and actually tile the floor, figure 4.87.

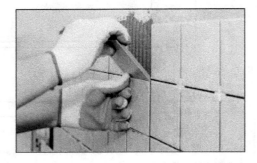

Figure 4.87 Floor tiling   Figure 4.88 Wall tiling

Let us now change the requirements somewhat: tile the wall of a bathroom. This, almost always, employs the straight tile pattern (if you've ever tiled you'll know exactly why), its implementation being shown in figure 4.88. But this example also carries an important message; for different jobs we might use just one design pattern but employ different build techniques.

In the context of software patterns, floor tiling might be analogous to programming in Java whilst wall tiling is the C++ version.

Summarizing things so far: patterns, for our work:

• Are primarily plans to act as production guides.
• Need to have their requirements to be complete, concise and accurate (if they are to be effective).
• Do not normally dictate precisely how things are to be constructed.

Now that we've established some fundamentals, we can look at patterns in the context of software development. This, it turns out, contains two distinct key aspects: program-level and system-level development work.

4.7.2 Program-level patterns.

The most important points about 'classical' program-level patterns are that they:

• Describe very specific program operations.
• Are depicted in structural (architectural) form using class diagrams and associated OOP constructs.
• Are intended to be implemented using an OO language.
• Do not normally specify how the implementation should be done.

The ideals underlying the use of these patterns can be simply explained using the analogy to the process of cooking, figure 4.89. We begin with a specific requirement, figure (a): how to make a Thai curry? To answer this our first port of call is to get hold of a cookbook (figure (b), specifically one relating to Thailand. This gives us a whole set of recipes or 'implementation guides', from which we can produce the dish of our choice (figure (c).

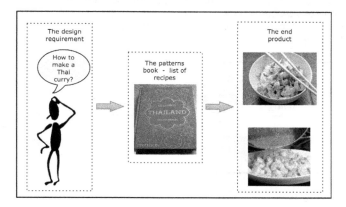

Figure 4.89 Cooking analogy

This neatly highlights the fact that there may be a number of ways to implement a single requirement. Moreover, we're not constrained to slavishly follow the recipe: it can always be adapted as we wish.
    Note that as our requirement become more detailed, the range of possible solutions narrows. For example, changing our cookery requirement to 'a recipe for Thai shrimp curry' will result is a fairly limited list; adding 'cook in under 30 minutes' will further restrict our choices.
    But that isn't the complete story. Another very important point concerning patterns can be deduced from the recipe itself, figure 4.90.

Figure 4.90 Recipe details.

Here the recipe description consists of two elements:

• A pictorial description of the item to be produced (the pattern) and
• Detailed text instructions concerning the cooking process.

Without the written instructions patterns don't really tell us how to actually carry out the job.
    Let us now see how this works for software. One of the core books on this topic is 'Design Patterns', by Gamma, Helm, Johnson and Vlissides (originally published in 1994); this is an important read if you intend to actually use patterns. Since then an enormous amount of material has been published on the topic. The example we'll look at here - the Singleton - is quite simple, chosen because it needs little knowledge of classes to understand it.
    The design requirement: create an object dynamically from its class specification, but make sure that only one can ever be produced. The way to create an object dynamically in, say Java and C++, is to use the *new* operator. This, a straightforward and simple process, also enables us to create many objects of a single class.   And yet, to meet our specific requirement, this is something we *must* prevent. Enter the Singleton pattern.
    Its role as a pattern is shown in figure 4.91, acting as a code specification that restricts class instantiation to a single object.

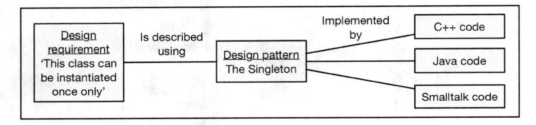

Figure 4.91 Role of the Singleton

The Singleton pattern devised by Gamma et al is shown in the class diagram of figure 4.92.

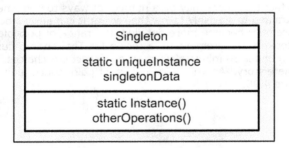

Figure 4.92 Singleton class - generic description

What we have here is a general or generic class description, the wording used being essentially a form of pseudocode. If you were proficient in OO programming you'd probably make a good guess as to its intent: but it would be a guess based only upon your interpretation of the pseudocode. In fact the central aspect is that the Singleton object can *only* be created by executing the code of the Singleton class. *In other words the class itself is responsible for controlling its instantiation.* The way that the Singleton class achieves it's aims is by:

1. Hiding the constructor of the class (by making it a private item, here *EngineMonitor*) and
2. Making the class hold its own instance (here *EngineDataMonitor*) and
3. Defining a public operation (*getEngineDataMonitor()*) that returns the sole *EngineDataMonitor* object to a client caller (here *Controller* object). This enables the client to get and use this single object.

We realise that you may not, unfortunately, be familiar with any of the OO languages. In that case treat this as an appreciation exercise of pattern definition and implementation.

The class diagram for this is given in figure 4.93, which should be self-explanatory.

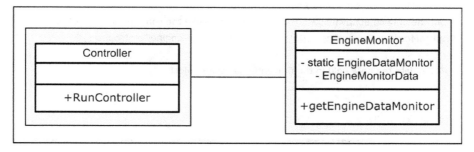

Figure 4.93 Singleton class application

The essential code (core aspects) for these is shown in figures 4.94 and 4.95.

Program level patterns have, in practice, turned out to be both useful and popular. As a result many new ones have been devised, some designed for implementation in non-OO languages such as C. For more details and information on these newer offering we suggest that you search the Web to see what's out there.

```
EngineMonitor.java
public class EngineMonitor
{
   //Declare the object EngineDataMonitor of EngineMonitor class.
   private static EngineMonitor EngineDataMonitor;
   //Make the constructor private so that EngineMonitor class cannot be
instantiated.
   private EngineMonitor(){}
   // Declarations of any singleton data
   // Declarations of any additional functions
   // Create a public operation to be used by clients.  In this case it also invokes
   // the creation of the object on its first use ('lazy instantiation').
   public static EngineMonitor getEngineDataMonitor
   {
     if (EngineDataMonitor == null)
     {
```

Figure 4.94 Basic code of the Singleton class EngineMonitor

```
Controller.java
public class Controller
{
    public static void main(String[] args)
    {
        //Just for info: if you were to use the new operator like this you would get a
        //compile time error, illegal construct: The constructor EngineMonitor() is not visible.
        //EngineMonitor object = new EngineMonitor();
        //Get the only object available.  This call will also invoke the constructor EngineMonitor.
        EngineMonitor CurrentEngineData = EngineMonitor.getEngineDataMonitor();

        // Manipulate the data held in the CurrentEngineData object
        // etc.
    }
} // End class controller
```

Figure 4.95 Outline code of the client class Controller

4.7.3 System-level patterns for real-time embedded systems.

System-level patterns are sometimes described as being Architectural patterns.   A well-known definition is that they are 'Stereotypical ways of organising the architecture of a particular type of software system'. One example, shown in figure 4.96, is that of a particular type of industrial process control system. Please note: this is an adapted version of an original example produced for a software engineering textbook. Now for the really important question: 'just how useful is this process

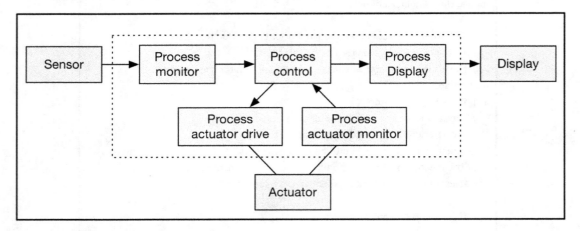

Figure 4.96 Temperature control system pattern

control system pattern?'. There's no doubt that it can be used to describe, at a very high level, the architecture and functioning of the control system. But there is a problem in using it as an implementation guide; real systems can be quite diverse, as demonstrated in figure 4.97 (note: these examples haven't been dreamed up. They are based on three systems that I have personally been involved with).

	Sensor type	Actuator type	Actuator monitor	Display type
JPT control	Thermocouple	Servovalve	Rotary variable differential transformer	Full graphics (cockpit display)
Liquid temperature control	Platinum resistance thermometer	Variable-speed dc motor	Pulse sensor (Hall effect)	Bar graph (on the system digital controller)
Freezer temperature control	Thermistor	Switched ac motor	None	Multi-segment A-N display (on freezer)

Figure 4.97 Example - attributes of some temperature control systems

If you look up the definition of stereotypical in the Oxford dictionary you'll find it says:

Stereotypical: Relating to a widely held but fixed and oversimplified image or idea of a particular type of person or thing.

The key word here is 'oversimplified'; this certainly is the case with the process control system pattern. In practice much more detail is needed to make this useful as a software design guide for real systems. Thus it is best described as a 'meta-pattern', i.e. a pattern of patterns. In this role it could contain a set of very specific patterns, each applicable to a very restricted domain. More of this in a moment.

   This leads into the topic of detailed design patterns, their practicality and their usefulness. The pattern shown in figure 4.98 is an adapted version of an Anti-skid braking system pattern, also taken

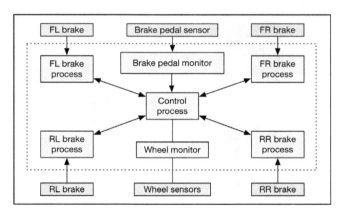

Figure 4.98 Anti-skid braking system pattern 1

from a software engineering textbook. This, in its intent and application, is much more focussed (specific) than the generic control system pattern. Now compare this with figure 4.99. This was used earlier (see figure 4.77) to illustrate a functional flow based design 'specification' for the software

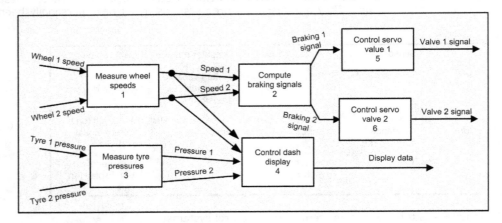

Figure 4.99 Anti-skid braking system pattern 2

of an anti-skid braking system. It doesn't take much stretch of the imagination to define this as a software pattern. Yet there is a profound difference between these two patterns, which isn't obvious from the diagrams themselves. It is, in fact, all to do with *how* these were devised in the first place. Pattern 1 has been developed from a somewhat abstract view of anti-skid braking systems; pattern 2 has been derived from a very specific set of requirements. And here is the first key question; if you are developing software for real systems, is pattern 1 actually helpful/useful as a software specification method? Well, this is where the ideal world meets the real world: and fails to make the grade. The reason is that real systems, even within specific technology sectors, are often quite diverse. Take, for example, the vehicles shown in figure 4.100.

Figure 4.100 A diverse range of vehicles

All use anti-skid, anti-lock braking systems, yet it's clear that a 'one size fits all' approach just won't work. This point is reinforced by the architectural diagram of an actual commercial system, figure 4.101. Note: this is not for the complete vehicle as it shows one calliper only. There will, of course, be a multiplicity of these on the target vehicle (take your pick: 4, 6, 8, etc.). So you can pretty-well guarantee that the structure of specific target systems will differ significantly from that of pattern 1.

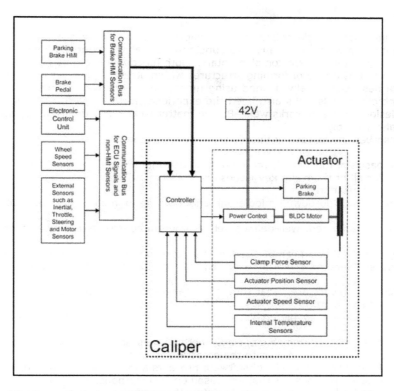

Figure 4.101 Architecture of a commercial anti-skid braking system (part - one calliper only shown)

Consider now a second key question: 'is there a fundamental difference between using program-level and system-level patterns?' The answer is a definite yes. Program-level patterns are *software*-centric; what the software is intended to achieve at the *system* level has little bearing on pattern usage. In contrast, software for real-time embedded software is shaped by *system* requirements. And, as you have seen, even in specific sectors there can be considerable architectural differences between implementations.

Next, let's revisit the question about the intent of patterns. Fundamentally they are used to define proven, reusable ways to build software structures that solve specific design problems. System-level patterns, in this role, are 'hardly fit for purpose' (to use a well-known phrase).

Finally, what of the use of system-level patterns for educational or training purposes? You *could* argue a case for it as a way of introducing students to the concepts of architecting software structures.   But if you think this really qualifies them to take on the design of embedded systems (especially mechatronic systems), take a reality check.   Any company developing such systems will want their software engineers to:

• Be proficient and experienced.
• Have a good understanding of important system aspects such as function, structure, safety and behaviour.
• Understand clearly the role of software in the greater scheme of things.

before trusting them to take responsibility for the design work.

Once they have attained this high standard, patterns really don't have much to offer.

4.8 Review.

The various design methods described in this chapter should not be seen as mutually exclusive techniques (a statement which may cause OO purists to froth at the mouth). All have strong and weak points, and, in many instances, are complementary. Both functional and data flow methods can be (in fact, have been) used as a way of forming structures within objects. In other applications the overall system structure has been initially defined using functional flow methods: these subsequently being translated into object models. It's also been the experience from Matra Space that a hierarchically-structured OO design approach works well. But no matter what methods are used, the fundamentals of good design always apply.

If you have absorbed the lessons of this chapter you should now:

- Understand the basics of functionally structured, object-oriented and functional flow design methods.
- Appreciate that for all of them the key issues are those of problem abstraction, problem structuring and software modularization.
- Know what the terms top-down, middle-out and bottom-up mean when applied to the design process.
- See how the use of a limited, well-defined set of program constructs can help in producing quality software.
- See how coupling and cohesion can be used as indicators of the quality of a software design.
- Realize that the software of a real-time system can be grouped into two layers; application and service.
- Know what these two layers are, what they do, what benefits are obtained by using this approach and how to implement them.
- Understand what is meant by hierarchical structuring, and see how it may be applied as part of software design.
- Know what is meant by the terms object, class, method, message, subclass, superclass, inheritance.
- Feel confident to apply CRC techniques to the object identification process.
- Realize that the functional flow model of software presents a materials flow view of the process.
- Be competent to assess real designs that are based on FFD methods.
- See the need for, and use of, specifications to define the execution order of software machines.
- Understand the fundamentals of patterns: what, why and how.
- Realize why design requirements play such an important role in the development of patterns.
- Appreciate that patterns don't normally prescribe an implementation solution.
- Understand that a pattern may be implemented in a number of ways.
- Know what a program-level pattern is and what it aims to achieve.
- Know what a system-level pattern is, what it aims to achieve and how it differs from a program-level one.
- Appreciate that program-level patterns have been widely used and why this is so.
- Appreciate that generic system-level patterns have not been particularly successful.

4.9 Exercises.

1. Produce a functional flow design solution for the software of the system described below:

The primary function of the attitude sensor system is to measure the degree of tilt ('slant angle') and the magnetic bearing ('slant angle bearing') of an oil well logging tool. Basic measurements are made by triaxial accelerometer and magnetometer assemblies. From these the actual slant angle (SA) and slant angle bearing (SAB) values are computed.   Temperature monitoring of the sensor mounts is carried out so that errors caused by dimensional changes due to the high operating temperatures can be corrected for.   These are called 'misalignment errors'.   The order of processing the input accelerometer signals is as follows:

1. Correct raw signals for static misalignment errors.
2. Apply temperature compensation to the results.
3. Compute the SA and SAB values using appropriate trigonometric formulae.

Attitude data is transmitted to the surface on a serial transmission system that uses a carrier encoding scheme. The sensor unit is required to interface to the line modem using standard logic level signals.

A secondary function of the unit is to provide support for field maintenance of the equipment. It enables an operator to perform a series of tests using a laptop computer linked to the unit via an RS232 serial communication link. These features include:

- System calibration.
- Input signal validity check.
- Display of all input and computed values.
- Operator help information.

First, produce an object-oriented design solution for the attitude sensor system.
Second, produce a data-flow design solution for the attitude sensor system.

Compare and contrast the two solutions, as follows:

(a) Determine the advantages and disadvantages of the various techniques.
(b) Evaluate the degree of modularization inherent in these approaches.
(c) Compare the effectiveness of their coupling and cohesion.
(d) Evaluate the impact of the methods on the later development, integration and test of the software.

4.10 Useful reading material

(a) IMPORTANT FOUNDATIONS.

Turing machines and languages with only two formation rules, C.Bohm and G.Jacopini, Communications of the ACM, Vol.9, No.5, pp366-371, May 1966.

Go To statement considered harmful, E.W.Dijkstra, Communications of the ACM, Vol.11, No.3, pp147-148, March 1969.

Principles of Program Design, M.A.Jackson, Academic Press, 1975.

Engineermanship, a Philosophy of Design, L.Harrisberger, L.Harrisberger,
(An essential read. Out of print but available on Amazon.)

Object Oriented Analysis and Design with Applications, 2nd Ed., G.Booch, 1994.

Structured Programming (in Software Engineering Techniques), E.W.Dijkstra, Nato Science Committee (Eds. J.N.Buxton and B.Randell), pp99-93, Rome, 1969.

Objectifying Real-Time Systems, J.R.Ellis, SIGS books, New York, 1994.

A practical guide to real-time systems development, S.Goldsmith, 1993.

Strategies for Real-time System Specification, D.Hatley and E.Pirbhai, Dorset Publishing House, ISBN 0-932653-04-8, 1988.

Software Engineering - A Practitioner's Approach (8th Ed.), R.S.Pressman and B.R.Maxim, 2015.

Object-oriented modelling and design, J.Rumbaugh et al, 1991.

Software Engineering, I.Sommerville, (10th Ed.), 2015.

Structured Development for Real-Time Systems, P.T.Ward and S.J.Mellor, Vols. 1,2,3, 1985.

Using CRC Cards, N.M.Wilkinson, 1995.

(b) GRAPHICAL TECHNIQUES.

LabVIEW 2017   -   A graphical programming tool for developing test, measurement, and control applications.
http://www.ni.com/en-gb/shop/labview/labview-details.html

MATLAB - A platform for data analysis, algorithmic development and model creation.
https://uk.mathworks.com/discovery/what-is-matlab.html

Scade Control Software Design.
http://www.esterel-technologies.com/products/scade-suite/

(c) PATTERNS.

Design Patterns - Elements of Reusable Object-Oriented Software, E.Gamma, R.Helm, R.Johnson, J.Vlissides, 1994.

Design Patterns for DUMMIES, S.Holzner, 2006.

Real Time Design Patterns, Olah Medvedyev, https://www.slideshare.net/GlobalLogicUkraine/realtime-design-patterns

END OF CHAPTER

Chapter 5

Multitasking systems - an introduction

The purpose of this chapter is to describe the basics of multitasking systems, setting out to describe:

• What the tasking model of software is.
• The benefits of modelling software as a set of collaborating tasks - a multitasking structure.
• How interrupts can be used as a mechanism for implementing concurrency.
• What, in general terms, a real-time operating system (RTOS) is and what it does.
• How the RTOS can be used as a mechanism for implementing concurrency.
• How task execution is controlled - scheduling principles.
• Problems that may be met when tasks share resources, and show how these can be resolved.
• Features needed to enable tasks to communicate with each other - intertask communication.

5.1 The task model of software.

5.1.1 Modelling - what and why.

This opening section might, at first, seem to be somewhat academic, far removed from the reality of software and software engineering. Not so. It does, in fact, deal with a very practical and important topic: the use of models as part of the design process. However, before going further we need to answer two key questions:

1. What is a model and
2. Why doe we use models?

A model, in our view, is a 'representation of reality'. Though that sounds pretty abstract (and not especially helpful) it actually gets to the heart of the matter. Now let's make it more meaningful by looking at some tangible items, figures 5.1, 5.2 and 5.3.

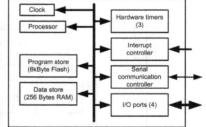

Figure 5.1 Clay model of a car

Figure 5.2 Functional scale model of a marine craft

Figure 5.3 Block diagram model of a microcomputer

In the auto industry it is common practice to produce models of new or proposed vehicles using clay, figure 5.1 (even in these days of cutting-edge CAD systems). This model is used for a number of purposes, a key one being to assess the vehicle's styling (and hence its customer-appeal). Otherwise it doesn't actually do anything; it's inanimate. By contrast the marine craft model of figure 5.2 *is* animate (in the sense that it is an operational unit). This particular model, a scaled version of a proposed craft, is used mainly for proof-of-concept work. The third example, figure 5.3, shows a block diagram of a specific microcomputer. It might, at first, seem odd to think of this as a model: but it is. It represents the reality of the microcomputer structure and parts, their functions and their interactions. This model allows us to understand and explain the structure, qualities and function of the device; it is an abstract view of the micro's reality.

From this you can see that models come in many forms, being used for a variety of purposes. And, of course, any single item may be represented by a variety of models. Take the marine craft, for example. Suppose we wished to explain the structure and functioning of the propulsion system: what's the best way to do this? In all likelihood we would probably describe this using block diagrams together with supporting text. This example highlights a truly important point when a 'system' can be modelled in a number of ways. Here it is *essential* that you always use the most appropriate model for the work in hand.

So, in summary, a specific model:

- Is a particular representation of some reality.
- Allows us to reason about and evaluate the qualities of this reality.
- May not be a the only way to represent the reality — if all depends on what qualities you want to model.
- Is usually a simplified version of the real item.

A final point: a model that doesn't correctly represent reality may be worse than useless.   For example, using it to predict behaviour may well produce results that subsequently turn out to be nonsense (weather modelling?).

Now that we've laid the out key aspects of models (and modelling), let's see how we can apply these to software.

5.1.2 Modelling executing software - the single task structure.

Suppose that we're asked to implement the computer software for the simple system shown in figure 5.4. Let us also assume that this is the only job that the computer has to perform.

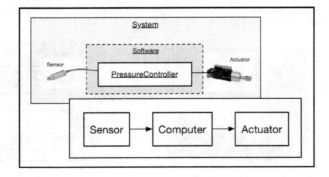

Figure 5.4 A simple processor-based real-time system — pressure control system

Here the requirement is to control a gas storage tank's pressure by varying the pressurisation rate. This is done by:

- Measuring a tank's pressure using a pressure sensor.
- Comparing this with the desired pressure value, and then
- Generating a control signal to set the position of an actuator that controls pressurisation rate.

The software has to perform:

- Data acquisition.
- Signal linearization and scaling.
- Control calculations.
- Actuator drive.

There is no unique code solution, but it certainly will be of the following form (listing 1.1):

```
Loop;
    MeasurePressure;
    LinearizeSignal;
    ScaleSignal;
    ComputeControlSignal;
    SetActuatorPosition;
    DelayUntilTime = xx milliseconds;
```

Listing 1.1

What we have is an example of 'application-level' code, here formed as a _single sequential program_ unit.   Note this well: a single sequential program unit.   In line with good design and programming practices the top level 'operations' (e.g. *MeasurePressure*, *ComputeControlSignal*, etc.) would be implemented using subprograms; these also hide all low-level code details.

With structures like this we can reason about the processor's run-time behaviour by walking our way through the code.   This is true because the route through the program is entirely predictable — a deterministic 'single thread' of code execution.   This holds even when the program contains selection and iteration operations.   In such cases there are a number of possible routes through the code: but only one route can ever be executed at a time.

At this point our objective is to produce a model that represents the run-time structure of the program.   To understand how we developed this model consider an analogy with the process of cooking food, figure 5.5.

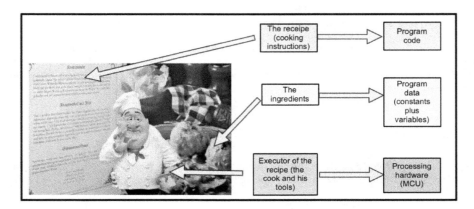

Figure 5.5 Code execution — a cooking analogy

Most of you will be familiar with the hows and whys of cooking so little need be said about the process details. However, if we modelled the kitchen system itself we would need to show that it (the kitchen) contains a working cook. Note that at this level we aren't concerned about recipe details, ingredients used or cooking techniques; we merely wish to show that cooking is taking place.

As you can see from figure 5.5 the software equivalent of the 'working cook' model comprises three component parts:

- Program code — analogous to the recipe.
- Program data — analogous to the ingredients.
- Processing hardware (the Microcomputer Unit) — analogous to the cook and his tools.

After a program is compiled its output is downloaded and stored in the target system in digital format (as a bit, byte or word pattern, for example). This is stored in the memory devices of the MCU (ROM and RAM, as appropriate). Nothing more happens until the CPU is started, activated by some form a reset signal. All subsequent operations take place at the electronic level, being dictated to a large extent by processor decisions. And what we now want to show (in our software system model) that such activities are taking place. This run-time description we define to be the task model of software, denoted by a parallelogram symbol of figure 5.6a.

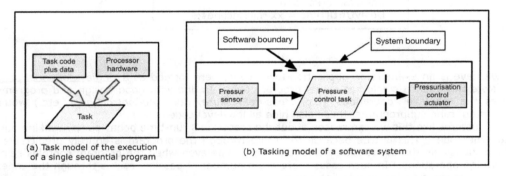

(a) Task model of the execution of a single sequential program

(b) Tasking model of a software system

Figure 5.6 The task model of software

The tasking model for a complete software system (in this case the pressure control system of figure 5.1) is shown in figure 5.6b. Observe that this is directly equivalent to defining that a kitchen has a working cook present.

Note: we normally show any connections between the internal software and external devices on tasking diagrams.

For the example discussed here the tasking diagram is somewhat trivial; its role can be performed perfectly well by a context diagram   However things are quite different when a software system contains multiple tasks. In such cases the tasking diagram forms a key (in our view essential) part of the software development process.

5.1.3 Multiple tasks — why?

It's a rarity to find a software system that performs only a single function. For example, our simple pressure control system may, in practice, also be required to:

- Control the plant switching operations for start up and shut down (sequencing control).
- Provide alarming functions.

It may be extremely difficult to achieve all these objectives using just a single task (single 'thread') program. The code can easily become lengthy, complex, difficult to understand and quite difficult to maintain. How can we simplify things and make our life a easier? The answer, it turns out, is to use a number of tasks, not just one.

Conceptually it is simple to develop a multiple task software design, the *multitasking* model, figure 5.7 (the problem comes with its implementation: more of that later).

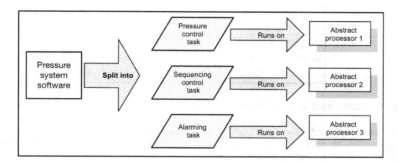

Figure 5.7 Multitasking model — an ideal abstract solution

The first step is to split the overall system functions into sensible groups, then allocate them to specific tasks. This, the *most* important step in the development process, is carried out as a high level design decision. As such it is beyond the scope of this work; we will accept (and work with) the specified tasking structure. So what figure 5.7 shows is that the overall system functionality is performed by three tasks. We assume, for the moment, that each task has its own processor, an abstract or 'pretend' one. Each task is then implemented as a single sequential program, having well-defined objectives. This is basically a 'divide and conquer' technique which simplifies the job of programming the individual tasks.

Well, this is fine in theory, but how do we get the system to actually work. One method would be to replace each abstract processor by a real one, a multiprocessor implementation. While this, at first, might seem to be quite straightforward, it unfortunately brings some new challenges with it. These are, in some cases, quite complex (when compared with single processor designs). The subject matter is beyond the scope of this book; hence we will consider single processor systems only.

In the abstract model of figure 5.7 each task does its own thing, and can run at the same time as any (or all) other tasks. That is, they can run simultaneously or 'concurrently'. Clearly, in any real single processor unit only one sequential program can run at any one time (i.e one task at a time). So what we have in reality is a form of 'pretend' concurrency (also known as *quasi-concurrency*). And now for the key question: how can we make this work in practice?

The solution is to employ a mechanism to decide which task can run and for how long. Simply put, we need some form of 'execution engine' to decide how to share the processor's time between the various tasks. And that's the topic of the next two sections.

Please note: from here on the term 'concurrent' implicitly means 'quasi-concurrent'.

5.1.4 Using interrupts to concurrent task operations.

One of the simplest ways to provide task concurrency is to use interrupts as a task activation mechanism, figure 5.8. In this particular example three separate timer-activated ISRs are used, one per task. Each ISR houses its related task code: ISR1 implements the functions of the Pressure control task, ISR2 the Sequence control task and ISR3 the Alarming task. This makes it relatively

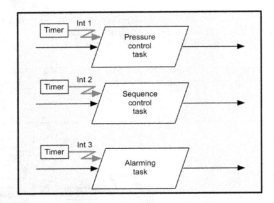

Figure 5.8 Using interrupts as a task activation mechanism

straightforward to develop each task function as a cohesive unit of source code. Each code unit can (*in this simple example*) be programmed and tested as an individual, separate item; there's no need to concern ourselves with the code of the other tasks.

Well, that was the good news: now for the difficult bit. We, as designers, must choose both the timer settings and the ISR priority values. In many cases these are critical to providing secure and timely operation of the complete system. This is especially true of hard-fast systems. So give great thought to the overall problem and system requirements when arriving at your decisions.
You should now see that interrupts:

• Are key-enabling mechanisms in multitasking designs.
• Simplify the code design of the individual tasks.
• Simplify the handling of tasks vis-a-vis different timing and response requirements.

What we have then are three synchronous (periodic) tasks, as described in figure 1.14. Here we may, if we're really lucky, be able to run the tasks in non-overlapping time slots. This eliminates contention between interrupts, producing one major benefit; it enables us to predict the run-time behaviour of the system. Unfortunately, most real embedded systems don't turn out to have such a neat solution. There are two complicating factors.   First, tasks often interact by, for example, using the same hardware devices or by sharing common data. Second they often deal with asynchronous (aperiodic) signals such as operator inputs, network message arrivals, etc.   These, by their nature, occur at random times; thus we can't predict in advance when we'll have to respond to them.   As a result multitasking system temporal (time) behaviour is unpredictable, which can be a truly major problem.
If you wish to implement a multitasking design for a small system, the interrupt technique can work quite well. However this technique doesn't scale easily; it can be quite challenging to use it effectively in larger systems. So this is when we need to use a different execution engine: the operating system.

5.1.5 Introduction to the operating system.

The central function of an operating system is to simplify the work needed to implement a multitasking design. It is intended to screen the complexities of the computer (such as interrupts, timers, analogue-to-digital converters, etc.) from the programmer, Thus the OS can be treated as a 'virtual' machine, one which provides facilities for safe, correct and timely operation.
Taking into account the factors discussed earlier, the operating system software must support:

- Task structuring of programs.
- Task implementations as logically separate units (task abstraction).
- Parallelism (concurrency) of operations
- Use of system resources at predetermined times.
- Use of system resources at random times.
- Task implementation with minimal hardware knowledge.

Nowadays most designers of embedded systems use 'third party' OSs (essentially a collection of code units) rather than producing their own home-grown versions. During the development process the OS software must be integrated with your own software.

So, what should the OS provide in terms of functionality and facilities?   First, we have to decide WHEN and WHY tasks should run — 'task scheduling', figure 5.9.

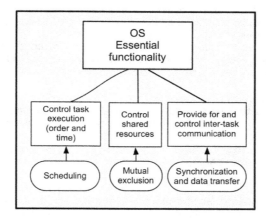

Figure 5.9 OS essential functionality

Second, when tasks share resources, there is always a danger that they might inadvertently corrupt data, cause system malfunctions, etc. Hence there is the need to police the use of shared items — 'mutual exclusion'. Third, as tasks must be able to 'speak' to each other, communication facilities are needed — 'synchronization and data transfer'.

In OS-based embedded systems the fundamental relationship between the various major software units is shown in figure 5.10.

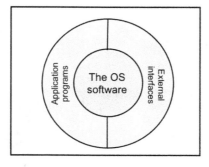

Figure 5.10 OS-based embedded system software structure

These consist of the OS software itself (or, for brevity, the 'OS'), the Application programs and the External interfacing software.   Although this is a simplistic view of things it is sufficient for our purposes.

(a) The OS.

The overall functioning of the processor system is carried out under the control of the operating system.   Now, it is difficult to define precisely what an OS does and how it does it: real systems vary considerably in terms of their functionality and behaviour.   Moreover, our area of concern is the use of OSs in real-time embedded systems: Real-time Operating Systems (RTOSs).   Many such RTOSs are intended to be used in micros that have a limited amount of RAM and ROM; as such they are designed to use a minimal amount of memory (i.e. having a small memory 'footprint').   But in each and every case they *must* (at the very least) provide the essential functionality shown in figure 5.9.   In tiny RTOSs (such as the AvRtos one, http://avrtos.sourceforge.net/) which uses only 1 Kbyte of flash memory, that's about all that you get.   Slightly larger ones (e.g. 2 to 5 Kbyte code size) such as ThreadX, (https://rtos.com/solutions/threadx/real-time-operating-system/) provide software having additional features: create a task, delete a task, start a task, etc..

The software which delivers these core services is commonly called a real time 'Kernel'; for small systems the words RTOS and Kernel are often used interchangeably.   Just to add to the confusion some RTOS vendors use the term 'Executive' instead of Kernel.

(b) The Applications programs.

These programs are the ones that *you* produce, ones that actually implement the functionality of the application (hence the name).   The emphasis here is on the work needed to be done to make the system work correctly; the responsibility for running the software is delegated to the RTOS.   The application software calls on the RTOS resources using a set of subprograms (functions) called application programming interfaces (APIs).

(c) External interfaces.

These consist of software that interfaces primarily to the hardware of the system.   However there may, in some cases, be software interfaces, such as those used to access and manipulate databases (see, for example, eXtremeDB, https://www.mcobject.com/extremedbfamily/).   It is a relatively simple job to interface to such software products, but hardware is a different matter.

The problem here is that embedded systems contain a vary large and diverse range of devices: programmable timers, configurable I/O ports, serial communication devices, ADCs, DACs, etc..   Moreover, there can be considerable differences between individual devices that perform exactly the same function; an Analog Devices ADC is likely to be quite different to a Maxim unit.   Thus the software needed to control ADC type 1 isn't going to be the same as that used to control ADC type 2.   Hence, if we change our hardware (replacing ADC1 with ADC2, for example), we'll also need to change the related API calls in the application software.   This is highly undesirable; we really want the application software to be as stable as possible.   Here is where the external interfacing software comes in.   Its sole purpose is to provide *standard* software routines for the handling of real-world devices.   Using this approach the API function calls for ADC1 and ADC2, for instance, would be exactly the same.   As a result changes to the hardware do not affect the application software; if it was right in the first place it will still be right after any hardware changes.

That's fine as far as the application software is concerned.   However, we still need to make sure that the correct device is selected when the API is invoked.   Many RTOS vendors provide the necessary mechanisms in what is called a Board Support Package (BSP).   See the following video for a brief introduction to BSPs: https://www.youtube.com/watch?v=yptC8ZXOm0I

If you don't have a BSP it is likely that the RTOS itself doesn't support external interfacing operations.   It is then up to you to supply the software needed to implement the necessary interfacing functions.   Consider, for example, the system shown in figure 5.6, and assume that we need to measure the tank pressure.   Assume also that this is an analogue signal which must be digitized using an ADC.   Further assume that two types of ADC may be used (ADC1 and ADC2), the choice being dependent on the hardware build. How do we go about implementing this requirement? Here's an outline of a sensible, workable and flexible solution.

First, develop a measuring function to be used by the application software. Call this *MeasureTankPressure*. Next, develop two data acquisition functions, one which uses ADC1, the other ADC2. Let's call these *GetADC1Value* and *GetADC2Value*. Insert calls of these functions in the body of the function *MeasureTankPressure*. Include some mechanism to select the correct data acquisition function for your specific hardware build. This can be done in a number of ways; one technique is to use compilation directives to define the function to be included in the software build. Thus conceptually, while we have two data acquisition functions, only one is included at compilation time (the correct one, we hope). This is a language-dependent operation, not within the scope of the current work.

Observe also that even where the RTOS supplies interfacing APIs we can still directly invoke the device-specific software.

5.2 Controlling task execution - scheduling.

5.2.1 Scheduling and time slicing operations.

As pointed out earlier, one of the primary jobs of the RTOS is to share out the processor time between the various tasks. This is defined to be task *scheduling*. To do this the RTOS contains a function that decides when a task should run and for how long: the *scheduler*. Such decisions are based on a set of rules called a *scheduling algorithm*. Over the years many algorithms have been developed; there's much to choose from. However, in practice, real-time systems use a very restricted set, ones that we'll look at shortly. First, though, let's revisit the topic of the run-time behaviour of tasks, specifically their temporal aspects.

Consider the Pressure control task shown in figure 5.6b, and its related pseudocode listing 1.1. We can model its time behaviour using a state transition diagram such as figure 5.11.

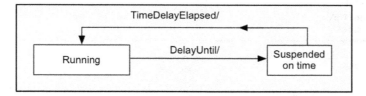

Figure 5.11 Task state — pressure controller

In this particular case the task was suspended in order to implement a sampled-data control system. There are, of course, systems that don't *have* to be suspended; thus they run continuously. But in multitasking design each task *must* suspend in order to allow others to run (a pretty-obvious statement, really).

Figure 5.11 describes the classic behaviour of a periodic task, specifically one in a real-time embedded system. Now let us consider a multitasking design that consists of a number of such tasks. What would be a simple, effective way to schedule the execution of such tasks? Let us start by considering one of the simplest scenarios: the tasks don't perform especially critical functions. Also, we wish to make it *appear* to the real world that tasks run continuously. In cases like this we can simply run the tasks in a timesliced fashion, as shown in figure 5.12. Here we run each task for a predefined period of time, the so-called *time slice*. At the end of a slice a new task is dispatched, by the scheduler software, to the processor. It then runs for the next time slice, as demonstrated in figure 5.12 for a simple. three-task system. The 'time beat' of the system is set by a specific timer called the *Tick* clock. This is a key component, is always provided by RTOS vendors and is user-settable.

Figure 5.12a shows the situation where each task completes its software function precisely within its time slice. Not a realistic situation at all; life is never like this. In practice we are going to be faced with one of two outcomes. First, a task completes before its time slice has expired. Second, a task still has code to execute when it reaches the end of its slice. In the first case, as soon as a task finishes, the scheduler usually loads up the next one (most RTOSs work in this fashion). However, in the second case the problem is more complex. When a task splits across two (or more) time slices, the underlying assumption is that correct system behaviour will be preserved (certainly as far as the outside world is concerned). From the software point of view task code should appear to execute seamlessly; that is, whether it completes in one or more time slices, the results will be the same. To do this, when the task recommences, conditions must be exactly the same as when it left off. This can be achieved by saving the task's information (its *context*) when it is switched out, figure 5.12b. Then, the next time it is dispatched, *and* before it begins executing, the context information must be restored.

Now for just a bit of terminology:

1. The time duration between one task ending and the next one starting is call a *context switch* time.
2. The time slicing technique is called 'Round robin scheduling'.

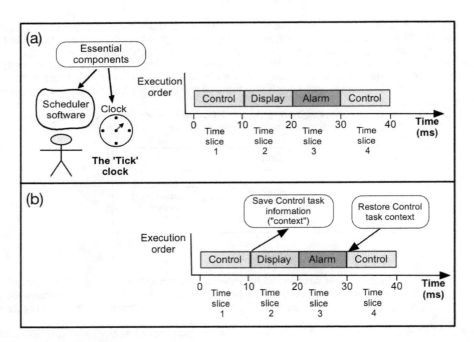

Figure 5.12 Time slicing of tasks

5.2.2 Scheduling and priority-driven operations.

In many applications it is extremely important that once a task is started (dispatched) it executes all its code: i.e., it runs to completion.   Examples include closed loop control, plant sequencing operations, and alarming functions. Clearly round robin scheduling isn't suitable for such applications; we need an alternative.

Let us start by looking at what the outcome is if we use a first-come-first-served (FCFS) technique. To illustrate this assume we have a two task system, having the following attributes:

Task 1: Execution time = 20ms, Periodic time = 50ms
Task 2: Execution time = 20ms, Periodic time = 60ms

Suppose that on start-up (time T_0) the scheduler dispatches task 1, which then begins executing, running to completion. Task 2 now, at time T_{20}, begins its run, ending at T_{40}. Given these timings then if the tasks were run *individually* the restart times for the tasks would be as follows:

Task 1: T_0 , T_{50} , T_{100} , T_{150} , etc.
Task 2: T_{20} , T_{80} , T_{140} , T_{200} , etc.

However, when both are scheduled to run, we meet a problem at T_{150}. Task 1 wishes to restart but, at that instant, task 2 is half way through its run. Thus, although task 1 is ready to run it will not be dispatched; task 2 must first run to completion (at time T_{160}). Only then will task 1 begin executing. In this case the behavioural model of task 1 is as follows, figure 5.13:

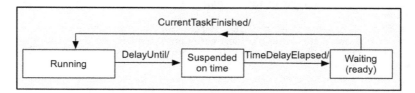

Figure 5.13 Task states in first-come-first-serve scheduling

Hence, as the system runs, the periodic times of the tasks will not be constant; we say they suffer from 'jitter'.
    As more tasks are added to the system the timing variations are sure to increase and, in practice, becoming unpredictable. Now, if this isn't a problem for your application then FCFS scheduling (which is easy to understand and implement) works very well.   But in realistic multitasking designs only a small number of tasks can tolerate significant jitter; for the rest it is important to maintain timing correctness.
    In our specimen problem one factor that hasn't been discussed so far is the issue of task importance.   What if the requirements here were amended to say that task 1 timing must be maintained under all conditions (even if this degrades that of task 2)?.   What this clearly implies is that as soon as task 1 is ready to run it *must* be dispatched. As a result task 2 gets replaced by task 1, even though it hasn't finished current run. We say that task 1 has *pre-empted* task 2 (figure 5.14), putting task 2 into a waiting state.   Once task 1 finishes task 2 is re-dispatched, and runs to completion.

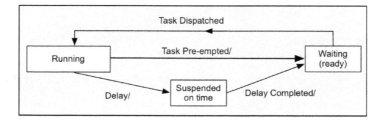

Figure 5.14 Task states with pre-emption

The question we now have to consider is how best to control task scheduling taking into account task importance. Fortunately the solution to this turns out to be relatively simple. Assign each task a priority, then ensure that higher priority tasks take precedence over those lower in the order. So let's consider how our specimen system behaves when priorities are used, with task 1 having the higher priority.

At time T_{150} :
1. Task 2 is executing (running) at priority Low, 10ms into its run.
2. The delay timer signals the scheduler that task 1 is now ready to run (it is now in the ready state). In effect it calls the function 'reschedule'.
3. The scheduler compares the priorities of the two tasks. As a result task 2 is removed from the processor and placed in the ready state; task 1 is dispatched and commences execution, running to completion.

At time T_{170} :
1. Task 1 is goes into timed suspension.
2. Task 2 is dispatched and re-commences execution, running to completion.

For this to work correctly the context of task 2 *must* be saved when it is pre-empted, then restored when it is re-dispatched.

What happens if task 1 is running when task 2 is readied? In this case a reschedule is called, as in the previous case. Once again the scheduler software compares the relative task priorities. However, as task 1 has the higher priority it is allowed to run to completion; task 2 is left in the ready state.

So far the reason for task suspension has been the need to go to 'sleep' for a period of time. But we will also meet situations (see later) where tasks go into suspension until some event occurs. So, taking this into account the <u>general</u> state model of task behaviour is as follows, figure 5.15:

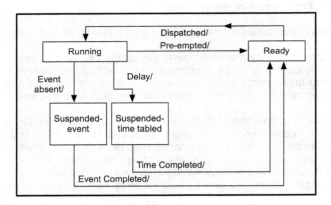

Figure 5.15 Task states — general model

Note: this is a model for each and every task. Some tasks get suspended on time only, others on events only and some for both reasons.

It is stating the obvious to say that practical systems contain a number of tasks. One, and one only, can be in the active (running) state; all others are either ready or suspended. And this situation continuously changes as the system runs. So it is essential that the RTOS software handles all operations (dispatching, suspending, readying) efficiently and quickly. One widely used solution to this requirement is to use *queues* of tasks, as shown in figure 5.16. This will be discussed in general terms only; implementation aspects are quite detailed, outside our remit.

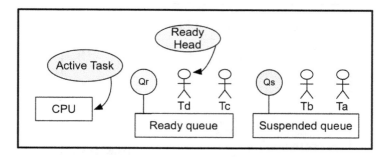

Figure 5.16 Ready and suspended queues

Basically the RTOS software contains two queues, one holding ready tasks, the other holding the suspended ones.   Tasks in the ready queue are organized according to their priority, that with the highest being placed at the front. This is defined to be the *Ready Head*. When a suspended task is readied (either due to a time or event signal) it is inserted into the ready queue at the correct position (determined by its priority). Thus when a reschedule is called the scheduler only has to compare the relative priorities of the Ready Head and Active tasks.

5.2.3 System responsiveness and mixed scheduling policies.

The priority pre-emptive scheduling algorithm has, for many years, been widely used in real-time operating systems. It:

- Is simple to implement.
- Is fast and efficient in operation and
- Imposes little time or memory overheads.

Without a doubt most modern RTOSs use this as *the* primary scheduling policy. To reiterate: with this scheme each individual task is allocated a specific priority level, being run in a priority pre-emptive mode. But there are cases where designers may consider that some tasks should be run at the same priority level (this is especially true of the less critical ones). Hence, when more flexibility is needed, the primary policy may be augmented with one or more sub-policies. Here, where a set of tasks have the same priority, they are run using other algorithms: typically round-robin or FCFS (details are RTOS-specific).

So, across the task set the normal priority pre-emption rules apply; within the individual priority level the rules of the sub-policy are enforced.

One weakness of the priority pre-emptive policy is that there are no real rules for setting task priorities; it's all up to the programmer. If poor choices are made then the resulting system performance is also likely to be poor. The situation is further complicated when a system contains aperiodic tasks; these introduce random disturbances into the run-time operations.   In most applications the RTOS is notified that an aperiodic task needs servicing; it is unusual to poll for such situations.   The notification method is usually implemented using interrupts, either hardware or software types.   Such aperiodic tasks almost always need to be handled very quickly, overriding existing conditions.   Thus, to make sure that they get prompt attention when activated, they must have the topmost priorities, figure 5.17.

In general the priorities of periodic tasks are set lower than those of the interrupt-driven ones. Mostly these are activated by event or time signals (unless a FCFS policy is used, that is).

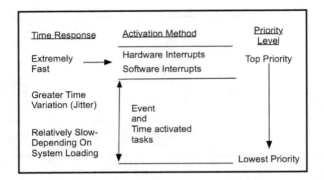

Figure 5.17 Relating responsiveness, activation methods and task priorities.

High-priority periodic tasks aren't likely to suffer much from time jitter.   Unfortunately the same cannot be said of tasks lower in the priority pecking order: these may well experience significant jitter.
    What this tells us is that multitasking systems cannot deliver deterministic behaviour when they include aperiodic tasks.   Moreover, as you increase the work load of the processor (increasing its utilization) temporal behaviour becomes less and less predictable.   So if want to minimize the unpredictability factor (especially in hard-fast systems), you *must* design to have a low utilization. Fact of life: you can't have high utilization *and* good predicability.   Research has indicated that utilization should be kept below 20%; I personally know of a real-time distributed multicomputer system that limited the utilization of critical nodes to 3%.

5.3 Sharing resources in multitasking systems.

5.3.1 Problems with sharing resources.

Up to this point our example systems have consisted of separate, independent tasks; these perform their functions without any interaction with other tasks.   In reality this situation is rarely met in practical systems; tasks almost always influence each other in some way or means.   Let's look at the most common reason for this: task intercommunication, figure 5.18.

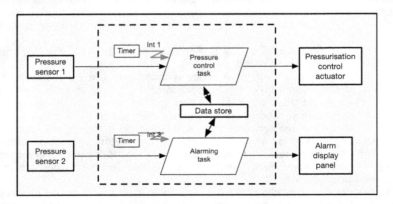

Figure 5.18 Sharing resources in a multitasking system - example 1

Assume that the design requirement of this Pressure control system calls for the Control and Alarming tasks to exchange and share information. To support such operations we now include a data store, one which can be written to and read from. Stores like this are frequently formed as records (structs) and/or data arrays, being located in RAM.

Sharing resources in a multitasking system is not, in itself, a problem. What can be a problem is tasks are allowed to use these in an uncontrolled fashion. A very important point: task scheduling is in no way linked to resource sharing. When the RTOS decides to do a reschedule, then that's exactly what's going to happen — irrespective of the current state of the system. Hence, when tasks share resources the following scenario can lead to behavioural problems:

1. A task (say Task1) is part way through using a shared data resource when it gets switched out (preempted or time sliced).
2. The new task (Task2) begins to execute and, at some time needs to use the same resource.
3. It changes the information contained in, or the state of, the resource.
4. Task2 completes its work of gets switched out.
5. Some time later Task1 is dispatched, and immediately pickups up from where it left off (using the shared resource).

What happens now is anybody's guess; it depends on the changes made by Task2. But in some cases behaviour like this in medical equipment has led to the deaths of patients (I recommend that you read Nancy Leveson's book 'Safeware', ISBN 0-201-11972-2).

Now let's rewind a bit: assume that there isn't any requirement for the tasks to share/exchange information. In such cases it would seem reasonable to assume that the tasks are truly independent. With the example here this is certainly true as far as the software is concerned However, this may not also be the case at the hardware level: tasks could well be sharing the use of the MPUs devices.

The example systems of figure 5.18 contains two pressure sensors, assumed in this case to be analogue types. Hence their signals must be digitized for use by the processor software: i.e. the MPU must perform analogue to digital signal conversion. Suppose now that we decide to implement this design using, for example, an STM32F411VE MCU. This microcontroller has, regrettably, only one on-chip ADC; thus this must be shared out between the two pressure sensors, figure 5.19.

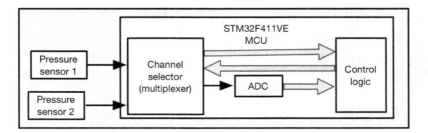

Figure 5.19 Sharing resources in a multitasking system - example 2

When using the shared hardware resource (the ADC) we could run into the following problem:

1. The Pressure control task is currently executing and, at this point, requires the pressure reading from sensor 1. It selects the sensor 1 channel and then calls 'start conversion'.
2. Before conversion has finished the task gets preempted by the Alarming task.
3. This begins executing, and then decides to acquire the pressure signal of sensor 2. It selects the sensor 2 channel and then calls 'start conversion'. Conversion completes successfully and the Alarming task continues with its execution until a new task is dispatched.

4. Some time late the Pressure control task becomes the active one, picking up from where it left off - waiting for and end of conversion signal.

What happens now depends to very much on the software design. If we're lucky we may detect that unusual behaviour has occurred, and take defensive action. Unfortunately two other outcomes are possible. First, the conversion software hangs. Second, the Pressure control tasks acquires an incorrect pressure data value. In either case things don't look promising. There is a simple, powerful message here; uncontrolled sharing of hardware devices is definitely not a good idea.

It is clear that when tasks share resources their usage of such resources must be controlled. Put simply, when a task is using a shared resource other tasks must be prevented from accessing that resource. Thus what is needed is an access control mechanism that:

- Determines whether a task can use a resource in the first place, then
- Allows a task, once it has acquired a resource, to use it until the task has finished with it.

Possible solutions fall into two categories: busy-wait and busy-suspend methods. Simple analogies: waiting for your order in a fast food outlet is busy-wait; you don't do anything else apart from waiting for your number to appear. Alternatively customers can to be given pagers, used to inform them that the orders are ready. No checking is required, which means that the customer can do absolutely nothing while waiting: wait-suspend.

Whichever method is used, it is essential that the access control mechanism is:

- Secure and safe.
- Simple to implement.
- Easy to use and
- Efficient in operation.

Many operating systems incorporate busy-wait methods, implemented using flag techniques. However, as this approach wastes processor time (nothing else is done during the wait-check period), it's best to avoid it for real-time working. By contrast, the busy-suspend technique is much more efficient. With this method each individual shared resource is allocated its own access controller, which operates as follows:

==
Scenario 1 - A task wishes to use the resource *and* the resource is free.
1. First, the task asks the controller for permission to use the resource.
2. The controller allows the task to proceed and use the resource.
3. When the task finishes with the resource it signals the controller that it (the resource) is once more free for use.

Scenario 2 - A task wishes to use the resource *but* the resource is in use.
1. The task asks the controller for permission to use the resource.
2. The requesting task is suspended.
3. When the resource becomes free the task is taken out of suspension and readied (and, if conditions are right, dispatched to the processor).
==

In the following sections we are going to look at three types of access controller: the semaphore, the mutex and the simple monitor. First to consider is the semaphore, which actually comes in two versions: the binary semaphore and the general (or counting) semaphore.

5.3.2 The binary semaphore.

The semaphore is basically a program flow control mechanism, *not* an access controller. Its purpose? Simply put: to automatically stop program execution and later to automatically restart it.

 The semaphore data type is defined by the RTOS vendor; it is up to us to create variables of this type (*semaphores*) for use in our code. All internal features are hidden; we just need to know how to use it. A binary semaphore has two states: *free* and *locked*; it also has a queue associated with it, used to 'hold' tasks. When employed as an access control technique it must be initialized to the free state. From that point on all operations are controlled by just two APIs: one to lock the semaphore, the other to free it up. We use these to control access to resources, the so-called *critical* or *protected* sections of code. Each task that intends to use the resource contains the following code (pseudo-code form):

```
/* Start of the protected code section */
    Lock the semaphore.
        Execute the code of the protected section.
    Free the semaphore
/* Finish of the protected code section */
```

It is up to the programmer to decide where to insert this into the source code.

 A practical example code implementation using FreeRTOS is as follows:

```
/*———————————— Start of the protected code section ———————————— */
    osSemaphoreWait (CriticalResourceSemaphoreHandle, WaitLong);
        RunProtectedCode();
    osSemaphoreRelease (CriticalResourceSemaphoreHandle);
/*———————————— End of the protected code section ———————————— */
```

Both *osSemaphoreWait* and *osSemaphoreRelease* call on functions that are provided by the RTOS software. The responses to such calls are controlled entirely by this software.

 Now let us revisit the two scenarios outlined earlier, describing them using semaphore actions. To simplify the explanation assume that the system contains two tasks only. Taking semaphore operations into account, the overall behaviour of each task can be modelled as shown in figure 5.20. For ease of understanding the following two scenarios are modelled separately.

===
Scenario 1 - A task wishes to use the resource *and* the resource is free.
1. First, the task checks if it can proceed executing: it calls *wait*.
2. The wait function changes the semaphore state to *locked*, then finishes executing. Program control returns to the calling code (the calling task).
3. This then proceeds to run the protected code to completion.
4. At this point the task informs the semaphore that it has finished with the resource by calling *release*. The release function changes the semaphore state to *free*. The task itself carries on with executing its (unprotected) program code.

Scenario 2 - A task wishes to use the resource *but* the resource is locked.
1. The task (say $Task_1$) checks with the semaphore to see if it can proceed: it calls *wait*.
2. The wait function first suspends $Task_1$, placing it in the the semaphore's queue. It then invokes a reschedule.
3. A reschedule is performed, the ready head task being dispatched (i.e. $Task_2$).
4. At some point $Task_2$ (which locked the semaphore in the first place) unlocks it by calling *release*. The release function then readies the suspended task, $Task_1$. Next it invokes a reschedule. At this

point tasks recommence executing, under the control of the scheduler. When Task1 is once again dispatched it immediately executes the protected code.

5. When it has finished executing the protected code Task1 calls *release,* which sets the semaphore state to *free.* It (Task1) continues running, executing non-protected code.

==

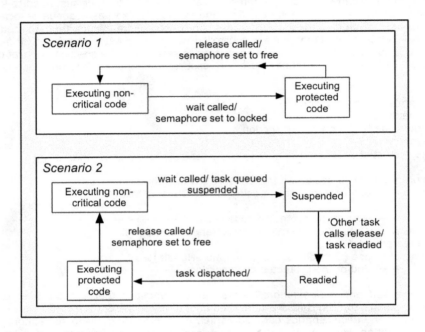

Figure 5.20 Task states when using the semaphore

5.3.3 The general or counting semaphore.

Suppose that our single shared resource is restructured so that it now consists of a number of items. Each item is identical, providing a specific service. For instance, it could be a set of data stores, used to store objects for later collection by other users. Given this arrangement it is safe to let more than one user into the controlled area: provided they don't access the **same** store.   To support this the semaphore construct is altered so that:

• It has a range of values (say 0 to 5); initially it is set to the maximum value (5).
• Each value corresponds to a specific instance of the provided resource, zero indicating all devices in use.
• When a user wants to access the store it first checks that the resource is available (not a zero value). If access is granted it decrements the semaphore value by 1 (one), and proceeds to use the resource facilities.
• When the user has finished, it increments the semaphore value by 1 and exits the store.

```
(*Part of function wait on semaphore NetworkQueue *)
        IF (NetworkQueue) >0) THEN
                NetworkQueue := (NetworkQueue - 1);
        ELSE SuspendTask;
```

```
        END;

(*Part of function 'signal on NetworkQueue *)
        IF (TaskIsWaiting) THEN
                WakeupTask;
        ELSE NetworkQueue := (NetworkQueue + 1);
        END;
```

The value of 'NetworkQueue' controls access to the resource and defines the item which can be used; it is never allowed to go negative.

Note in passing that *wait* and *signal* are also called P and V, derived from the Dutch *Passeren* and *Vrygeven* (named by Edsger Dijkstra, the originator of the semaphore).

5.3.4 Semaphore weaknesses.

It is a fact that poor use of semaphores has led to many, many run-time problems in multitasking systems. It would seem that these stem from just one particular problem: programmers not properly understanding the limitations and weaknesses of the semaphore construct. These can be summarized as follows:

1. Semaphores are not automatically connected with the protected items.
2. The operations wait and signal form an essential pair. But there is no automatic enforcing of such pairings; each can be used without regard to the other. So, for example, a semaphore locked by one task could be unlocked quite incorrectly by another.
3. Semaphores must be visible and in scope to all tasks that share the protected resource. This means that any task can issue semaphore calls at any time — and they will be acted on (even if they produce nonsense actions).
4. The semaphore does not *guarantee* to prevent unauthorised access to protected resources. This comes about because the semaphore does not *hide* the resource; in reality it is visible and in scope to all the user tasks. Thus tasks can by-pass semaphore locks and directly use critical resources.

5.3.5 The mutex.

The semaphore, as mentioned earlier, is merely a flow control mechanism, not an access control technique. By contrast the mutex was specifically designed to ensure that critical resources could be used by one, and only one, task at any one time. In other words it ensures that tasks use critical resources in a **mut**ually-**ex**clusive fashion.

A mutex is used in a very similar way to the semaphore. In order to access a resource which is protected by a mutex the calling task must first get (take) the mutex. When it has finished with the resources it must then release (return) the mutex. A successful get operation locks the mutex; likewise the release unlocks it. A practical example of its use is given in the following code snippet, based on the ThreadX RTOS mutex.

```
/*———————— Start of the protected code section ——————————— */
        /* Assume that a mutex SensorMutex has already been created */
        Tx_mutex_get (&SensorMutex, TX_WAIT_FOREVER);
                ReadSensor(); // protected resource
        Tx_mutex_Put (&SensorMutex);
/*———————— End of the protected code section -——————————— */
```

The overall behaviour of the mutex is exactly as described in figure 5.20.   What this doesn't show, however, is a key feature of the mutex; a mutex can be unlocked *only* by the task that locked it in the first place.   In reality this is only a relatively small improvement on the semaphore; all the other weaknesses also apply to the mutex.

5.3.6 The simple monitor.

The original monitor construct was developed to monitor system resources and performance in computer systems.   This was a quite complex item, providing many features not needed in embedded applications.   The simple monitor is a 'slimmed down' version of this, which:

- Provides protection for critical regions of code.
- Encapsulates data *together* with operations applicable to this data.
- Is highly visible.
- Is easy to use.
- Is difficult to misuse.
- Simplifies the task of proving the correctness of a program.

Fundamentally the simple monitor prevents tasks directly accessing a shared resource by:

- Encapsulating the resource with its protecting semaphore/mutex within a program unit.
- Keeping all semaphore/mutex operations local to the encapsulating unit.
- Hiding these from the 'outside' world, i.e. making them private to the program unit.
- Preventing *direct* access to the semaphore/mutex operations and the critical code section.
- Providing means to *indirectly* use the shared resource.

From a conceptual aspect the simple monitor can modelled as shown in figure 5.21.

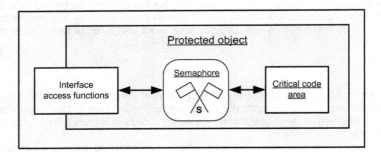

Figure 5.21 The simple monitor

This denotes that the semaphore and the critical code area are encapsulated within a program unit. As before, access to the critical code area is controlled by a semaphore.   Encapsulated items are not visible to external software; all accesses to them has to go via an interface function.   How this is implemented in practice depends on your programming language.   With C++, for instance, this would be based on the class construct.   Here the semaphore/mutex and the critical code section would be private to the class, access to these being controlled by public functions.

5.4 Contention problems in multitasking systems.

5.4.1 Resource contention and deadlocks.

The previous section has shown that tasks can safely share resources as long as we employ robust mutual exclusion techniques. Unfortunately there is the possibility that the use of these mechanisms can accidentally produce serious run-time problems (the law of unintended consequences?). For us the two most important ones are *deadlock* and *priority inversion*. But (and this is a significant but) these problems cannot arise where tasks share one resource only; they must share at least two resources.

Deadlock is the subject of this section; priority inversion is dealt with in the following one. To illustrate these effects we'll look at the run-time behaviour of the example system shown in figure 5.22.

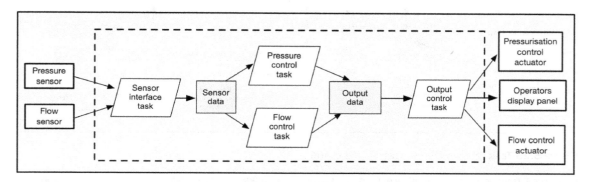

Figure 5.22 Example system tasking diagram

Its operation should be self-explanatory but please check that you do understand it. The scheduling policy is a priority preemptive one, task priorities being:

• Highest: Sensor interface task
• High: Pressure control task.
• Middle: Flow control task.
• Lowest: Output control task.

A run-time situation that leads to deadlock is shown in figure 5.23, which we'll work through carefully. To simplify the explanation the Sensor interface and Output control tasks are both assumed to be in timed suspensions. Also, to keep the diagram relatively simple and clear, they aren't included in figure 5.23.

As the scenario begins both the Flow control (FC) and Pressure control (PC) tasks are in timed suspensions. Later, at time T_1, the FC task completes its suspension time, is readied and then dispatched (set running). It immediately accesses and locks the Sensor data resource This continues until time T_2, when the PC task, on completing its suspension time, is readied and preempts the FC task (as it has the higher priority). The FC task is thus placed in the ready queue, with the Sensor data resource left in a locked state.

Moving on: at time T_3 the PC task accesses and locks the Output data resource. It (the task) continues executing until, at time T_4 it attempts to access the Sensor data resource. However, as the resource is already locked the PC task is suspended and a reschedule called. This results in the FC task being dispatched to become the active task. All continues without problem until the FC task tries to access the Sensor data resource at time T5. This resource, remember , was locked by the PC task and is still locked. Consequently it (the FC task) gets suspended. It is now impossible to get the

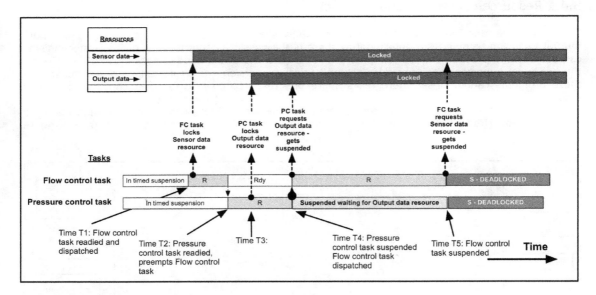

Figure 5.23 Task interaction — deadlock situation

resources unlocked; the 'keys' are held by suspended tasks.   Hence they will remain in suspension from this point on (and you should be able to work out that we'll soon end up with *all* tasks in suspension). This is not only a disastrous situation; it's also one that we can't recover from. Here is where the watchdog timer comes into use; if it works correctly it will force a program restart. Unfortunately system problems may occur during the deadlock period; the real world devices are operating in an uncontrolled manner.   Also, the program restart sequence itself may generate problems.

So let's see how we can eliminate deadlocks. You'll be able to see from figure 5.23 that deadlocking wouldn't have happened if:

1. There hadn't been a task switch (a reschedule) at time T2. This would have allowed the FC task to finish its use of the Sensor data resource, so unlocking it.
2. The FC task had to release and unlock the Sensor data resource before trying to acquire the Output data resource.
3. The FC task acquired both the Sensor data resource *and* the Output data resource simultaneously. In such a case it could have completed all the processing that required use of these resources.

The way to implement solution 1 is to stop rescheduling operations when a task acquires a shared resource: we disable all tasking. This can be done by disabling interrupts during the access period, a very simple and easy to use technique. Its downside is that stopping the scheduler effectively stops the execution of concurrent units; all multitasking ceases. So, when using this technique, get in and out of the shared item as quickly as possible.

Generalizing solution 2: a task must release any locked resource before it tries to access another one. In other words a task may hold one resource only at any one time.

Moving to solution 3: this leads to the general rule that a task must acquire *all* required resources (at the appropriate time, of course) before it continues executing.

Both solutions 2 and 3 can be implemented easily and simply in the source code of the task's program: a pre-runtime or *a priori* solution. Both have been widely used in embedded applications; the one to use is the one that provides best temporal performance (behavioural analysis needed here).

5.4.2 The priority inversion problem.

Solving the deadlock issue is not, unfortunately, the end of our problems. There is still the possibility that a situation called *priority inversion* can arise. Let's look at a simple example of this in action for the system shown in figure 5.22.

Assume that the Flow control task is the active one, all others being in timed suspension. Further assume that this task has accessed the Sensor data resource and so has locked it. A short time later the Pressure control task finishes its suspension time. As a result it is readied, a reschedule is called, causing the PC task to preempt the FC task. Subsequently during its run it tries to acquire the Sensor data resource but fails to do so (because this is locked): it gets suspended, waiting for the resource to come free. At this point the FC task is dispatched to become the active one. In effect it blocks the progress of the PC task, even though its priority is lower. The system behaves as if the priorities have reversed, a case of priority inversion. This, though, is not abnormal behaviour; *it's exactly what we designed the system to do.* But now let us examine a situation that involves three tasks as shown in figure 5.24.

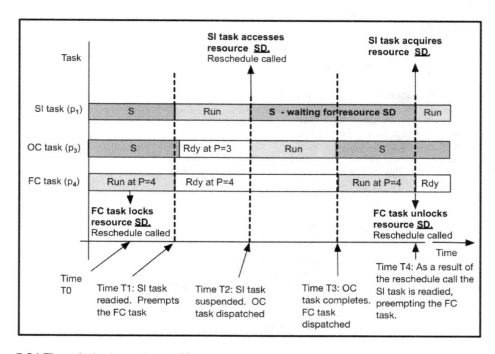

Figure 5.24 The priority inversion problem

For simplicity assume that during the scenario shown in figure 5.24 the PC task is in suspension. So it changes nothing to leave if off the diagram. Also, reschedule calls that don't change the state of the system aren't noted on the diagram. Lastly, the relative priorities of the tasks are as shown, where the SI task has the highest (1) and the FC task the lowest (4).

Please read through and analyze the diagram detail: the added notes should make things clear. The most important point to highlight here is what happens between times T_2 and T_3. At T_2 the SI task tries to access the SD resource. However, as this has already been locked by the FC task (which, note, is currently in the ready state) the request fails. The SI task gets blocked, being suspended until the SD resource once more comes free. The resulting reschedule call dispatches the OC task (as it has the highest priority in the ready queue), this now becoming the active one. It runs to completion at time T_3, at which point the FC task is re-dispatched. The task resumes executing from where it left off, finally finishing with the use of (and unlocking) the SD resource. This has the effect of awakening - readying - the SI task: the end result is that it preempts the FC task to become the active task.

For the SI task, its suspension between T_3 and T_4 is exactly what is intended; the FC task is using the shared resource SD. However its suspension between T_2 and T_3 is completely unintended, one which, unfortunately, produces an unwanted extra delay. It is, though, merely a consequence of using priority preemptive scheduling. Note that during the period between T_2 and T_4 the SI task behaves as if it has the lowest priority.

In this design the SI task was given the highest priority because it is an important one. Yet it has been forced to wait for *all* other tasks to execute, because of the mutual exclusion locks. The challenge now is to see how we can prevent such unwanted delays (which inevitably degrade system responsiveness).

It turns out that the solution to this problem is to raise the priority of the task that locks the resource: but only under specific circumstance and for a limited time. Two techniques can be used, the *priority inheritance* and the *priority ceiling* protocols. The priority ceiling protocol is the more widely used technique in modern RTOS so we'll have a brief look at how it works.

5.4.3 The priority ceiling protocol.

When using shared resources there is a simple way to minimize blocking delays; just allow the blocking task to use the resource as quickly as possible. What this means is that once a task has acquired resource it cannot be interrupted, with one proviso; only tasks that actually share the resource are taken into account. For example, the Sensor data resource is shared by the SI, PC and FC tasks: the Output data resource by the PC, FC and OC tasks. With the priority ceiling protocol each resource is given a priority value, this set by the highest priority of the accessing tasks. Let us assume that the tasks of figure 5.22 have the following priority settings:

SI task - priority 1 (highest).
PC task - priority 2.
OC task - priority 3.
FC task - priority 4 (lowest).

Thus the priority value assigned to the Sensor data resource is 1; for the Output data resource it is 2.

Now let us look at an example use of this protocol, specifically for an interaction that involves the Sensor data resource, figure 5.25. Initially the SI and PC tasks are in suspension while the FC task is running, at priority 4. At time T_1 the FC task accesses the resource, locking it in the process. A reschedule is called but the FC task continues as the executing task, with one major change; its priority is now raised to 1. As such it cannot be preempted by any other tasks *that share the SD resource*.

At time T_2 the SI task finishes it timed suspension and is readied. Although a reschedule is invoked there is no change of system state; the FC task remains the active one. It continues executing until, at time T_3, it unlocks the resource. This action causes its priority to return to normal (i.e. 4); the resulting reschedule causes it to be preempted. Thus the SI task becomes the active one. This task (SI) proceeds with the execution of its code, which may involve use of the SD resource (not especially important as it has no bearing on operations).

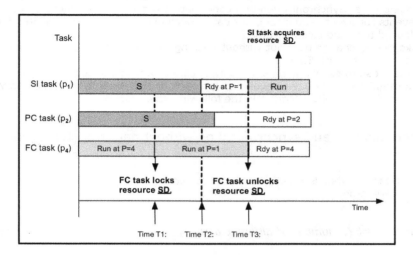

Figure 5.25 Priority ceiling protocol in use

Observe that the PC task was readied soon after T_2, but the resulting reschedule action allowed things to continue as before.

As you can see we have achieved our goal; blocking times are reduced to a minimum. There is, though, a price to pay for this. Implementing the protocol causes the RTOS software to become more complex and (more important) more time consuming.

5.5 Intertask communication.

5.5.1 Introduction.

The topic of intertask communication was introduced in an informal way in figure 5.18. As shown there two tasks 'communicate' by transferring data using a shared read/write data store. However, it turns out that this is just one of three communication techniques used in embedded systems, figure 5.26.

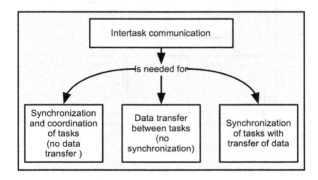

Figure 5.26 Intertask communication features

First, tasks may need to communicate in order to synchronize and/or co-ordinate their activities *without* exchanging data. Synchronization and coordination requirements generally occur where tasks are linked by events (or event-sequences), not data. Such events include time-related factors such as time delays, elapsed time and calendar time.

Second, tasks may exchange data but without needing to synchronize operations, as demonstrated in the tasking diagram of figure 5.22.

Third, tasks may wish to exchange data but only at carefully synchronized times.

Separate mechanisms have been developed for each of the three functions to provide safe and efficient operation. Their details are given in the following sections.

5.5.2 Task coordination and synchronization without data transfer - general aspects.

First, let us by clear by what is meant by the terms coordination and synchronization.   These are defined by Chambers to be:

Coordinate:
To integrate and adjust (a number of different parts or processes) so as to relate smoothly one to another.
Synchronize:
Cause to happen, move or operate in exact time with (something else or each other).

Different constructs are used to support software coordination and synchronization, these being condition flags, event flags and signals (figure 5.27). The following operations can be used with these constructs:
(i) Condition flags: Set, Clear and Check (read).
(ii) Event flags: Set, Get and Check (read).
(iii) Signals: Wait, send and check (read).
Please note that there isn't a standard definition of RTOS operations; these are the ones we choose to use.

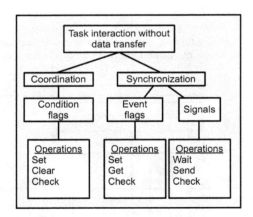

Figure 5.27 Coordination and synchronization constructs

5.5.3 Task interaction without data transfer.

(a) Task coordination and the simple condition flag.
Here we will first look at coordination operations, considering synchronization aspects later.

A flag is merely a simple binary signalling method, usually being implemented as a single bit or byte. The value it shows at any time has, in itself, no meaning; it depends on *how* it is being used (i.e. its meaning within the application). When used to coordinate activities it is called a *condition* flag (or simply, a *flag*). An illustration of flag usage is given in the tasking diagram of figure 5.28a, showing signalling between an HMI task and a Motor control task.

This, from an abstract point of view, is very easy to understand. From a practical point of view it leaves one important question unanswered: just how are these commands implemented in the application program? Remember, they must be in scope and visible to both tasks? Well, the information shown in figure 5.28a implies that *Start motor* and *Stop motor* signals are global variables. But the use (misuse, really) of globals is known to be a major contributor to software unreliability; seasoned programmers avoid them like the plague. What is needed is a defined signal handling construct which is *not* global to the programs.

The solution to this requirement is to employ a coordinating flag to connect the tasks together (figure 5.28b). We, as designers, define that a cleared flag indicates the motor should be stopped: when set it denotes the motor should be started.

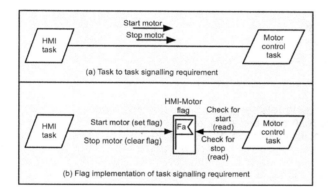

Figure 5.28 Simple use of a flag for coordination

Note that it is up to the application programmer to decide when the sending and checking operations are performed. Clearly the Motor control task should check for a start command *only* while the motor is stopped: likewise a stop command check should be done only while the motor is running.

As this is a coordination activity then the Motor control task always proceeds past the check points (irrespective of the interrogation results).

The key features of the flag construct are that it is:

• A precisely defined and named communication component.
• Located in a specified location (e.g. a file that holds the system's communication components).
• Not an uncontrolled global item. Its visibility can be controlled by the appropriated use of include directives in the code of the tasks (e.g. the communication file must be included in a task's program before the flag can be used).

(b) Task synchronization using event flags — the unilateral rendezvous.
The unilateral ('one-way') rendezvous is a form of synchronization that can be very effectively used to support ISR-driven operations, figure 5.29. The ISRs are sender tasks, the others being receivers. Note that these receiver task are aperiodic ones. Normally they are in a suspended state, waiting to

be woken up by (waiting to *rendezvous* with) the sender tasks. By contrast, the sending tasks do not wait for synchronization with the receivers; they merely signal that a synchronizing condition has been met. As depicted in figure 5.29:

- ISR1(2) is a sender task. Task1(2) is its corresponding receiver.
- The event flag is initialized to the cleared state (flag value = 0).
- When a receiver task calls *Get* on a cleared flag it is suspended.
- When a receiver task calls *Get* on a set flag (flag value = 1) it clears the flag and continues executing.
- When a sender task calls *Set* on a cleared flag it sets that flag, then continues executing. If a task is waiting suspended on that flag it is woken up (readied).
- When a sender task calls *Set* on a set flag it just continues executing.

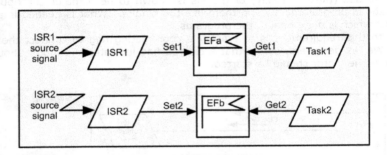

Figure 5.29 Event flags and unilateral synchronization

(c) Task synchronization using signals — the bilateral rendezvous.
In the scenario shown in figure 5.30 both tasks A and B wish to synchronize their activities. Each task has a defined synchronization point in its code, this being inserted by the programmer. At run time, however, it isn't usually possible to predict which task will reach its sync point first; the synchronizing order is unknown. This is where two-way or bilateral interaction synchronization must be provided, in our case by using signals. The resulting behaviour is called a *bilateral rendezvous*.

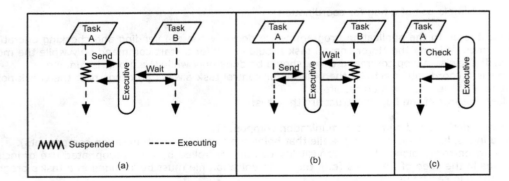

Figure 5.30 Task synchronization - the bilateral rendezvous

Signalling activities are the responsibility of the executive; to the user such operations (described below) are transparent.

First consider the Send action, figure 5.30(a). Here task A executes its program and reaches a point where it sends a signal (calls the API 'send').   At that instant no tasks are waiting to receive this signal; consequently task A is suspended. Some time later task B generates a Wait request (an API call 'wait') for the signal sent by A. It (task B) picks up the signal and carries on executing. The wait request also restarts Task A.

What happens if B generates the wait before A has sent the signal, figure 5.30(b)? The result; task B is suspended until A sends the signal.   At this point task A wakes task B and then continues executing.

Flexibility can be added to the signal construct by allowing tasks to decide if they wish to get involved in synchronization.   The *Check* operation, figure 5.30(c), surveys the status of the signal but does not itself halt task execution. Such decisions are left to the checking task (a technique that can be used very effectively for polling operations).

5.5.4 Data transfer without task synchronization or coordination.

There are many occasions when tasks exchange information without any need for synchronization or coordination.   This requirement can be implemented by using a straightforward data store incorporating mutual exclusion features.   In practice two data storage mechanisms are used, *Pools* and Queues, figure 5.31a. Queues are also known as channels, buffers or pipes.

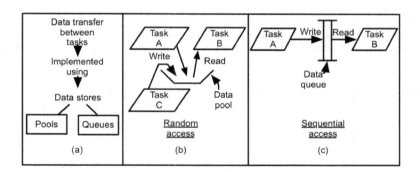

Figure 5.31 Transferring data between tasks

(a) Pools.
Pools (Fig 5.31b) hold items which are common to a number of processes, such as coefficient values, system tables, alarm settings, etc. The notation used here shows tasks A and C depositing data into the pool, with B reading information out. This is not a destructive read-out, i.e. information within the pool is unchanged by the read action.   The pools consist of sections of read-write memory, usually RAM (or for read-mostly operations, flash memory).

In practical systems it makes sense to use numerous pools, as and when desired.   This restricts access to information, so avoiding problems related to using global data.   Even so, it is still essential to control pool usage via a mutual exclusion mechanism like the monitor.   Note that the monitor is used to support data transfer activities; it is not **itself** a communication mechanism.

In general, commercial RTOSs do *not* provide the pool component; fortunately they can be constructed easily and simply using predefined data types such as the C struct (a record structure).

(b) Queues.
Queues are used as communication pipes between processes, normally on a one-to-one basis (figure 5.31c). Here, task A deposits information into the queue, task B extracting it in first-in first-out style.

The queue is usually made large enough to carry a number of data words, not just a single data item. As such it acts as a buffer or temporary storage device, providing elasticity in the pipe. Its advantage is that insertion and extraction functions can proceed asynchronously (as long as the pipe does not fill up). It is implemented in RAM. The information passed between processes may be the data itself; in other cases it could be a pointer to the data. Pointers are normally used for handling large amounts of data where RAM store is limited. Two techniques are used to implement queues, a linked list type structure and the circular buffer. For smaller embedded systems the preferred choice is the circular buffer. This is normally assembled using a fixed amount of memory space, being designed to hold a specific number of data units (bytes or words). Normally the buffer size is programmable, being defined at queue creation time.

Under normal circumstances tasks A and B proceed asynchronously, inserting and removing data from the queue as required. Task suspension occurs only under two conditions, queue full and queue empty. Should the queue fill up *and* task A tries to load another data unit, then A is suspended. Alternatively, if the queue empties and task B tries to remove a data unit, then B is suspended. In many implementations suspension does not occur; instead an error exception is raised.

There is an important difference between the pool and the queue. In the first, reading of data does not affect the contents. In the second, though, queue data is 'consumed' when read, i.e. a 'destructive' operation (this is really a conceptual view of things; in reality the reader pointer has merely moved on to the next location).

5.5.5 Task synchronization with data transfer.

In practice situations arise where tasks not only wait for events, but also use data associated with those events. To support this we need both a synchronization mechanism and a data storage area. The structure used is the 'mailbox', this unit incorporating signals for synchronization and storage for data, figure 5.32.

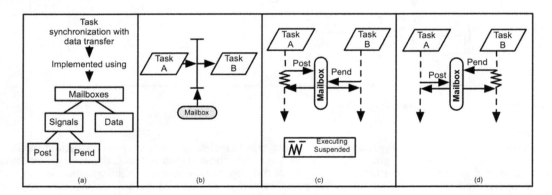

Figure 5.32 Data transfer with task synchronization.

When a task wishes to send information to another one it 'posts' the data to the mailbox. Correspondingly, when a task looks for data in the mailbox it 'pends' on it. In reality, *Post* and *Pend* are signals. Moreover, the data itself is not normally passed through the mailbox; a data pointer is used. Even so, no matter how large the data contents are, the data is treated as a single unit. Thus, conceptually, we have a single-store item. Task synchronization is achieved by suspending or halting tasks until the required conditions are met, Fig 5.32(c),(d). Any task posting to a mailbox that hasn't got a pending task gets suspended. It resumes when the receiver pends for the information. Conversely, should pending take place first, the task suspends until the post operation occurs.

5.6 Review.

In this chapter you have seen how the nature of software design changes when we use multitasking techniques. If you have taken these lessons to heart you will now:

- Have a good grasp of the basics of task-based designs.
- Understand the rationale for structuring software as a set of cooperating tasks - multitasking.
- Appreciate the advantages gained by using a multitasking design approach.
- Know the format, content and use of the tasking diagram.
- Understand that enabling mechanisms are needed to implement multitasking designs.
- Understand the role of interrupts and RTOSs as enabling mechanisms.
- Appreciate the role of scheduling in the operation of an RTOS.
- Understand the basics of FIFO, Round-Robin and Priority Preemptive scheduling policies.
- Know why, in practical multitasking systems, resource sharing always takes place.
- Realize what problems arise from using shared resources: contention, performance, data corruption, deadlocks, and priority inversion.
- See how and why flags, semaphores and monitors are used as protection mechanisms for shared resources.
- Understand the need for task communication, co-ordination and synchronization, together with the role of the various supporting components: flags, pools, channels and mailboxes.

In your readings you may come across the term *livelock*. This is outside the scope of our work as it applies to situations where tasks are truly concurrent (e.g. multiprocessor/multicore systems). It is similar to deadlock in that, as a result of resource contention, tasks are 'halted'. As you have seen, when deadlock occurs tasks get suspended. However, this is not the case with livelocks; here each task goes into a continuous busy-wait loop, waiting for the resource to become free.

5.7 Background reading material.

(a) Important concepts.
Cooperating sequential processes, E.W.Dijkstra, Technological University, Eindhoven, Netherlands 1965 (reprinted in Programming Languages, ed F Genuys, Academic Press, New York, 1968).
Dynamic priority ceilings: A concurrency control protocol for real-time systems, M.I.Chen. and K.J.Lin, Int. J. Time-Critical Computer Systems, Vol.2, No.4, pp 325-345, Nov.1990.
Monitors: an operating system structuring concept, C.A.R.Hoare, Communications of the ACM, Vol 17, No 10, pp549-557, October 1974.
Real-Time scheduling theory and Ada, L.Sha. and J.B.Goodenough, IEEE Computer, Vol.23, No.4, pp 53-63, April 1990.

(b) Books
MicroC/OS-III The Real-Time Kernel, Jean J. Lacrosse.
See: https://www.micrium.com/books/ucosiii/
Real-time Concepts for Embedded Systems, Qing Li, CRC Press 2003-01-06, ISBN 1578201241
https://www.slideshare.net/doreh/realtime-concepts-for-embedded-systems-pdf
Real-Time Embedded Multhreading Using ThreadX and ARM, Edward L. Lamie, 2005
https://www.amazon.co.uk/Real-Time-Embedded-Multithreading-Using-ThreadX/dp/1578201349
Real-time Operating Systems: Book 1 - The Theory, Jim Cooling, 2017
https://www.amazon.com/dp/B00GO6VSGE

END OF CHAPTER